W9-DFG-112

Roots of Crisis

Roots of Crisis:

AMERICAN EDUCATION IN THE TWENTIETH CENTURY

CLARENCE J. KARIER
University of Illinois

PAUL C. VIOLAS
University of Illinois

JOEL SPRING
Case Western Reserve University

Theodore Lownik Library
Illinois Benedictine College
Lisle, Illinois 60532

RAND McNALLY & COMPANY • Chicago

RAND McNALLY EDUCATION SERIES

B. Othanel Smith, *Advisory Editor*

370
.973
K18r

Figure 6.2: From *General Psychology* by Henry E. Garrett, copyright 1955 by Litton Educational Publishing, Inc. Reprinted by permission of Van Nostrand Reinhold Company.

Copyright © 1973 by Rand McNally & Company
All Rights Reserved
Printed in the U.S.A. by Rand McNally & Company
Library of Congress Catalog Card Number 72–7850

CONTENTS

Roots of Crisis

INTRODUCTION

Friedrich Nietzsche once said: "You can only explain the past by what is highest in the present. Only by straining the noblest qualities you have to their highest power will you find out what is greatest in the past, most worth knowing and preserving."[1] History is inevitably written from a particular perspective of the present. The historian can no more divest himself of the present than he can live in the past. To accept these conditions is not, however, to assume a position of historicism.[2] Although history is an imaginative creation of the past, it is not a fictional creation. Its validity is derived from both the artifacts of the past and the meanings it illuminates in the present. History, we believe, is an art. The historian as an artist is different, however, from the painter as an artist. While both are ultimately judged by the meaning achieved in the present, the evidence with which the historian works must itself be validated by

[1] Oscar Levy, ed., *Complete Works of Friedrich Nietzsche*, vol. 5 (New York: Russell & Russell, 1964), p. 55.
[2] For a particularly sharp critique of John Dewey's and George Herbert Mead's use of the past, see Arthur O. Lovejoy, "Present Standpoints and Past History," *Journal of Philosophy* 36:477–489.

reason, logic, and empirical analysis.[3] Context, internal consistency, cross-referencing, authenticity of documentation—all are tools with which the historian shapes and colors his picture of the past.[4]

In many ways the mind of man is timeless. While he lives in the present, he transcends the barriers of the future and the past through imagination. Yet here also the imagination that allows one to wander in the future is different from that which works on the past. The imagination recreating the past must grapple with not only the artifacts of a past world, but also with values and structure of that past which are a part of a living present. The past is thus inescapably linked to the present, and any truly human quest for meaning involves a particular creation of a past. Historical inquiry is therefore an exciting fundamental search for meaning that imaginatively adds space, time, and dimension to one's existence.

While one might profitably concern himself with the questions of why one historian views the past differently from another and why some people regard one past superior to another, perhaps a more fundamental question might be: why does the historian write history? We submit that the historian cultivates the art of history to add meaning to his present existence, and that people prefer one history over another because it is that history which most satisfies their quest for meaning.[5] The art of historical scholarship, like the art of painting or sculpture, necessarily reflects the *Weltanschauung*

[3] For a unique analysis of the ways a historian utilizes evidence, see R. W. Winks, *The Historian as Detective* (New York: Harper & Row, 1969).

[4] Extended arguments supporting the above position will be found in Carl Becker, "What Are Historical Facts?" in *Philosophy of History in Our Time,* ed. by Hans Meyerhoff (New York: Doubleday, 1959), pp. 120–137; R. G. Collingwood, *The Idea of History* (New York: Oxford University Press, 1946), pt. 5; William H. Dray, *Laws and Explanation in History* (London: Oxford University Press, 1957), chs. 4 and 5; W. B. Gallie, *Philosophy and the Historical Understanding* (London: Chatto and Windus, 1964), esp. chs. 3, 4, and 5.

For opposing arguments, see Carl G. Hempel, "The Function of General Laws in History," in *Theories of History,* ed. by Patrick Gardiner (New York: Free Press of Glencoe, 1959), pp. 344–356; John Passmore, "The Objectivity of History," in *Philosophical Analysis and History,* ed. by William H. Dray (New York: Harper & Row, 1966), pp. 75–94; and Ernest Nagel, *The Structure of Science* (New York: Harcourt, Brace & World, 1961), pp. 547–606.

[5] A sensitive and convincing case for this function of history is developed by Hayden V. White, "The Burden of History," *History and Theory* 5, no. 2 (1966):111–134. A less extensive treatment is located in Isaiah Berlin, "The Concept of Scientific History," in *Philosophical Analysis and History,* ed. by William H. Dray (New York: Harper & Row, 1966), pp. 5–53, esp. sect. T and U.

in which the artist lives.[6] Accepting this, we can then attempt to understand and see, as well as feel, the relationship between Renaissance painting and Renaissance culture just as we can understand, see, and feel the relationship between liberal historians and liberal progressive culture in twentieth-century America.[7] The intellectual, cultural, and educational histories of Merle Curti, Henry Steele Commager, Richard Hofstader, and Lawrence Cremin fundamentally reflect certain common assumptions about the world in which these men moved. Those assumptions guided their perceptions, which in turn framed the picture of reality they created. Although each painted pictures depicting different aspects of the conditions of modern man, all held fairly similar assumptions about the ideas of progress, rationality, community, science, and technology.

Broadly speaking, these men reflected a neo-enlightenment world view that emerged out of the intellectual debates over Spencerian–Darwinism combined with a pragmatic progressive temper. This combination produced a kind of liberal humanitarianism that came to dominate the vital center of American social, intellectual, and political life for half a century. These liberal historians believed in the American dream of progress. Progess was not seen as inevitable, but it certainly was seen as possible. Accordingly, through a process of social melioration, institutions might be so adjusted as to usher in a more satisfactory future. All these liberal historians believed that through the intelligent use of science and technology a better life for mankind might be achieved. They further believed in a meritocracy in which the professional expert would play an ever increasing role in using both state and corporate power to meliorate man's condition. They were not, however, naively optimistic, either with respect to the social condition or the use of power to meliorate those conditions. In general, they viewed the straits of blacks, southern European immigrants, Mexican Americans, the In-

---

[6] Even the staunch positivist Karl R. Popper recognized this in his *Poverty of Historicism* (New York: Harper & Row, 1964), esp. sect. 31; while the impact of *Weltanschauung* on social science is forcefully examined in Leon Bramson, *The Political Context of Sociology* (Princeton: Princeton University Press, 1961), esp. ch. 7.

[7] For a persuasive discussion of such relationships, see Carl Becker, *The Heavenly City of the Eighteenth-Century Philosophers* (New Haven: Yale University Press, 1932), esp. ch. 1; and J. Huizinga, "The Idea of History," in *The Varieties of History*, ed. by Fritz Stern (New York: Meridian Books, 1957), pp. 290–303.

dians—in short, the disinherited—with compassion. Nevertheless, they saw the solution to the problems of the disinherited not in questioning the system that cut people out, but rather in allowing more of the disinherited to enter a growing middle class in America. Although some historians might have wished at times to radically change the system, their own pragmatic realism, applied especially to power situations, inclined them to advocate gradual change within the established system.

The world in which these historians moved was a world of growing power in international and national affairs. That progressive alliance between government and corporate wealth welded together during World War I, and further developed during the Great Depression and World War II, came to full fruition in the postwar decades in the form of the military-industrial state. This was a world of burgeoning government bureaucracies effectively allied with corporate wealth, which fashioned a mass system of schooling to maintain corporate security at home and abroad. The world the liberal historian viewed was sometimes his own creation, sometimes "out of joint," and at other times "accidental." Most, however, agreed that as much as they might disagree with current trends, this social system was the best that could be wrested under circumstances that were, at best, difficult. Like other historians, these men could not escape their own value orientations. More important, they could not escape the fact that many of their own personal values were embedded in that corporate liberal state that they helped make intelligible if not justifiable. Given the assumption that the society in which they moved was basically sound, it was almost inevitable that their histories would track along progressive lines. Under these circumstances, the bloody violence and acts of repression committed against minority groups were not part of the mainstream of American history. In a similar vein, expansion of schooling for the masses was usually viewed as a progressive step forward, one generated by humanitarian motives. The possibility that the school was in fact a vehicle of control and repression escaped analysis. Schooling in American history was viewed as a positive "good" largely because educational historians viewed schooling as a positive necessity. Once again the present world accounted for a particular interpretation. Other examples might be cited. For instance, the liberal world of Lawrence Cremin allowed him to fashion *The Genius of American Education* in the 1960s amidst the literal collapse of urban education and the burning of the cities. We do in fact live in different worlds, and we do therefore see our past differently.

Every new present, however, creates a need to reexamine our past. Those who still believe in the American dream and the basic soundness of this social system will still find meaning in the liberal progressive picture of the past. However, if one views the present world more critically, liberal history will be found short on meaningful criticism and long on apology. If one believes this society is *not* structured to enhance the dignity of man but rather fosters a dehumanizing quest for status, power, and wealth, then the liberal histories fail to explain how we got where we believe we are. Under these circumstances, liberal history does not connect with and add meaning to our present world. If one starts with the assumption that this society is in fact racist, fundamentally materialistic, and institutionally structured to protect vested interests, the past takes on vastly different meanings. The authors of these essays write from such a conception of the present, which shapes their own view of the past. Given these assumptions, new material long ago passed over as unimportant takes on significance as indeed older data requires fresh interpretation. The reader will therefore find not only new materials in these essays, but also a more critical treatment of the movers and shapers of American educational thought and practice in the twentieth century. The verbal paintings presented are cast in a different context than the one normally portrayed by liberal historians. In addition to the many arguments over context, documentation, and fairness of use, the ultimate test of these essays in the history of American education will be how well they in fact connect with and add meaning to our present world. This will of course depend on whether or not we have captured that which is "greatest in the past, most worth knowing and preserving." The reader will judge.

CHAPTER 1

BUSINESS VALUES AND THE EDUCATIONAL STATE

Clarence J. Karier

The school, as a formal vehicle of education, exists as an instrument of social and economic power for the most influential elite groups as much as for the political and social organizations through which the society is managed. Thus, in the twentieth century, schools became important instruments of power under capitalism and fascism, as well as under communism. The educational state that emerged in twentieth-century America did so ultimately as an instrument of those economic and political elites who managed the American corporate state. The values and attitudes making up the complicated matrix of that school system are, to a considerable extent, products of the economic and social development in American culture. Although none of the authors of these essays accept an economic deterministic position, they do agree that economic concerns have played a major role in shaping our values and attitudes which, in turn, shape our perception of ourselves and our community.

Perhaps Karl Marx was never more insightful than when he pointed to the intimate relationship between man's production and his life-style:

> As individuals express their life, so they are. What they are, therefore, coincides with their production both with what they

produce and with how they produce. The nature of individuals thus depends on the material conditions determining their productions.[1]

Not only *what* men produce, but *how* they produce is important in considering the creative act of production in which men create themselves as they shape their environment. In the most profound sense, both play and work enter into man's productions and represent the ways in which man recreates himself and his world. Whether we consider education as a process of creating a free man in the full dimension of that term, or merely one of training him for specified tasks, the link between man's production and his education is simultaneously obvious and subtle. It is obvious with respect to training skilled workers to man the machines; it is subtle with respect to inculcating the important social-psychological value requisite to the maintenance of a particular economic social system.

American education in general has provided an effective service function to the business community in the training of both producers and consumers. It also has served as the vehicle through which the basic values of a commercial culture are transmitted from generation to generation. Although peripheral values have come and gone and the schools and the business community have changed during the past century, the basic values transmitted have remained fairly constant. When peripheral values change there is social reform; when basic values change there is social revolution. This nation has never undergone a social revolution. Even though America has moved from a *laissez-faire* capitalism to a state welfare capitalism, and the norms of this society have changed from those of producers to those of consumers, the basic values necessary for the maintenance of a capitalist society remain the same. It is my contention that the schools throughout the history of American education have been used as instruments to teach the norms necessary to adjust the young to the changing patterns of the economic system as well as to the society's more permanent values. I further contend that much of the historical evidence seems to indicate that if any major change in the basic core values occurs, it will result from a fundamental shift in the economic system. Starting, then, with the assumption that work and education are fundamentally linked, I intend to trace historically certain selected relationships between the

[1] Quoted in Erich Fromm, *Marx's Concept of Man* (New York: Ungar, 1961), p. 10.

business community and the education of youth so as to delineate some of the key problems now emerging.

Considering the long span of history, there have been relatively few periods in which a basic transformation of values has occurred. In the West, the last such transformation took place during the Reformation. Within that period, one can identify a fundamental change in attitude toward poverty, work, and wealth. In a society of economic scarcity, controlling institutions may reconcile themselves to the economic realities and operate a social system in such a way as to help people accept limitations. Or they may attempt to mobilize the energy of the people to overcome them. The former approach is best represented by the medieval church's caution against fretting about tomorrow and its advocation of the model of God, who through nature takes care to "feed the birds and clothe the lilies of the field." The latter approach is best represented by John Calvin, preaching at Geneva the gospel of work, sobriety, and diligence. The difference represents a profound transformation of values ushering in a capitalistic era. Attitudes toward poverty, work, and wealth, premised on scarcity and shaped during the Reformation, have remained the cornerstone of much of American educational practice.

Increasingly, however, many of these values are becoming irrelevant, especially to those groups that have overcome the original problem of scarcity. For the children of those groups, reared in an affluent environment free from the older system's moral demands, the possibility of a fundamental transformation of values exists. Given the likelihood of affluence for greater numbers, we may be on the verge of a transformation of values unparalleled since the Protestant Reformation.[2] The moral demand system premised on scarcity cannot survive in an affluent age.[3] To whatever extent capitalist economics demands a value system premised on scarcity, one is forced to conclude, paradoxically, that the success of capitalism

[2] See Paul Goodman, "The New Reformation," New York Times, Sept. 14, 1969. To be sure, other nations have achieved varying degrees of affluence by following other historical routes than that utilized in the West. See, for example, David C. McClelland, The Achieving Society (Princeton, N.J.: Van Nostrand, 1961). My discussion here, however, is confined to the historical development of American capitalism.

[3] See Philip Rieff, The Triumph of the Therapeutic (New York: Harper & Row, 1966). See also Charles A. Reich, The Greening of America (New York: Random House, 1970).

will be responsible for its demise. The possibility of such a demise represents the real danger as well as the promise for the last third of this century—danger, because out of fear or panic those in power may erect a repressive regime against those who threaten the security of those holding the traditional value system; promise, because of the possibility of developing an economic and social system that enhances something other than men's materialistic competitiveness.

THE SCHOOLS AND THE PURITAN ETHIC

The early development of modern capitalism was tied largely to the new urban bourgeoise that found expression for its life-style in the church. Especially in Calvinist urban centers, the new business class struggled to find a kind of political and social environment conducive to its own world view. Education always has been the concern of the dominant institution. Therefore, education remained largely a church function until the rise and consolidation of the nation-state.[4] The major transformation of values from a medieval to a capitalistic ethic therefore took place within a religious institution that used education to foster the ethical values of the new business elites.

Both the medieval Catholic church and the Puritans who reflected the new business ethic appreciated the sinful nature of man. The medieval church was reluctant, however, to support the businessman's quest for material goods and capital, whereas Calvin and most Puritans who followed him looked upon this quest as a possible way of honoring and glorifying God. If the community could maintain tight control over the uses of wealth, and if the individual's self-interest was harnessed to a keen sense of duty to God and community, the City of God might yet rise in this world. Always suffering from the acute tension between the ideal and the real, the Puritans hammered out both the logical and the psychological values that came to undergird a capitalistic nation.

Accumulation of capital requires savings. Such savings might be achieved by overt, coercive government action through forced savings—as in the contemporary case of the Soviet Union—or it might be achieved by a more subtle, manipulative approach—through education. By inculcating in each individual a fear of poverty, a desire for wealth, a respect for work, a need for thrift, and a keen sense of

---

[4] This occurred at different times in different nations. In most cases when it occurred, heresy ceased to be a crime punishable by death. Treason took its place.

duty to be a productive, useful citizen of the community, education produces an ethic conducive to the accumulation of capital. When poverty was no longer seen as a virtue but a vice, a fundamental shift in values had occurred. "Begging," one result of the medieval attitude toward poverty, and once seen as a fruitful lesson in humility and charity by members of medieval mendicant orders, now came to be viewed as self-destructive and antisocial. The Puritan knew that God, in His almighty wisdom, had predestined some men to heaven and some to eternal damnation. He also knew that only God knew who was saved. Never certain of salvation, but always looking for a sign, the Puritan acted as though he were a child of the elect. From this point, it was not hard to go on to read the hand of God into one's material success. While wealth was viewed as a sign of election by some, others recognized the dangers to the spirit of religion that might result if community controls over the uses of wealth were ever relaxed. John Wesley put it well when he said:

> I fear wherever riches have increased, the essence of religion has decreased in the same proportion. Therefore I do not see how it is possible, in the nature of things, for any revival of true religion to continue long. For religion must necessarily produce both industry and frugality, and these cannot but produce riches. But as riches increase, so will pride, anger, and love of the world in all its branches.[5]

By the end of the eighteenth century, Puritanism as an organized religious influence had all but disappeared in America. What remained was a secularized way of life for an emerging capitalistic nation. Brought up in the Puritan tradition by a strict Calvinist father, Benjamin Franklin personified the secularization of the Puritan tradition and its blend with the Yankee dream of success. Franklin lived in the shadow of the biblical injunction: "Seest thou a man diligent in his business? He shall stand before kings" (Prov. 22:29). Franklin did indeed stand before kings. With his pen and wit, Franklin captured the core of the American dream of success and those perennial values that underlie the basic structure of this society. His Poor Richard maxims pointed the way to economic success. He, like

---

[5] Max Weber, *The Protestant Ethic and the Spirit of Capitalism* (New York: Scribner's, 1958), p. 175.

so many educators before and after him, equated wealth with virtue. As he said, "Industry multiplied by Frugality gives the product
Wealth, which equals Virtue."[6] It was very much in the Franklin tradition that Edward L. Thorndike and other educators in the twentieth century drew "scientific" correlations between men of wealth
and good character.[7]

The Franklin maxims "time is money," "credit is money," and
"money is of a prolific generating nature" also taught that work and
thrift are rewarded by wealth, which is the keystone to success in
any capitalistic society. Franklin argued that begging was to be
shunned and poverty despised. Values expounded by Franklin reap-
peared again and again in children's readers as well as in popular
adult literature throughout the nineteenth and twentieth centuries.
America was, after all, a capitalistic society, and the values necessary
to sustain a competitive materialistic world view for both producer
and consumer were necessarily a fundamental part of a citizen's
education.

The establishment of common schools followed the triumph of
the nation-state. Their mission was to impart the new common values in order to prevent political, social, or economic revolution. The
common school was, in fact, perceived by many as a form of police
action to protect the system. Daniel Webster said public education
is a ". . . wise and liberal system of police by which property, and
life, and the peace of society are secured."[8] Horace Mann, a key
proponent of the common school, viewed its chief social and economic function as "a balance wheel of the social machinery," bal-
ancing conflicting interests and thus preventing violent revolution.
The common school would protect the rights of property, first by
teaching the children of the propertyless to believe that the economic system was reasonable and just, rewarding people according
to natural abilities and for real contributions to society, and second
by teaching that if the student practiced Puritan virtues, he, too,
could be successful.[9] Horace Mann, himself a Whig politician and a
former corporation lawyer, was very clear about the social impact

---

[6] Benjamin Franklin, *Poor Richard's Almanac* (New York: Doran, 1928), p. xvii.

[7] See Merle Curti, *The Social Ideas of American Educators* (New York: Scribner's,
1935).

[8] As quoted by Charles Burgess in "The Educational State in America" (Ph.D. diss.,
University of Wisconsin, 1962), p. 146.

[9] See Horace Mann, *Twelfth Annual Report* (1848).

such a school might have on revolutionaries. In making his case for common schools to the business community, he said:

> Finally, in regard to those who possess the largest shares in the stock of wordly goods, could there, in your opinion, be any police so vigilant and effective, for the protection of all the rights of person, property and character, as such a sound and comprehensive education and training as our system of common schools could be made to impart; and would not the payment of a sufficient tax to make such education and training universal, be the cheapest means of self-protection and insurance?[10]

Mann repeatedly reacted to the danger that illiterate Irish immigrants might destroy the business and social institutions of Massachusetts by arguing that the best insurance policy would be an effective common school. The state would use public education as a vehicle of social control and order. Repeatedly the American public turned to the public school to inculcate the common elements of American culture into the children of the "strangers in the land," whether those strangers were Irish, Indian, black, southern European, or simply Catholic. This cultural indoctrination was, in fact, what the King Kleagle, Pacific Domain of the Knights of the Ku Klux Klan, had in mind in 1922 when during the Oregon parochial school controversy he said:

> . . . it is the settled policy of the Ku Klux Klan and with its white-robed sentinels keeping watch, it shall for all time, with its blazing torches as signal fires, stand guard on the outer walls of the temple of liberty, cry out the warning when danger appears and take its place in the front rank of the defenders of the public schools.[11]

Religious values taught in the common school were Protestant; social values, white Anglo-Saxon; and economic values, Puritan. Little wonder that the KKK would be such a staunch defender of the common school.

---

[10] Quoted in Lawrence A. Cremin, *The Republic and the School* (New York: Bureau of Publications, Teachers College, Columbia University, 1951), p. 53.

[11] David Tyack, "The Perils of Pluralism: The Background of the Pierce Case," *American Historical Review* 74(October 1968):74–98.

TEACHING BY TESTING

Although the economic and social situation changed and the role of public education was dramatically extended, schools nevertheless continued to transmit the values necessary for the maintenance of a business ethic. Evidence of this abounds in the texts and tests used in schools, businesses, and the armed forces. The army Alpha Test, used to classify over 1.7 million men in World War I, included questions explicitly reflecting the business ethic. For example, although a medieval mendicant might have difficulty with the following question, neither Franklin nor a graduate of the common school would.

Form D. **10.** Why should you not give money to beggars on the street? Because
it breaks up families
it makes it hard for the beggar to get work
it takes away the work of organized charities
☒ it encourages living off of others

Reminiscent of Poor Richard saying, "Sloth makes all things difficult, but Industry all things easy," the army tester asked:

Form E. **1.** If a man gets tired of his work, he should
throw it up
☒ keep at it till the work is done
run away and loaf
make someone else do it

Poor Richard said, "An Honest Man will receive neither Money nor Praise that is not his due." The army tester asked:

Form D. **6.** If the grocer should give you too much money in making change, what is the thing to do?
take the money and hurry out
☒ tell him of his mistake
buy some candy with it
give it to the next poor man you meet

In good Puritan fashion, the army tester was concerned about keeping one's accounts straight right to the grave as he asked:

Form C.   **4.** If a man knew he would die in two weeks, he
should
blow in all his money
☒ make his will and straighten out his accounts
go dig his grave
start out on a sight-seeing trip[12]

Most intelligence tests utilized in schools and factories in America in the twentieth century broadly reflect the dominant Puritan ethic. For example, the Stanford-Binet, a commonly used intelligence test, counts the following answers as "plus" to the question, What is the difference between work and play?

You work to earn money and you play for fun. One is for amusement and the other for a living. Play is a pleasure and work is something you should do, your duty. Work is energy used for doing something useful and play is just wasting energy. One's recreation—and one's labor. I mean play is an enjoyment and work is something you have to do. Sometimes you enjoy it and sometimes you don't. When you're working you're generally doing something that has to be done—when you're playing you're just doing what you feel like. One is something that most people like to do and the other is a duty. The attitude towards whatever you're doing—if you're playing baseball and don't like to play baseball then it's work—if you're working at mathematics and you like to do it—then it's not work to you anymore. Work you take seriously and play you don't.[13]

The youngster who answers the question correctly must view work as a means of earning money, as distasteful labor, irksome, serious, useful, and duty bound. He must associate play with fun, and view it as amusement, pleasure, a waste of energy, enjoyment, and lacking in seriousness. The correct answer clearly reflects a Puritan ethical attitude toward work and play that has persisted throughout the history of this society. The Stanford-Binet test, far from being culture free, is in fact a clear reflector of the common elements of

12 Robert M. Yerkes, *National Academy of Sciences—Memoirs XV* (Washington, D.C.: U.S. Government Printing Office, 1921), p. 215.

13 Lewis M. Terman and Maud A. Merrill, *Stanford-Binet Intelligence Scale* (Boston: Houghton Mifflin, 1960), p. 213.

American culture. It is an accurate predictor of success in a system of education based on these same common cultural elements.

Schools not only help perpetuate those attitudes toward work, wealth, and success necessary in a materialistic, competitive society; they also serve to rationalize and justify the current class system. One second-grade social studies text used in American schools today summarizes the lessons taught as follows:

> What Did We Learn?
>
> **1.** We go to school to learn about other people.
> **2.** We learn that people look different from each other.
> **3.** People speak different languages.
> **4.** Some people have more than others. Some have less.
> **5.** Some people know more than others. Some know less.
> **6.** Some people can learn a lot. Some people can learn only a little.[14]

From this the second-grade child learns that some people look different and speak differently from others, and that some know more, learn more, and have more wealth than others. Differences in wealth seem to be associated with both knowledge and ability, and they are treated as phenomena as natural as differences in speech or appearance. If the second grader learns this lesson well, he has taken an important step in his socialization—the acceptance and justification of an economically determined social system. The school in both the nineteenth and twentieth centuries not only taught those values that normally sustain a commercial culture, but it also effectively taught the social myths necessary to maintain the social-class system that was a product of the economic order.

THE SCHOOL AND ITS FUNCTIONS

The Marxian thesis holding that changes in the means of production result in significant changes in social institutions and life-styles is demonstrated in American educational history. The growth of large urban centers after the Civil War; the development of the American high school (an urban school); the decline of the academy (appropriate for a rural environment); the development of industrial education, manual training, and vocational guidance and

---

[14] Lawrence Senesh, *Our Working World: Neighbors at Work* (Chicago: Science Research Associates, 1965), pp. 177–178.

training, as well as the decline of the apprenticeship system; and the enactment of child labor and compulsory education legislation—all are historic developments directly traceable to the newer forms of production that this society adopted.

The creation of a system of mass education followed the shift from handicraft to mass production and the adoption of production-line techniques. Before the turn of the century, the common school was sufficient to maintain what Mann considered the necessary "balance within the social machinery." After the turn of the century, there was an extensive consolidation of capital[15] and a tremendous growth of mass production industries. These events in turn stimulated urbanization, the importation of cheap labor from southern Europe, and the growth of urban ghettos. It was apparent that a new "balance" within the social machinery was needed, one that could provide a systematic and rationalized control of the labor force. Child labor legislation went hand in hand with increased determination to enforce compulsory education laws, many of which were revised upward. Regular school attendance by masses of students in America, however, is a relatively recent phenomenon. In 1900, for example, approximately 10 percent of the high school age group (14–17) was in school; but by 1970, approximately 90 percent of that age group was in school. By then, too, although the compulsory education ɔv did not extend beyond high school, increasing occupational requirements had made college compulsory in fact for a large number of youth.

The American system of mass education functioned along three distinct but overlapping lines. First, there was the training function. This, in cooperation with business and industry, assisted youth to fulfill occupational requirements in an increasingly complex system. Second, there was the testing and sorting function, an operation based on economic privilege, a fact fairly well obscured by various myths propounded by the educational testers. Third, there was the holding function. The school not only kept children off the labor market, but it also maintained a viable manpower pool for almost every conceivable occupation. In *What Doctrines to Embrace*, Merle Borrowman and Charles Burgess persuasively argue that the rhetoric

---

[15] In 1897, the total capitalization of all corporations individually valued at a million dollars or more came to only $170 million. Three years later, the same figure for total capitalization stood at $5 billion, and in 1904 at over $20 billion. Charles Forcey, *The Crossroads of Liberalism* (London: Oxford University Press, 1961), p. xiv.

of educational reform in the twentieth century shifts from consumer to producer values as shortages occur in the total manpower pool.[16] When, for example, the reformer's rhetoric advocates a child oriented–consummatory function, he is serving, in effect, the need of the system to hold potential workers in the educational institution and off the production line. When, however, the rhetoric advocates a society oriented–productive function, he is serving the need of the system for trained personnel on the production line. In either case the educational reformer is a servant of the system. If one considers this thesis in the light of demographic projections of manpower surplus in the decade of the seventies, one might expect the reform rhetoric to be child oriented–consummatory. Despite its intentions, however, the school is having increasingly serious difficulty maintaining its holding function. The increased numbers of "phantom" schools[17] in large urban areas is empirical testimony to the difficulty of pursuing the holding function when myths involving academic achievement and occupational opportunities are no longer considered credible.

Although schools have always played some role in training and selection for the economic and social system, it was not until the latter part of the nineteenth century in Germany and the first half of the twentieth century in America that they became the major vehicle for economic and political control. With the unification of the German states, it was clear that the newly industrialized nation had ignored Von Humboldt's warning about the dangers to human freedom inherent in the positive state.[18] The new Germany used coercive political machinery to resolve all sorts of economic and social problems created by new mass production industries. The idea of the compulsory state and its corollary, compulsory education, was born in Germany. The many thousands of American students who attended German universities in the nineteenth century carried it to America. In Germany, political leaders used state power to head off radical socialist demands by ameliorating the condition of the workers. In America, state authority was utilized to curb radical

---

[16] Charles Burgess and Merle L. Borrowman, *What Doctrines to Embrace* (Glenview, Ill.: Scott, Foresman, 1969), pp. 113–137.

[17] Phantom schools are those schools with an absentee rate so high that they operate most of the year without students.

[18] See Wilhelm Von Humboldt, *Limits of State Action,* ed. by J. W. Burrow (New York: Cambridge University Press, 1969).

populism[19] as well as radical labor agitation.[20] The major impetus of progressive reform, whether political or educational, was to make the system work efficiently and effectively. Progressives were willing to use the compulsory power of the state to achieve that end. Progressive reform was indeed conservative.[21] So, for that matter, were many state socialists. They were conservative in their quest for efficiency and orderly change and in their desire to maintain the system. By World War I much of the progressive reformers' work had been institutionalized in the form of government regulation of commerce, labor, industry, and banking.

Like members of the eighteenth-century Enlightenment, twentieth-century progressives called not only for improvement of the economic-political system, but also for the perfectibility of the race. Laws prohibiting racial intermarriage increased as sterilization of the mentally unfit and the criminally insane also became part of the twentieth-century progressive reform era.[22] The eugenic movement in America, very much an outgrowth of the progressive era, was functionally related to the testing movement that proved its utility during World War I. From testing the mentally unfit and criminally insane, testers moved to testing army officers and to classifying over 1.7 million men. After the war, men like Thorndike, Goddard, Terman, and Yerkes applied what they had learned to millions of children in the rapidly expanding public school system. Under the guise of "scientific objectivity" the testers measured millions of students against their own peculiar model of a successful man. The model usually turned out to be white, Protestant, and middle class. The early testing movement reflected the strong elitist and racist values of the testers[23] as well as of the general culture. The testers repeatedly found strong correlation between intelligence, wealth, and character. Little wonder! Thorndike best represented that tendency when he said, "To him that hath a superior intellect is given also on

[19] See Norman Pollack, *The Populist Response to Industrial America* (New York: Norton, 1962). See also William Appleman Williams, *The Roots of the Modern American Empire* (New York: Random House, 1969).

[20] See James Weinstein, *The Corporate Ideal in the Liberal State, 1900–1918* (Boston: Beacon Press, 1968).

[21] See Gabriel Kolko, *The Triumph of Conservatism* (New York: Free Press, 1965).

[22] See Mark H. Haller, *Eugenics: Hereditarian Attitudes in American Thought* (New Brunswick, N.J.: Rutgers University Press, 1963), p. 158.

[23] For one example, see Edward L. Thorndike, "The Psychology of the Half-Educated Man," *Harper's* 140(April 1920):666–667.

the average a superior character; the quick boy is also in the long run more accurate; the able boy is also more industrious."[24] "Scientific" testers also helped standardize and rationalize the school along business lines. The business community used their work to classify and manage labor,[25] and Congress found it useful in developing a rationale for restricting the immigration of southern Europeans in 1924.[26] In teacher education, the test and measurement movement helped develop and perpetuate the myth of "scientific professionalism" as well as the use of the I.Q. test as a device for organizing schools along social-class lines.

Utilizing the works of Lester F. Ward, Albion Small, and E. A. Ross, such educators as George D. Strayer (school administration),[27] David Snedden (vocational education),[28] and Frank Parsons (vocational guidance)[29] sought to develop education for social efficiency. By the 1920s, industrial education as well as general education was organized and developed along lines of social efficiency and control.[30] Tester, administrator, and guidance counselor—all seemed dedicated to rationalizing and standardizing the system of mass education, adjusting the child to the needs of the system. Throughout the early decades of the twentieth century, most guidance counselors considered it their chief function to match native and acquired

[24] Edward L. Thorndike, "Intelligence and Its Uses," *Harper's* 140(January 1920):233.

[25] See Loren Baritz, *The Servants of Power: A History of the Use of Social Sciences in American Industry* (New York: Wiley, 1960).

[26] For the extremely questionable data and its use, see Kimball Young, "Intelligence of Certain Immigrant Groups," *Scientific Monthly,* 15(1922):444; H. H. Laughlin, *An Analysis of America's Melting Pot,* House Committee on Immigration and Naturalization, 68th Congress, 1st sess., March 8, 1929, p. 1311; House Committee on Immigration and Naturalization, *Europe as an Emigrant-Exporting Continent and the United States as an Immigrant-Receiving Nation,* by H. H. Laughlin, 68th Congress, 1st sess., March 8, 1924, p. 1311. For the inferiority of the racial groups, see T. R. Garth, "The Intelligence of Mexican School Children," *School and Society* 27(June 20, 1928):794; also R. A. Schwegler, "A Comparative Study of the Intelligence of White and Colored Children," *Journal of Educational Research* 2(December 1920):846.

[27] See Raymond E. Callahan, *Education and the Cult of Efficiency* (Chicago: University of Chicago Press, 1932).

[28] See Walter H. Drost, *David Snedden and Education for Social Efficiency* (Madison: University of Wisconsin Press, 1967).

[29] See Howard V. Davis, *Frank Parsons* (Carbondale: Southern Illinois University Press, 1969).

[30] See Bernice M. Fisher, *Industrial Education* (Madison: University of Wisconsin Press, 1967).

talents with the system's manpower needs, thus increasing the efficiency of both the individual and the system. Frank Parsons said:

> Superior efficiency flows from natural fitness—education, special and general, physical, intellectual and moral—and the influence of feelings which produce enthusiastic and painstaking labor. A sensible industrial system will therefore seek to make these feelings factors in every piece of work, to put men, as well as timber, stone, and iron, in the places for which their natures fit them—and to polish and prepare them for efficient service with at least as much care as is bestowed upon clocks, electric dynamos, or locomotives.[31]

Industry, allied with schools, would "polish and prepare" the young for efficient service. Owing to the difficulty of providing up-to-date training in a rapidly changing industrial system, while some youth received skill training in vocational technical schools, most were trained on the jobs. Actually, American industry operated the largest vocational technical-training school in the world. Although the extreme efficiency rhetoric of the earlier part of the century became subdued during the depression of the 1930s, public schools, from the kindergarten through the vocational technical and graduate schools, continued to serve the manpower needs of the business community by providing large numbers of trainable people who would easily fit into the industrial system.

Maintaining the System

The development of the Cold War and the creation of the military-industrial complex caused an acute shortage of skilled manpower. Now a second phase of the social efficiency movement in American education emerged. Those persons who once thought in terms of social efficiency now talked of manpower models, as they saw the school at all levels as an instrument to serve the manpower needs of a new technetronic society. Just as the stopwatch and Taylor symbolized the early efficiency movement, so the computer, cybernetics, Norbert Wiener, and systems analysis came to symbolize the new efficiency thrust. Among those who thought in terms of the overall needs of society during the Cold War, James B. Conant was perhaps the most influential figure. His influence was

---

[31] Frank Parsons, *The City for the People* (Philadelphia: C. F. Taylor, 1900), p. 68.

due partly to his prestigious career, and partly to his association with the Carnegie Foundation and the role that foundation had played in shaping educational policy at all levels of education. Foundations have played a major role in maintaining the corporate liberal state as well as in shaping educational policy to serve the interests of that state.[32] In virtually all of his published work on education in the post-World War II period, including *The American High School, The Junior High School,* and *Slums and Suburbs,* Conant repeatedly expressed his central concern for the maintenance of what he perceived as a democratic society. Reflecting the new efficiency values, Conant called for a national testing program that could provide an educational achievement index that was much like a gross national product.

Conant's educational recommendations directly followed from his conception of the good society. That was the competitive, open society where hard, honest work would be rewarded. Conant personified those Franklin virtues of work and diligence as well as a sense of calling and duty to the larger community. He was a Yankee pragmatic liberal who, like John Dewey and others, reflected the strength as well as the weakness of the liberal tradition. As an astute student of the possible, Conant turned moral questions into tactical survival problems. Avoidance of moral issues by emphasizing practical expediency was, however, as American as *Poor Richard's Almanac.* American pragmatic philosophy was functionally useful in developing a capitalistic system, but it failed to deal with the moral issues of the day. Thus Dewey did not find a moral issue in reporting how to effectively manipulate the Polish laborer in the national economic interest any more than Conant found a moral issue in the development of gas as a lethal weapon, or the dropping of the atomic bomb on Hiroshima. Pragmatism was a philosophy dedicated to the system's survival. Although some people questioned Conant's judgment, no one impugned his loyalty to the system and his dedication to making it work. His recommendations in *The American High School* and *The Junior High School* and *Slums and Suburbs* were to make the schools more vocationally efficient and more effective in sorting and holding students. Thus, Conant called for increased federal support for vocational guidance.

---

[32] See David W. Eakins, "The Development of Corporate Liberal Policy Research in the United States, 1885–1965" (Ph.D. diss., University of Wisconsin, 1966). Also see Merle Curti and Roderick Nash, *Philanthropy in the Shaping of American Higher Education* (New Brunswick, N.J.: Rutgers University Press, 1965).

Turning to the problem of the urban ghetto, Conant again saw vocational training and guidance as solutions to problems. Very much like Horace Mann a hundred years before, Conant argued that if the ghetto dweller could be trained and guided into the mainstream of American economic life, the "social dynamite" might be defused and the system saved from serious disruption. Interlaced throughout the discussion of American racism during the sixties was Conant's argument about cooling off the social dynamite through training for economic opportunity. The Kerner Report, for example, clearly and decisively indicted white America as racist, then failed to take the next logical step and call for an effective educational program for the children of white Americans in order to eliminate that racism. Instead, the Report proposed special education for black children.[33] One might conclude from the Kerner Report simply that the problem was not white racist attitudes, but rather black failure to meet sufficient standards to enter the economic system.[34] The burden of performance thus fell on black children. Interestingly, the economic opportunity argument could be used not only to support the idea of cooling off social dynamite, but also to transfer guilt within the system from those who held power to those who were victimized by that power.

By the end of the 1960s, both conservatives and liberals joined in common cause to protect and maintain the system. One could observe such a strange phenomenon as Milton Friedman (an avowed conservative economist) advocating such liberal, if not socialist, measures as guaranteed minimum family incomes in the interest of the system's maintenance. When both economists and manpower experts began to speak of an "acceptable" level of unemployment,[35] it was evident not only that unemployment was here to stay, but even more important, that managers considered it essential to the efficient operation of the system. The unemployment pool was, in effect, a shock absorber for the economic system. For that shock ab-

---

[33] See Bernard Spodek, "So It Doesn't Whistle," *Illinois Schools Journal* 49(Spring 1969):49.

[34] For an interesting discussion of the way Americans implement their commission findings, see Catherine Caldwell, "Social Science as Ammunition," *Psychology Today* 4(September 1970):38+.

[35] One always wonders, "acceptable" to whom? For an interesting analysis of the relationship of unemployment and education, see Willard Wirtz, "Remarks of the Honorable W. Willard Wirtz" in *Proceedings* of the Symposium on Employment, Washington, D.C., 1964, sponsored by the American Bankers Association.

sorber to function effectively, certain conditions were necessary. Those unfortunate enough to be caught in the pool had to be actively striving for employment, thus guaranteeing employers a ready and eager labor supply. In order to facilitate that condition, a graduated income was proposed. Employers of both production and service industries could then readily obtain employees and release them to the pool whenever their services were no longer required. In an interesting way, Conant's manpower-oriented educational proposal for urban slum dwellers was the complement of Milton Friedman's welfare proposal. Both served to create a manpower pool that would efficiently serve the system, and at the same time defuse the social dynamite with the least possible disruption. Neither proposal was seriously designed to eliminate the urban ghetto or the unemployment pool itself. The major threat to the system came when the Black Panthers and black nationalists generally refused to be co-opted. These groups then represented an uncontrollable threat, and therefore came under direct police action.

A key Conant recommendation for the American high school was the establishment of extensive vocational guidance services. When federal funds were increased over the following decade, they were used to support a guidance movement that increasingly directed its major efforts at psychological therapy rather than vocational guidance. The difference between the work of Frank Parsons in vocational counseling and Carl Rogers in nondirective therapy is indicative of that trend.

Individual as well as group therapy was used to overcome the alienation and depersonalization resulting from the workings of the complex bureaucratic machinery. By the late fifties and early sixties, sensitivity training as developed by such educators as Benne, Bradford, and Lippitt was found useful in overcoming and alleviating some of the personnel problems in industry and education, as well as in the churches.[36] Problems of alienation in the technetronic world were acute. Few workers—production-line, blue-collar, or white-collar—were fortunate enough to find their work intellectually, socially, and psychologically satisfying. For most, "work" was a period of lost time, an experience from which one needed peri-

---

[36] See Leland P. Bradford, J. R. Gibb, and K. D. Benne, eds., *T-Group Theory and Laboratory Method: Innovation and Re-education* (New York: Wiley, 1967). See also Chris Argyris, *Explorations and Issues in Laboratory Education* (Washington, D.C.: National Training Laboratories, N.E.A., 1966).

odic escapes. The schools reflected the meaninglessness and help-lessness that infected the world of technetronic change.

A high percentage of the 59 million students now in school have learned to live by the bell and passively tolerate boredom, irrelevance, and absurdity in their educational lives in order to achieve future material rewards accruing from selected occupations. Some thinkers have suggested that students therefore have been well trained and effectively prepared for the life they will be expected to live within the system. Many observers reject such preparation as a goal and argue for a more relevant curriculum and better teachers. The problem lies deeper than that. It lies in the very nature of this particular culture, in its values, and in the way it uses its educational system. For example, there may be something inherently contradictory between trying to "educate" for individual growth, and at the same time trying to select the "best" for the economic system. Karl Popper suggests that the latter is an impossible task with which an educational system should never be burdened. As he said:

> This should never be made their task. Their tendency transforms our educational system into a race course, and turns a course of studies into a hurdle race. Instead of encouraging the student to devote himself to his studies for the sake of studying, instead of encouraging in him a real love for his subject and for inquiry, he is encouraged to study for the sake of his personal career; he is led to acquire only such knowledge as is serviceable in getting him over the hurdles which he must clear for the sake of his advancement. In other words, even in the field of science, our methods of selection are based upon an appeal to personal ambition of a somewhat crude form. (It is a natural reaction to this appeal if the eager student is looked upon with suspicion by his colleagues.) The impossible demand for an institutional selection of the intellectual leaders endangers the very life not only of science, but of intelligence.[37]

Schools from the kindergarten to the university in the twentieth century negated the goal of educating for personal growth by playing a selecting and sorting role. More disturbing still, they became a manpower holding institution for the economic community. It is

[37] Karl R. Popper, *The Open Society and Its Enemies* (Princeton: Princeton University Press, 1950), pp. 133–134.

probably no overstatement to suggest that of the 59 million students now in school, at least 20 million are physically and mentally capable of manning most of the occupations that now exist. We have reached the absurd height of requiring twelve years of formal schooling for such occupations as clerk or night watchman. Such was not the case in the world of Benjamin Franklin. The young Franklin could move from occupation to occupation with relative ease. To be sure, in the two centuries that separate Franklin from the youth of today, American society has created a complicated technological system with a vast array of specialties. Most of these specialties, however, require minimal skills that can be learned in a relatively short time. Educational requirements are usually grossly inflated. They are concocted more in the interest of controlling labor supply than in satisfying job requirements. Employers have used inflated job requirements also to veil racial discrimination. The cooperation of educational institutions to inflate job requirements in order to delay entrance into the world of adult work creates a kind of institutional hypocrisy that seriously impairs the role of the school as a credible vehicle of education. To many students and observers, the school has become a part of the overall bureaucratic structure that imprisons people's lives. Youthful protest literature often repeats the theme of imprisonment. For example:

> the grammar school—high school—university mass education —death trip. Little classrooms, cramped with sitting, suffocating children.

> "Don't talk, children, sit there and listen to me for the next six hours, for the next five days, for the next forty weeks. If you successfully pass through the first eight years imprisonment, you can do four more years in high school. Then, if you are intelligent, fortunate, and have money enough, you can do four more years in a university. Then you can graduate and proudly be imprisoned in offices, factories, and institutions throughout the world until, at long last, you are sixty-five. Then you are free to take off more than two weeks in a row." ("Don't ask stupid questions")

> ("I'm busy right now")
> "Amen brother."[38]

---

[38] Jesse Kornbluth, *Notes from the New Underground* (New York: Viking Press, 1960).

Delaying the young's entry into adult life produces profound so-cial-psychological consequences. Franklin knew no adolescent cul-ture, largely because he lived in a society that put youth into the labor market as quickly as possible. "Youth culture," with its unique psychology, sociology, economic needs, and tastes, is largely a by-product of the social conditioning used to delay entrance into adult life. The youth culture phenomenon is related to the needs of an industrial society to delay adulthood and increasingly to standard-ize, control, and create consumer demands among various discrete age groups from childhood to adulthood. The decline of the family as an educational unit, the rise of the peer group, as well as the pro-liferation of offerings through the mass media are all parts of the youth culture syndrome. The process, it seems, is one of creating, through means of mass media, a self-image and a set of behavioral expectations that effectively set the age group apart from the con-trol of the adult. The process replaces adult control with peer group control, which is fairly susceptible to commercial manipulation. Here, again, as in the earlier efficiency movement, psychologists and sociologists played a facilitating role. While psychologists devel-oped their own psychology of adolescence, educational sociolo-gists such as Robert J. Havighurst spoke of "developmental tasks." Presumably based on both the psychological and sociological life of the child, each age group had its own tasks to be learned. Here, then, was an educational ladder up which the young might slowly climb out of the immature status to which the overall system had confined them. Each rung of that ladder was polished with the suc-cess-oriented achievement values of middle-class America, all of which held little meaning for children of the rich or the poor.

Children at both the top and the bottom of the socioeconomic ladder threatened Havighurst's middle-class world. Children of the affluent, free from the threatening sanctions of the system, found they could afford the luxury of their ideals. Radical white youth challenged the system by arguing that institutions, like men, ought to behave with moral purpose. The suggestion, for example, that the university was a moral institution and ought therefore be self-conscious about the moral implications of its decisions seemed to strike fear in the hearts and confusion in the minds of trustees and administrators of most institutions of higher learning. Affluence not only led radical youth to question some of the basic Franklin virtues of success, but it also provided freedom from the controlling de-mands of career preparation. Radical questioning of the system occurred in the arts colleges, seldom in the professional schools, mainly because of the conservative effect of the latter's vocational orientation. People bending every effort to make it within a system cannot afford the luxury of criticizing that system. They may well put their careers in jeopardy. The arts college student, all other things being equal, was in a considerably freer position than other university students.

MEANS BECOME ENDS

For most Americans, the possibility of gaining the economic and social requisites to exercise independent social criticism remained little more than a distant hope. The desire to maintain the economic-social value system without serious confrontation with its moral bearings continued to be an important characteristic of this society. American society, driven by anxious materialistic private-profit motives and narrow self-interest, did not disappear with the prosperity of the post-World War II period, nor did a transformation of values occur. On the contrary, World War II and the Cold War that followed gave birth to the warfare state. This phenomenon had the effect of postponing any serious confrontation with the system's purposes. The economic system was now maintained by a kind of military capitalism which under the guise of public interest, increasingly developed a larger control, not only over foreign affairs, but over the internal economic and social affairs of the nation.[39] With military expenditures at well over $1,000 billion in the postwar period and with 63 percent of all American scientists, engineers, and technicians working on defense projects, by 1970 it was clear that the American economy depended on a military budget for its survival. If peace broke out and military spending halted, it has been estimated that the unemployment rate of 5 percent would increase to approximately 15 percent—a level fairly close to that of 1939.[40] Since universities were the prime source of power directing the scientific and technological developments in the Cold War decades, their interests intertwined with those of government and industry.[41] With scientists employed by the industrial-military complex for national security reasons, the question of a society driven by private-

---

[39] For an interesting discussion of this problem, see Ithiel de Sola Pool's article in *Scientific Research*, Sept. 15, 1969.

[40] See Seymour Melman, *Pentagon Capitalism: The Political Economy of War* (New York: McGraw-Hill, 1970).

[41] See James Ridgeway, *The Closed Corporation* (New York: Random House, 1968).

profit motives and its self-destructive character seemed irrelevant. Increasingly, many observers came to agree with Michael Harrington that things seemed out of control and that this has been *The Accidental Century*—a century driven by the apparent necessities of technical efficiency, yet guided by no overriding humane philosophy. All kinds of artists in the postwar era repeatedly expressed the despair, chaos, and helplessness of man in a technocracy substantially out of human control.[42] A society driven by anticommunist hatreds and guided by the technologically possible had little inclination to reflect in terms of a philosophy of man or society.

The alliance of industry, government, the military, and education produced an age of considerable affluence for an ever larger middle class. As America both ideologically and practically out-materialized the Soviet Union, the American way of life came to mean little more than a vast and continuous consumption of goods and services. Fewer and fewer voices in the great middle class—most members of which existed as kept agents of the system—were heard asking the naive question, What truly humane purposes does the system serve? Most people seemed concerned only with keeping the system going and extending its co-opting benefits to minority groups that remained outside.

As population and cybernation increased, many thinkers envisioned an educational state processing people from the cradle to the grave by the end of the century. Thus, by the late sixties, Xerox, R.C.A., General Learning Corporation, C.B.S., I.B.M., and many other corporations entered the "knowledge industry" field, eager to capture a share of a market estimated at possibly $50 billion a year.

The new efficiency movement emerging served both the industrial-military complex and the educational establishment. In this movement, Rand and Systems Development Corporation played an active role. Fresh from his experiences with Systems Development, Robert Boguslaw wrote about *The New Utopias* (1965) he envisioned. There was no need, he argued, for concern with the nature of man or, for that matter, his psychological needs. Simply plug man into the system and he would adjust to whatever demands the sys-

---

[42] Interestingly, even our utopian literature has become antiutopian. Aldous Huxley's *Brave New World* and George Orwell's *1984* were both a warning and a prediction of things to come. The future they projected held little hope for individual dignity and freedom. Most disturbing, however, was the fact that Huxley's world of "soma" and "test-tube babies" and Orwell's world of "double think" became more and more a part of the social reality of twentieth-century man.

tem makes. Boguslaw went on to point out that the purpose of human engineering was to eliminate the human factor as much as possible. Along the same lines, Norbert Wiener earlier suggested that the question of human purposes might also be settled by engineering techniques. Wiener argued, "As engineering technique becomes more and more able to achieve human purposes, it must become more and more accustomed to formulate human purposes."[43] Perceptively describing modern society, Jacques Ellul, in his *Technological Society,* pointed out that gradually the overall system takes over and techniques do become ends in themselves.

Means had become ends and the perfection of technique, not the perfection of man, had become the standard. As their lives increasingly became objectified, depersonalized, and systematized, and as the technological system was used more and more not only to create means, but also ends, independent of human will, Americans reached a critical stage in the idea of enlightened progress. The materialism that gave meaning to an earlier generation now appeared not only crass, but without meaning to some of the younger generation. The revolt of the younger generation became, in part, a revolt against the meaninglessness of middle-class life measured in terms of material fulfillment without human purpose. And that revolt holds the greatest promise for a transformation of values necessary for a humane age.

Historically, however, this has been a society that has rather consistently avoided examining its moral roots. If it had examined them, it might have pondered the wisdom of consistently respecting and honoring those who, from Franklin on, found success in materialistic, competitive, cunning, and self-seeking behavior. These are the Franklin virtues undergirding a capital-producing society that the schools, down to the present, have reinforced rather effectively. These values were productive in the development of the wealthiest technological state in the world, but counter-productive concerning development of a moral culture based on humane considerations. So we have both dilemma and promise in the present age. American society may yet move from the materialistic spirit of capitalism to a transformation of values. There might still be the time and the possibility in the affluent cybernated age of the future to usher in a humane age that will enhance the dignity of man.

[43] Norbert Wiener, *God and Golem, Inc.* (Cambridge, Mass.: M.I.T. Press, 1964), p. 64.

CHAPTER 2

EDUCATION
AS A FORM OF
SOCIAL CONTROL

Joel Spring

By the beginning of the twentieth century, industrialization and urbanization had severely eroded the influence of family, church, and community on individual behavior. As the power of these institutions waned, the school became increasingly important as a primary instrument for social control. It became *the* agency charged with the responsibility of maintaining social order and cohesion and of instilling individuals with codes of conduct and social values that would insure the stability of existing social relationships. Although a preserving institution, the school was viewed as a form of internal control—and therefore more in the "democratic" tradition than such external forms as law, government, and police.

American sociologist Edward A. Ross, in a series of articles published in the *American Journal of Sociology* between 1896 and 1898, was the first to state explicitly the ideology of social control. The articles were later gathered together as a book under the title *Social Control* and attracted a wide audience among both sociologists and

This essay was first published at the Center for Intercultural Documentation, Cuernavaca, Mexico.

educators. In his study of social control mechanisms, Ross referred to education as an inexpensive form of police. In what was to become a traditional way of defining the concept, Ross divided social control into external and internal forms, stressing that future societies would probably rely more on internal or psychic than on external forms of social manipulation. Traditionally, Ross argued, internal forms of control had centered on the family, the church, and the community. The family and church had worked on the child to inculcate moral values and social responsibility to insure social stability and cohesion. The small community had provided the individual with a social context in which he saw his own interests as inseparable from those of others. In terms of social psychology, Ross believed, the individual developed within a small community a social self that was shared by other members of that same community.

SOCIAL CONTROL

Ross, writing from the perspective of the 1890s, when industrialization and urbanization were rapidly taking hold in America, arrived at the conclusion that it was precisely these institutions—the family, the church, and the community—that were disintegrating under the forces of modernity. To replace these deteriorating institutions Ross suggested new forms of control, such as mass media, propaganda, and education. Reliance on education as a new means of control, Ross argued, was in fact exactly what was becoming a characteristic of American society. More and more the school was taking the place of the church and the family. "The ebb of religion is only half a fact," Ross wrote. "The other half is the high tide of education. While the priest is leaving the civil service, the schoolmaster is coming in. As the state shakes itself loose from the church, it reaches out for the school."[1] In an extremely perceptive statement Ross saw quite clearly the parallel between the decline of the church and the rise of the school. "Step by step," he said, "with disestablishment of religion proceeds the establishment of education; so that today the moneys, public or private, set apart for schools and universities far surpass the medieval endowments of abbeys and sees."[2]

The advantages Ross saw in using the school as a central agency of control centered on his faith in the malleability of youth. In a startling and revealing statement, he argued that civilization was

[1] Edward A. Ross, *Social Control* (New York: Macmillan, 1906), p. 175.
[2] Ibid., p. 175.

reaching an understanding of the effectiveness of education for social control. "To collect little plastic lumps of human dough from private households and shape them on the social kneadingboard," he wrote, "exhibits a faith in the power of suggestion which few peoples ever attain."[3] Ross emphasized the process of schooling over curriculum content as the key to preparing the individual for society. And the advantage of the school over the home as a means of control lay in the fact that a public official was substituted for the parent. "Copy the child will, and the advantage of giving him his teacher instead of his father to imitate, is that the former is a picked person, while the latter is not." In school the child learned "the habit of obedience to an external law which is given by a good school discipline." The teacher, in Ross's terms, also represented a subtle form of authority that heightened the effectiveness of the school as an instrument of social control. He believed that "the position of the teacher gives him prestige, and the lad will take from him suggestions that the adult will accept only from rare and splendid personalities."[4]

The ideology of social control also found its place in the early university departments of urban sociology. Among the first and probably the most important was the University of Chicago Department of Urban Sociology founded by Robert Park. From here poured forth a flood of projects that influenced the whole course of urban studies in the United States. Park defined the breakdown of the neighborhood and family as the major problem of modern urban living. Deterioration of these social controls was causing social disorganization that could be halted only through the establishment of new institutional forms of control. To Park, for example, art museums and spectator sports represented means of calming the restlessness of the urban man. "It is at this point that sport, play, and art function," Park noted. "They permit the individual to purge himself by means of symbolic expression of these wild and suppressed impulses."[5] For Park the school was to have a central role in replacing the role of the neighborhood and family. Writing in the 1920s, Park concluded that indeed the school was already replacing family and neighborhood controls. "The school," he stated, ". . . has taken

---

[3] Ibid., p. 168.

[4] Ibid., pp. 164–165.

[5] Robert E. Park, Ernest W. Burgess, and Roderick D. McKenzie, *The City* (Chicago: University of Chicago Press, 1967), p. 43.

over some of the functions of the family. It is around the public school and its solicitude for the moral and physical welfare of the children that something like a new neighborhood and community spirit tends to get itself organized."[6]

The schools in the early part of the twentieth century were in fact expanding their responsibilities to act as effective instruments of control. It became common to say that the school was responsible for the whole child, which meant it had responsibility for all the child's activities. This led naturally to the idea that the school should expand its custodial functions beyond the classroom to include the child's entire social life. Play, dancing, and hobbies were to fall under the umbrella of schooling. The playground movement of the late nineteenth and early twentieth centuries had as its goal the ending of juvenile crime within the city. A Committee on Small Parks in New York City report in the 1890s claimed: "Crime in our large cities is to a great extent simply a question of athletics."[7] It seemed logical to the developers of playgrounds that the place to establish small parks was next to schoolhouses and that teachers be utilized to supervise play activities.

The role of the school expanded not only in terms of activities but also in terms of the amount of the child's time the institution occupied. This meant not only an expanded school day and year but also the institution of a summer session. Arguments given for summer schools show clearly how schooling was coming to be viewed more and more as an instrument of social control. The School Committee of Cambridge, Massachusetts, became in 1872 the first to ask for a summer school. The committee report for that year stated that summer was "a time of idleness, often of crime, with many who are left to roam the streets, with no friendly hand to guide them, save that of the police." Fifteen years later, the Cambridge superintendent wrote: "the value of these [summer] schools consists not so much in what shall be learned during the few weeks they are in session, as in the fact that no boy or girl shall be left with unoccupied time. Idleness is an opportunity for evil-doing. . . . These schools will cost money. Reform schools also cost money."[8]

---

[6] Ibid., p. 24.

[7] Sadie American, "The Movement for Small Playgrounds," *American Journal of Sociology* 4(1898):176.

[8] Sadie American, "The Movement for Vacation Schools," *American Journal of Sociology* 4(1898):291–296.

THE SORTING PROCESS

Maintaining social order represents only one aspect of social control ideology. The second role of the school as an instrument of social control consists of differentiating pupils so that their educational training prepares them for a particular social slot. Within this context, social efficiency results from the efficient allocation of human resources for the industrial needs of society. While a differentiated curriculum and vocational guidance have been important means to achieve this goal, a more important development historically was the writing of group intelligence tests for the "scientific" differentiation of students. Studying the development of group intelligence tests lends insight into what this aspect of the sorting process meant with respect to social control and schooling.

Everyone acquainted with psychology knows that there is no adequate definition of intelligence. In fact, the question of what is intelligence has been widely debated in the twentieth century. In the absence of definition, intelligence tests have been validated by correlating their results with other factors, such as social success and other tests. The selection of outside criteria for validating the tests introduces value judgments. As will be explained in more detail later, the criteria used to judge the results of the first major group I.Q. test was the ability to be a good soldier. Immediate questions about the nature of the selective process arise, of course, when these same tests are used by the schools.

The World War I army Alpha and Beta were the first major group intelligence tests developed and administered, and they became a model for the construction of future testing programs. After the armistice in 1918, the government flooded the market with unused Alpha and Beta test booklets, which educators immediately utilized. Guy M. Whipple, a leading psychologist of the time, reported in 1922 that the army Alpha test was most widely used in colleges because it was the first group test constructed by a team of well-known psychologists that had been tried on large numbers of men in the army, and because "the test blanks were procurable for several months after the armistice at prices far below what other tests could be produced."[9]

The committee of psychologists that developed the army tests first met at Henry Herbert Goddard's Vineland Institute in New Jer-

---

[9] Guy M. Whipple, "Intelligence Tests in College and Universities," *National Society for the Study of Education Year Book* 21(1922):254.

sey on May 28, 1917. Working with amazing speed the group completed its work by June 10 and after trying the tests in army camps, sent a copy of the examiner's guide to the printer on July 7. It was appropriate that the Vineland Institute was the site for this history-making event that still has a great influence on school organization. Goddard, director of Vineland, was primarily responsible for the translation and the introduction of French psychologist Alfred Binet's writings and tests into the United States. Binet had constructed intelligence tests as a vehicle for separating mentally retarded children from normal children at the behest of a commission organized by the French Minister of Public Instruction to establish standards for placing children in special schools.

From these intelligence tests Americans drew many of their ideas on test construction. Underlying the Binet test was a definition of intelligence both vague and relative. On the one hand Binet defined native intelligence as "judgment, otherwise called good sense, practical sense, initiative, the faculty of adapting one's self to circumstances."[10] On the other hand, Binet stated that intelligence was relative to the social situation of an individual. Thus "an attorney's son who is reduced by his intelligence to the condition of a menial employee is a moron . . . likewise a peasant, normal in ordinary surroundings of the fields, may be considered a moron in the city."[11] Confronted with the fact that his measurement of native intelligence varied with social class, Binet reflected the values implied in the test. While admitting that important differences in language ability between social classes might effect test results, he stated that social-class differences added validity to his test. "That this difference exists one might suspect," he wrote, "because our personal investigations, as well as those of many others, have demonstrated that children of the poorer class are shorter, weigh less, have smaller heads and slighter muscular force, than a child of the upper class; they less often reach the high school; they are more often behind in their studies."[12]

The army Alpha and Beta were developed with an equally vague definition of intelligence and depended for their validity on correlation with factors in army life. The team of army testers examined

[10] Alfred Binet and T. Simon, *The Development of Intelligence in Children* (Baltimore: Williams & Wilkins, 1916), pp. 42–43.

[11] Ibid., pp. 266–267.

[12] Ibid., p. 318.

over one million men during the course of the war, evaluating results in terms of the test's ability to select good soldiers. For instance, in one army camp officers were asked to rate their men according to "practical soldier value." Comparing these ratings to soldiers' test scores, examiners found a high correlation between an officer's rating and the results of the Alpha and Beta tests. Validating the tests with officer's ratings in other army camps, examiners placed the coefficient of correlation between 0.50 and 0.70. The head of the army psychological team concluded: "The results suggest that intelligence is likely to prove the most important single factor in determining a man's value to the military service."[13]

Army and School

What "practical soldier value" means in army life is the ability to follow orders and function within a rigidly disciplined and highly organized institutional structure. Instructions for the group examination for the Alpha test provide ample evidence that this was the meaning of intelligence that the test sought to measure, and the instructions were used almost word for word in subsequent examination booklets. For years after World War I, students taking tests were subjected to the same type of instructions given soldiers during the war. The instructions began: "When everything is ready E. [examiner] proceeds as follows: 'Attention! The purpose of this examination is to see how well you can remember, think and carry out what you are told to do. . . . The aim is to help find out what you are best fitted to do in the Army. . . . Now in the Army a man often has to listen to commands and carry them out exactly. I am going to give you some commands to see how well you can carry them out.' " In the schools these words might be translated into, "Part of being a good student is your ability to follow directions." Anyone who has taken such a test will recognize the instructions, "When I call 'Attention,' stop instantly whatever you are doing and hold your pencil up—so. Don't put your pencil down to the paper until I say 'Go! . . . Listen carefully to what I say. Do just what you are told to do. As soon as you are through, pencils up. Remember, wait for the word 'Go'."[14]

---

[13] Clarence S. Yoakum and Robert M. Yerkes, eds., *Army Mental Tests* (New York: Henry Holt, 1920), pp. 20–32.

[14] Ibid., pp. 53–55.

The army and the school are, of course, similar organizations. In a school, the superintendent sits as commander of the armies, the principal acts as field commander, the teachers as lesser officers, and below this command is a vast number of pupils. Orders flow from above and pupils, like soldiers, receive privileges but lack rights. Both organizations handle large numbers of recruits, which requires discipline and obedience to instructions. Soldiers must loyally obey commands and students must have faith that the directions they receive are in their best interests. Army test correlations with teacher ratings were very close to that of "practical soldier value." Reported correlations were between 0.67 and 0.82. Interestingly, correlations with officer ratings and teacher ratings were both higher than the 0.50 and 0.60 correlations with school marks.[15] If one assumes officer and teacher ratings depend more on character evaluation than marks, one could conclude that the group intelligence test might be more of a test of social character than of something called native intelligence.

Looked at within the context of social-control ideology, group I.Q. tests provided the mechanism for selectivity within the school. After World War I, the head of the army psychology team wrote, "Before the war mental engineering was a dream; today it exists, and its effective development is amply assured."[16] The dream of most psychologists, following their war experience, was to apply the selective procedures of I.Q. tests in all areas of society. After the war, Henry Herbert Goddard was willing to admit, "We do not know what intelligence is and it is doubtful if we even know what knowledge is." Even so, Goddard still insisted that "the efficiency of the human group is not so much a question of the absolute numbers of persons of high and low intelligence as it is whether each grade of intelligence is assigned a part, in the whole organization, that is within its capacity."[17] Selective differentiation in the school was to prepare students for selected social roles in society. The army model fit not only the school but also modern corporate structures dependent on a highly organized and stratified bureaucracy.

Quite obviously I.Q. tests, with their high degree of correlation

[15] Ibid., p. 20.
[16] Ibid., p. 197.
[17] Henry Herbert Goddard, Human Efficiency and Levels of Intelligence (Princeton: Princeton University Press, 1920), p. 35.

with "practical soldier value," did much more than differentiate individuals on the basis of something called native intelligence. Implied in the whole testing movement was judgment about individual character. Good performance on the tests was enshrined as having more social value than traditional yardsticks used to measure the worth of a man. At times in the history of Western man, qualities such as humility, honor, justice, and compassion have been considered standards by which men judged a person's social worth. Among test makers the new standard became test ability. Some test constructers, such as Edward L. Thorndike, went so far as to suggest that ability to do well on tests gave evidence of justice and compassion. From this point of view, those who were "intelligent" were also good. Thorndike tried to make his intelligence tests difficult and long so they would show not only an individual's intelligence but also "his ability to stick to a long and, at the end, somewhat distasteful task." A report received from one institution of higher learning using the Thorndike test in the early 1920s stated "that two or three students fainted under the three-hour strain, and the faculty became indignant at this alleged imposition of hardship."[18]

On the other hand, I.Q. tests discriminate against certain personality types. Tests such as Alpha and Beta that correlated with army life, and others that correlated with ability in school, discriminated against those who could not or would not function well in a highly organized institutional structure. Because the tests were validated in terms of an individual's success within such institutions, they became not so much a test of something called native intelligence but rather one of ability to perform well in organized institutions. If one assumes—and this assumption has not been proven or disproven—that engineers represent a more organizationally directed type of personality than doctors, one result of Alpha test lends support to the assumption. Army psychologists during World War I had difficulty explaining the fact that engineering officers scored one grade higher on the test than medical officers. The head of the army psychology team admitted, "There is no obvious reason for assuming that the military duties of the engineer demand higher intelligence or more mental alertness than do those of the medical officer."[19] Army psychologists tried to handle this result by arguing that there was an uneven distribution of intelligence among the various

---

[18] See Whipple, "Intelligence Tests," pp. 259–260.
[19] Yoakum and Yerkes, Army Mental Tests, p. 36.

branches of the service. They might have missed the point that medical men might have less "practical soldier" value than engineers, which after all was what the group intelligence tests were supposed to measure.

The quest for social control turned the school into a custodial institution designed to maintain the social order. It also led to differentiating and selecting students for social roles on the basis of tests validated primarily on success at institutional manipulation. All this placed extreme power in an institution that on the surface maintains the image of being benign and interested in helping the individual. The student, told it is for his own good, finds himself molded not in terms of personal needs but in terms of defined social needs and roles. The school has truly become an inexpensive form of police, one whose very authority is supported by the argument that it is a place that helps the individual, and that an individual's interests cannot be separated from social needs.

Testing as an important part of the social control mechanism fragments the individual personality by placing emphasis only on certain individual characteristics. Whether one sees I.Q. test as determining some quantity called native intelligence, or ability to conform and survive in an institution, the result is the same. Honor, justice, compassion, humility, and goodwill all fall by the wayside when this selective mechanism is applied in the school. The student learns to place the greatest importance on that quality of intelligence that best meets the needs of society, which generally means the needs of industry and the corporate structure. In the end, the loss of other qualities creates not only incompletely developed individuals, but also a society directed intelligently, but not necessarily humanely.

CHAPTER 3

‹

PROGRESSIVE SOCIAL PHILOSOPHY: CHARLES HORTON COOLEY AND EDWARD ALSWORTH ROSS

Paul C. Violas

Frederick Wiseman's film "High School" presents Northeast High in Philadelphia, picturing it as a depressing kaleidoscope of regimentation, conformity, and reverence for authority. The school does not encourage initiative, creativity, and individualism. Rather, it almost seems as though administration and faculty are engaged in a conspiracy to smother the excitement of learning while claiming to develop responsible citizens.

There are a number of ways to analyze this disturbing scenario, and they might be applied to the analysis of many contemporary social problems. Conditions at Northeast High developed under the tutelage of teachers and administrators weened on supposedly liberal educational philosophy and methodology. Perhaps, though, professional educators had little impact on this and other schools because of control exercised by the forces of tradition. Or perhaps the educators were not really liberal. On the other hand, perhaps the film was not valid; perhaps the scenario does not reflect the reality of American schools. All these possibilities offer some degree of comfort. They provide a refuge for those who can say with Professor Richard Hofstadter: "The tradition of Progressive reform is the one upon which I was reared and upon which my political sentiments were formed, as it is, indeed the tradition of most intellectuals in America."[1]

If one can assume that the problems of Northeast High either do not exist or are the result of too little progressive-liberal reform, then one is spared the discomfort born of searching criticism of cherished beliefs. It becomes most uncomfortable, however, to hear a person suggest that the roots of many contemporary problems reside within the progressive-liberal tradition. Such an irritating suggestion, nevertheless, may lead to efforts to understand present social issues. This essay will attempt to plumb some aspects of the progressive-liberal tradition through an examination of the social philosophy of two important progressive theorists, Charles Horton Cooley and Edward Alsworth Ross.

Cooley, one of the founders of the study of social psychology and professor of sociology at the University of Michigan, was a moving force in progressivism until his death in 1929. President Theodore Roosevelt's introduction to Ross's *Sin and Society*[2] suggests Ross's influence. The president stated that after being introduced to Ross's first book by Justice Oliver Wendell Holmes, he had sympathetically read all the academician's subsequent works.

David W. Noble suggested that progressive ideology represents a paradox because its advocacy of absolute freedom somehow accepted conformity.[3] The idea of paradox rests, of course, on the conviction that the progressives indeed championed freedom. If they did, then it might be assumed that repressive currents in American social history must have come from other sources. Richard Hofstadter has argued that these repressive currents were an outgrowth of "anti-intellectualism."[4] Close analysis of the social theories of Cooley and Ross, however, reveals a sophisticated intellectual justification for repression.

Cooley's and Ross's vision of the good society was that of a rationally organized, corporate state. Existential autonomy of the individual was considered dysfunctional. Their good society was grounded in the belief that man received his self, identity, and hu-

---

[1] Richard Hofstadter, *The Age of Reform* (New York: Knopf, 1955), p. 12.

[2] Edward Alsworth Ross, *Sin and Society* (Boston: Houghton Mifflin, 1907).

[3] David W. Noble, *The Paradox of Progressive Thought* (Minneapolis: University of Minnesota Press, 1958).

[4] Richard Hofstadter, *Anti-Intellectualism in American Life* (New York: Knopf, 1962).

manity from the social group. They assessed their era as one of rapid change requiring ever-increasing functional specialization and the articulation of such specialization in a rationalized social system. Resultant corporatism had significant implications for individuals. It required, Cooley and Ross argued, the establishment of a meritocracy and the assignment of each individual to the functional slot for which he was best suited. Social problems in an age of change could be intelligently attacked only if an expert elite was allowed to make correct social decisions. Education, they contended, would play a crucial role as the chief sorting agency in society.

The most serious threats to the Cooley-Ross good society were any factors that might lower the quality of the social raw material and disrupt social unity. They argued for immigrant restriction to exclude undesirables, for example, and advocated eugenics to improve the racial quality of native Americans. In constructing their ideal society, they systematically articulated nativistic racism and glorification of imperialism as an essential part of their social theories.

Social unity was essential to the efficient operation of their corporate society. Social unity in an age characterized by change, however, required that change occur within rational social structures in order to channel it in directions favorable to corporate unity. Cooley and Ross advocated equality of opportunity, social mobility, and a pluralism of social types as means of obtaining unity. Always, however, they championed controlled pluralism, and opportunity for mobility only within functional specializations. All of these parameters were determined by the corporate organism.

Ordered change in Ross's and Cooley's world could be achieved, they believed, only if a new kind of group-directed discipline was developed. The purpose of this discipline was to harness irresponsible individualism. It was considered much more effective than corporal discipline because it would control man internally. The group would stimulate and sanction not only man's actions, but his motives and desires as well. Perhaps the significant paradox of progressivism is that for so long it has been considered an ideology of freedom.

Both Cooley and Ross were seductive writers. Their fertile minds, possessing keen insights into the complexities of social life, rejected positivism and its rather simplistic mechanical models of man and society. Their sympathetic humanitarianism, which held that human nature was capable of responding to appeals other than brute force and terror, was reassuring when contrasted with the mechanistic evolutionary thesis of Herbert Spencer or William Graham Sumner. This melding of the more noble sentiments of nineteenth-century German idealism, the psychic evolution of Lester F. Ward, and the social melioration of the Enlightenment tended to disarm the potential critic of Ross's and Cooley's social philosophy.

THE ORGANIC SOCIETY

The foundation of the Cooley-Ross sociology was the organic concept of society. Both followed the commonplace turn-of-the-century practice of constructing a biological model for society. Ross argued that investigators must conceive of society as "something distinct from a bunch of persons! For we can regard this society as a living thing, actuated, like all the higher creatures, by the instinct for self-preservation."[5] Answering his own rhetorical question, "Is society anything more than the sum of the individuals?" in the affirmative, Cooley went on to state that "there is an organization, a life-process, in any social whole that you cannot see in the individuals separately. . . . You must see your groups, your social processes, as the living wholes that they are."[6] Both endowed this organic social order with such anthropomorphic attributes as mind, spirit, and will. In this living social organism, they said, each individual, as the cell in a physical body, had its stake, its life, and its future. The social order was the referent for validating all individual activity. The social parameters that Ross and Cooley prescribed for the actions of individuals were integrally related to this organic society. They rejected the simplistic notions of a mechanical positivistic relationship between the individual and society in favor of an organic, evolving, transactional process.

The Individual and the Social Group

One issue concerned the nature of the social boundaries within which the individual should function. Although both men agreed about the individual's need to accommodate to society, there was between them subtle divergence over the nature of the accommo-

---

[5] Edward Alsworth Ross, Social Control (New York: Macmillan, 1912), p. 67.

[6] Charles Horton Cooley, Human Nature and the Social Order (New York: Scribner's, 1902), p. 48.

dation. Cooley's individual was bound to the primary group, which was "fundamental in forming the social nature and ideals of the individual."[7] The primary group produced "a certain fusion of individualities in a common whole, so that one's very self, for many purposes at least, is the common life and purpose of the group."[8]

David Noble interprets Cooley as a spokesman for the individual's ability to transcend the matrix of his society and rely on the private self rather than conform to the public self. As evidence for this he cites Cooley's statement "a man does right as he follows his conscience."[9] Noble's interpretation, however, is less persuasive when one examines how Cooley believed the conscience was developed. Cooley asserted: "The individual and the group are related in respect to moral thought quite as they are everywhere else; individual conscience and social conscience are not separate things."[10] He was even more explicit when describing the formation of the conscience of those he called degenerates: "The group forms his conscience, and what it countenances or admires will not seem wrong to him."[11] Repeatedly the individual was viewed as simply part of a social group. Cooley went so far as to say that "the notion of a separate and independent ego is an illusion."[12] He consistently rejected the possibility of an individual distinct from or out of rapport with the social group. He considered such separation the basis of insanity. "The essence of insanity, from the social point of view . . . ," Cooley said, "is a confirmed lack of touch with other minds in matters upon which men in general are agreed."[13] Thus he regarded "the antithesis, society versus the individual, as false and hollow."[14] Cooley believed that "there is no general opposition between the individual and the social whole"[15] and that "the aims of the individual and of the whole are the same."[16]

[7] Charles Horton Cooley, *Social Organization* (New York: Scribner's, 1909), p. 23.

[8] Ibid.

[9] Noble, *Paradox of Progressive Thought*, p. 105.

[10] Cooley, *Human Nature*, p. 377.

[11] Ibid., p. 416.

[12] Cooley, *Social Organization*, p. 5.

[13] Cooley, *Human Nature*, p. 144.

[14] Ibid., p. 41.

[15] Charles Horton Cooley, "Reflections Upon the Sociology of Herbert Spencer," in *Sociological Theory and Social Research* (New York: Holt, 1930), p. 273.

[16] Charles Horton Cooley, "Personal Competition," in *Sociological Theory and Social Research*, p. 182.

Although Ross concurred with much of Cooley's analysis of the formation of the self, he did not believe it followed that the individual and society would necessarily have the same aims. He argued merely that the individual should be in concert with his society, and that society had diverse mechanisms at its disposal to enforce such harmony. Ross held that "from the interactions of individuals and generations there emerges a kind of collective mind evincing itself in living ideals, conventions, dogmas, institutions and religious sentiments which are more or less happily adapted to the task of safeguarding the collective welfare from the ravages of egoism."[17] The investigator who discovered the mechanisms of social control had a special responsibility to convey such knowledge only to "those who administer the moral capital of society" for "to betray the secrets of ascendency is to forearm the individual in his struggle with society."[18]

The individual that Ross posited embodied the possibility of a separate ego and identity apart from the social group in which they were formed. Cooley's individual, however, was significantly different, at least from a philosophical perspective. His individual embodied the social group in which he was formed. There could be no real conflict between the individual and the social group, because only in the social group, Cooley argued, could the individual become truly human. Cooley's construction was similar to the classical Athenian concept of the citizens' relation to the polis. This concept held, however, that the citizen gained his humanity in the polis in so far as both approximated some higher ideal. For Cooley, the ideal was grounded directly in the social group; from that the individual had no appeal. Regardless of the philosophical importance of this difference between Cooley and Ross, it made little practical difference in their social theories.

Complexity and Specialization

Both argued that the individual should act in harmony with his social group and that the social group ought to contribute to the larger social order. Such harmony was considered vital for a modern society becoming increasingly complex. Cooley and Ross were certain that this complexity required a multiplication of special functions and greater differentiation among individuals. The individual

[17] Ross, *Social Control*, p. 293.
[18] Ibid., p. 441.

would become dysfunctional, they believed, unless he acted as a member of a team and recognized that his contribution was structured by the team's requirement. Cooley's and Ross's major problem was how to determine the special function and contribution of each individual.

As was the case with so many intellectuals at the turn of the century, Ross and Cooley's survey of the contemporary social landscape produced both fear and optimism—fear of uncertainty bred by the breakdown of the stability they had perceived in nineteenth-century American society; optimism, indeed exhilaration, over the heights attainable by the human spirit if only technology could be applied as successfully to the social order as it had been to the material world. All progress depended on the health of the growing social organism, which in turn was conditioned by the effective activity of its individual units. Cooley, in an early paper on the theory of transportation, suggested an outline for such progress: "development or evolution, the organization of social forces, implies unification of aim, specialization of activities in view of a common purpose, a growing interdependence among the parts of society."[19] The future, he repeatedly asserted, would demand even greater specialization and differentiation than the past. This new differentiation would be different from older types in that it would require a continuous reorganization of persons. Ross's emphasis was also on the interdependence occasioned by the growing complexity of the social organism. And interdependence required the kind of trust in one's fellows and faithful execution of duties that could only be guaranteed, Ross believed, in a highly structured society. He argued that "a dense population lives in peace by aid of a protecting social order."[20]

Society's health, and hence the safety of the individual, Ross and Cooley believed, depended on efficient specialization. Such a condition would not result from accident or by chance. Each new function in society rested on all the others. Cooley argued that "the greater the complexity and interdependence of the social order the greater the need of soundness in all parts of its structure. The unreliable man is a public nuisance."[21] The more important the position

[19] Charles Horton Cooley, "The Theory of Transportation," in *Sociological Theory and Social Research*, p. 40.

[20] Ross, *Sin and Society*, p. 35.

[21] Cooley, "Personal Competition," p. 189.

occupied by the unreliable man, the increasingly dangerous he would become. This idea led both Cooley and Ross to consider social selection and assignment to function as significant problems for society. Cooley stated: "The theory of a free order is that everyone is born to serve mankind in a certain way, that he finds out through a wise system of education and experiment what that way is, and is trained to enter upon it."[22]

Unequality and Meritocracy

This theory of a "free order" implied that men are not equal. Both Cooley and Ross repeatedly stated that they did not consider men equal. Their belief in the basic inequality of men had important ramifications for their social philosophy, for they used it to justify salient restrictions on the masses. Cooley confessed: "I do not know how to talk with men who believe in native equality: it seems to me that they lack common sense and observation."[23] Similarly, Ross justified elitism in decision-making, in part because "associates are unequal in capacity."[24] He described the urban migration of superior individuals from southern Michigan and from Illinois and Wisconsin as "folk depletion," which left those areas "fished-out ponds populated chiefly by bullheads and suckers."[25]

Choosing a metaphor that likened the masses to lower species was hardly accidental. It represented a merger of nineteenth-century primitivism with Social Darwinism, which in turn yielded a view of human nature evolving along a continuum with some men still at the animal stage and an elite few as truly rational men. This concept had much currency among progressive intellectuals and both Cooley and Ross embraced it. Their development of this concept bears some interesting resemblance to the social theory that Sigmund Freud later developed in his *Civilization and Its Discontent*,[26] especially as he argued the necessary authority of the ego over the id. Cooley and Ross continuously pictured the masses as unable to reason because they were governed by emotion and other base drives. Ross made this point quite clear as he said, "Laws, hu-

---

[22] Cooley, *Social Organization*, p. 239.

[23] Ibid., p. 214.

[24] Edward Alsworth Ross, *Foundations of Sociology* (New York: Macmillan, 1905), p. 140.

[25] Edward Alsworth Ross, *The Social Trend* (New York: Macmillan, 1922), p. 47.

[26] Sigmund Freud, *Civilization and Its Discontent* (London: Hogarth Press, 1930).

man and divine, are addressed to a being who is able not only to calculate, but to anticipate penalties and overrule his impulses. But this reasonable person . . . is still far from common. . . . There is an unreclaimed jungle in man from which wild impulses break forth and lay waste the tilled fields. . . . Consequently, we must fight the devil with fire, quell one emotion with another, and supplement control by sanctions with control through the feelings."[27]

Cooley, in somewhat more restrained language, agreed: "Rationality, in the sense of a patient and open-minded attempt to think out the general problems of life, is, and perhaps always must be, confined to a small minority of even the most intelligent populations."[28] The masses, "people of much energy but sluggish intellects," were the "repositories of moral energy."[29] Although Cooley was certain that "the scientific point of view can never be that of most of mankind,"[30] he contended that "the ideal aim of intelligence seems to be the rational control of human life."[31] Reason was always to hold the reins: "What we judge to be right is simply the rational"[32] and, conversely, "the wrong, the immoral, is, in a similar sense, the irrational."[33] Ross agreed that few persons had reached the level of human rationality when he stated: "How few are competent to do their own social philosophizing!"[34] The implications were obvious, too, as Ross argued that the state was the best instrument of social control because "the state is an organization that puts the wise minority in the saddle."[35] If the irrationality of the common man was to be controlled through his feelings, it would be necessary to channel his emotions into convictions through a "social religion" and "nothing less than Genius is able to frame these convictions into a system that can lead men captive."[36]

---

[27] Ross, *Social Control*, pp. 196–197.
[28] Cooley, *Human Nature*, p. 80.
[29] Ibid.
[30] Ibid., p. 341.
[31] Charles Horton Cooley, *Social Process* (New York: Scribner's, 1918), p. 382.
[32] Cooley, *Human Nature*, p. 358.
[33] Ibid., p. 361.
[34] Ross, *Social Control*, p. 316.
[35] Ibid., p. 74.
[36] Ibid., p. 208.

The role of intelligence was to direct the social organism in its own best interests. Each man, Cooley argued, desires to have society function "in the best way possible, so as to express to the fullest that human nature that is in himself. And as a guarantee of this he demands that they (social functions) shall be conducted on an open principle, which shall give control of them to the fittest individuals."[37] Both Ross and Cooley believed that American society was emerging from a past in which the social order had been controlled for class interests. The new elite would avoid this because its members were not only rational scientists but an "ethical elite" that would promote the "general welfare."[38] This elite would be guided by the "laboratory spirit," which "is the moral capital of the expert, the divine spark that keeps him loyal and incorruptible."[39] As society became more progressive, concluded Cooley, "the more it needs leaders, men who know how to guide the forces, how to distribute them in the most effective order and to assign everyone to the duty that he can best perform."[40] Popular control over the expert was objectionable because, Ross argued, this expert would be "restrained by his professional conscience, strict control is nagging and hampering."[41]

These progressive sociologists' conception of the elite and the common man had a quite predictable effect on their view of democratic participation in society. Ross asserted that democracy "does not deny that men are as gold, silver and copper in relative worth."[42] He charged "one man, one vote does not make Sambo equal to Socrates in the state, for the balloting but registers a public opinion. . . . With modern facilities for mind influencing mind, democracy, at its best, substitutes the direction of the recognized moral and intellectual elite for the rule of the strong, the rich, or the privileged."[43] In somewhat less inflammatory language, Cooley expressed quite similar sentiment, saying that "collective judgments in literature, art

[37] Cooley, *Social Organization,* p. 147.

[38] Ross, *Social Control,* p. 316.

[39] Ross, *Social Trend,* p. 171.

[40] Cooley, "Personal Competition," pp. 191–192.

[41] Edward Alsworth Ross, *The Principles of Sociology* (New York: Appleton, Century, 1938), p. 282.

[42] Edward Alsworth Ross, *Changing America* (New York: Century, 1912), p. 4.

[43] Ibid., pp. 4–5.

and science . . . are democratic judgments, in the sense that every man has been free to take part in proportion to his capacity, precisely as the citizen of a democracy is free to take part in politics."[44]

Both men, however, retained some role for the masses—that of ultimate judgment on the results of expert planning. Cooley put it: "The rule of public opinion, then, means for the most part a latent authority which the public will exercise when sufficiently dissatisfied with the specialist who is in immediate charge of a particular function. It cannot extend to the immediate participation of the group as a whole in the details of public business."[45] This did not mean, however, that the expert should ignore the public, Ross argued, for "there ought to be an interchange of thought between those who have to determine policies and those who may be called upon to carry them out. The higher may well consult with the lower, while retaining the power to decide."[46]

The progress of humanity demanded experts able to organize and channel the emotional energy of the masses into socially desirable outlets. Therefore, the question of sorting individuals into functional roles was important to Cooley and Ross. They opted for the rationalization of individual and social life. Cooley stated the problem quite succinctly: "If we are to make the process of life rational there is nothing which more requires our attention than the adaptive organization of persons. At present it is, for the most part, a matter of blind experimentation, unequal from the point of view of individuals, and inefficient from that of society."[47]

This adaptive organization of persons, they contended, should preserve the individual's mobility, opportunity, and freedom. These terms, however, derived their meaning from the context of a complex social organism composed of interdependent but, nonetheless, unequal cells. Thus, opportunity logically became, according to Cooley, "such freedom of conditions that he [the individual] may find his natural place, that he may serve society."[48] He believed there was only one efficient way to assure such opportunity. "If we are really to have opportunity we must evidently make a science of

[44] Cooley, *Social Organization*, p. 125.

[45] Ibid., p. 131.

[46] Ross, *Principles of Sociology*, p. 253.

[47] Cooley, *Social Process*, p. 56.

[48] Ibid., p. 57.

it, and apply this science to the actual interworking of the individual with the social whole."[49] The preference of the common man would have little impact in the determination of his place in society and his life possibilities. This selection was to be determined according to the needs of society by experts best able to ascertain those needs and assess the capacity of individuals to fulfill them. Indeed, Cooley asserted that "a good administrative mind is a place where the organization of the world goes on. It is the center of the social process, when choices are made and men and things are assigned their functions."[50]

Scientific administration of occupational and social roles, Ross and Cooley insisted, could not be left to individual caprice. Unlimited individual choice was socially inefficient. Much time and effort was required to match one's ability to his functional role in society. Some individuals might never find the appropriate level and many would become demoralized by the pursuit of aspirations too grand for their capacities. Cooley argued that "an all wise despot would undoubtedly be the most efficient; and it is conceivable that he might give to men a great deal of personal liberty and provide for any amount of social change."[51] Although he rejected this ideal solution as unrealistic for American social conditions, it did contain the basic sentiment embodied in his realistic proposals. Some agency was required to sort men in an efficient manner, allow for optimal social change, and authorize socially acceptable amounts of personal liberty.

Both Cooley and Ross embraced the idea of the nation's schools as society's primary sorting agency. The efficiency of the selection process depended on an individual's completing schooling prior to attaining adulthood. They contended that schools should open to every child the possible careers for which he was suited, a plea to relate education to society that found continued reinforcement in liberal thinking during the twentieth century. John Dewey's praise of the Gary schools in Schools of Tomorrow[52] and James B. Conant's recommendations in The American High School Today[53] are both

[49] Ibid., p. 59.

[50] Ibid., p. 91.

[51] Cooley, "Personal Competition," p. 169.

[52] John Dewey and Evelyn Dewey, Schools of Tomorrow (New York: Dutton, 1915).

[53] James B. Conant, The American High School Today (New York: McGraw-Hill, 1959).

continuations of this theme. Progressives considered the public school the crucial institution in which to conduct society's scientific administration of personnel.

Cooley and Ross also embraced the cherished liberal faith in child study and individualized instruction. Contrary to the usual rhetoric describing these concepts, however, their major concern was not liberation of the individual as individual. Rather, they viewed the concepts as a means of increasing the individual's usefulness to society. Cooley advocated a "special study of each child with a view to making the most of him and teaching him how to make the most of himself."[54]

Both sociologists expected psychology to play a major role in the child-study movement. Foreshadowing the future scientism in the career-ordaining function of schooling, Cooley prophesied that "psychological tests should be of considerable help, and will no doubt become more and more penetrating and reliable."[55] Ross, even more emphatically, mapped the route the educational testing empire has since followed when he said, "When, furthermore, a technique has been worked out for testing the abilities and limitations of the pupil, the school will be able to discover which applicants have and which have not the traits requisite for success in a particular calling. When it can do this it will be charged with the responsibility of guiding youths into their vocations as well as imparting the skills which these vocations call for."[56]

The vocational function of schooling would not be limited to precollegiate education. Cooley suggested that "the universities should select and train men in all the more intellectual functions, including literature and the fine arts, inspiring them with ideals which, as members of special groups, they would uphold and effectuate for the good of society."[57] At all levels, apparently, education's main function was to sort and train.

Ross and Cooley repeatedly contrasted this system of social selection with a caste system. The advantages of schooling over heredity seemed obvious to both sociologists. The modern world was paced by change. Caste, however, was static and could not respond to

---

[54] Cooley, "Personal Competition," p. 183.

[55] Cooley, *Social Process*, p. 64.

[56] Ross, *Principles of Sociology*, p. 599.

[57] Cooley, *Social Process*, p. 392.

change. The Ross-Cooley system was keyed for change and could adapt to meet the vicissitudes of invention and fortune. It supposedly offered everyone the opportunity to develop capacities to their highest social usefulness. This system rested on the belief that men were unequal in abilities and that schools, aided by psychological tests, could fairly ascertain each individual's ability, assign him a vocational goal, and train him to become effective in it. Ideally, each individual was free to develop his capacity to its fullest as long as it was consonant with society's needs. Even this ideal, however, broke down under the weight of the authors' class, race, and ethnic biases. Their writings clearly reveal that they did not expect everyone to seize with equal dispatch all the possibilities for self-development. Cooley boldly proclaimed: "An Englishman or a German will seize upon all the opportunities in sight and demand more when an Italian or a Spaniard will perhaps make no use of those that are at hand."[58]

Racism and Ethnocentrism

The functional specialization of the rationally organized Cooley-Ross society required a redefinition of individualism to emphasize the importance of social efficiency and science. Their projected social ideal depended on successfully meshing interdependent units. Thus the quality of the raw material from which these units would be shaped was extremely important. Both Cooley and Ross viewed their raw material with alarm. Their analysis of non-Anglo-Saxon peoples accepted and transmitted to the liberal tradition much of the insidious racism and ethnic prejudice current at the turn of the century. Cooley was more tempered than Ross, probably because he seemed uncertain as to the origin of the inferiority of non-Anglo-Saxons. He argued that while "it is *even* possible to doubt whether there are any important innate psychical differences among the several branches of mankind, it is certain that different spirits are to be found in different races."[59] Nevertheless he was willing to offer racists proposals based on these psychical differences. Ross more emphatically stresed differences among races when he wrote that "races certainly appear to differ in the strength of these native propensities. . . . The Negro has a fiercer sex appetite than other men,

---

[58] Cooley, "Personal Competition," p. 170.
[59] Cooley, *Social Process*, p. 274 (emphasis added).

. . . the Southern Italian has a bent for murder, . . . the Irishman has an uncommon taste for fighting, the Jew for money-making."[60] Ross on the other hand emphasized that good environmental influences could render significant improvements when he reported that "the change a few years of our electrifying ozone works in the dull, fat-witted immigrant suggests that our proverbial alertness, cleverness and lucidity betoken stimulus rather than brain power."[61]

Both Cooley and Ross were disturbed by what Ross had called "race suicide." The superior race, native white American, was not as prolific a breeder as the "other half." The superior race's decline in relative numbers would have frightful consequences for the nation. "The cheap stucco manikins from Southeastern Europe," Ross lamented, "do not really take the place of the unbegotten sons of the granite men who fell at Gettysburg and Cold Harbor."[62] Because the "Slovaks," "Syrians," and "Italians" were "undersized in spirit, no doubt as they are in body, the later comers lack the ancestral foundations of American character, and even if they catch step with us they and their children will, nevertheless, impede our progress."[63]

Both sociologists argued that the inherent inferiority of certain immigrant stocks required new laws to exclude those who would debase the national stock. They lent the prestige of their "scientific analysis" of society to the mounting demand for legislation to restrict immigration according to racial and ethnic criteria. Unlimited immigration, according to Cooley, would weaken "that common spirit, that moral unity, that willing subordination of the part to the whole, that are requisite to a healthy national life."[64] Similarly, Ross charged that "cheap travel and full steerages make mock of this ideal of nationality. Any prosperous country which leaves its doors ajar will presently find itself not the home of a nation, but a 'polygot boarding-house'. . . . Coolies at the breech cloth stage of attire, such as you find in the back districts of the Far East, will jostle the descendents of the Puritans."[65] With uncanny predictive ability he forecast: "Travelers, officials, students, scholars, merchants, and artists will be

[60] Ross, *Principles of Sociology*, p. 60.

[61] Ross, *Foundations of Sociology*, p. 391.

[62] Ibid., p. 392.

[63] Ibid., p. 393.

[64] Cooley, *Social Process*, p. 280.

[65] Ross, *Social Trend*, p. 217.

able to go anywhere without molestation. It is only the broad masses that will be hindered from migration."[66]

Ross's and Cooley's writings carried through the implication of their racist sentiments for American attitudes toward non-Anglo-Saxon and non-Nordic peoples. One can find the intellectual defense of modern imperialism at the core of their progressive social theory. Their organic theory of society was simply extended to include the whole of humanity. Cooley claimed that "there is some attempt to sympathize with alien nations and races, civilized or savage, and to help them to their just place in the common life of mankind."[67] Their "just place" would undoubtedly be determined in the same fashion recommended for determining the social slot for the individual Americans. He offered the United States' treatment of Cuba as an example of a nation "acting upon generous principles which one may reasonably expect to expand as time goes on."[68] Ross, as usual, was more outspoken regarding the "just place" of "other peoples." In *The Social Trend* he stated: "The easy destruction of the dervishes by machine-guns at the battle of Omdurman settled it that henceforth the barbarian is out of the running save as the instrument of an advanced people."[69] He sketched the grim reality of modern imperialistic wars with frightening strokes as he elatedly asserted: "Now, in western Europe and in America, there exists an industrial technique which alters the face of society wherever it goes. . . . Nothing can check its triumphant expansion over the planet. . . . The white man of today spreads his economic gospel, one hand on a Gatling, the other on a locomotive."[70]

Eugenics

The menace of foreign ethnic and racial impediments to American progress represented only one side of the problem. The other was pollution resulting from native "degenerate types." Ross agreed with Cooley's dictum: "Social improvement and eugenics are a team that should be driven abreast"[71] Cooley also stated how eugenics

---

[66] Ibid., p. 13.

[67] Cooley, *Social Organization*, p. 181.

[68] Ibid., p. 323.

[69] Ross, *Social Trend*, p. 217.

[70] Ross, *Foundations of Sociology*, p. 365.

[71] Cooley, *Human Nature*, p. 15.

should be instituted. "Scientific tests should be made of all children to ascertain those that are feeble-minded or otherwise hopelessly below a normal capacity, followed by a study of their families to find whether those defects are hereditary. If it appears that they are, the individuals having them should, as they grow older, be prevented from having children to inherit their incapacity."[72] It is instructive to note the class bias in their conception of "degenerate." Cooley found great eugenic value in the "upper class," which "does, after all, contain a large number of exceptionally able families."[73] Ross also displayed his class bias as he argued that "from a quarter to a third of the paupers are hereditarily defective. Half or more of the chronic inebriates are victims of a bad heredity."[74] He recommended custodial care or sterilization for what he termed "the devil's poor."[75] This is not to suggest that either Cooley or Ross agreed with all the crude eugenic and sterilization proposals formulated during their time. It does mean, however, that their writing did lend a cloak of intellectual respectability to such dehumanizing projects.

Controlled Pluralism

It might seem that the demand to protect national unity through eugenics and immigration restriction rested somehow in contradiction with the widespread diversity that would supposedly result from Ross's and Cooley's campaign for increased functional specialization. The paradox evaporates, however, when one explores the proposed relationship among these specializations. They were all to be part of a larger spiritual and organic whole, each contributing to that whole. Surgery would be necessary only when a cell was dysfunctional to the organism. Such repressive measures were proposed only when an individual subgroup presented a threat to the larger society. A more typical response was to search for some way to socialize the recalcitrant unit and channel its energies into socially useful activities.

Cooley believed that "in an organized life isolation can not succeed, and a right specialization does not isolate."[76] Specialization

---

[72] Ibid., pp. 12–13.
[73] Cooley, *Social Process*, p. 223.
[74] Ross, *Principles of Sociology*, p. 17.
[75] Ibid., p. 399.
[76] Cooley, *Human Nature*, p. 150.

was to be related to the homogeneity of the social organism by the development of an understanding of its role. "We must be taught to do some one thing well," Cooley said, "and yet never allowed to lose our sense of the relation of that one thing to the general endeavor."[77] Ross suggested that national festivals could be used to secure necessary unity. The more complicated a society became, he argued, "the more it has need of magnificent and frequent festivals."[78] Similarly, Cooley believed that "everyone ought to have an alma mater" that he could frequently revisit to revitalize his social spirit.[79] He likened the resultant social devotion to a nationalistic religion. For this patriotic communicant, Cooley contended: "His country, for the time being, is the incarnation of God, and in some measure this is true of any group which embodies his actual sense of a greater life than that of his own more confined spirit."[80] Thus, the keynote of specialization was social unity and through that unity, social control.

Controlled pluralism, indeed, was built into all Ross-Cooley social philosophy. This was not a pluralism that would allow each component a separate identity to be developed according to its own internal needs and logic. No, it was ordered diversity in which each component developed according to the needs and logic of the whole and obtained its *raison d'être* from its contribution to that whole. The society would be composed of groups, each individual receiving his identity and direction from his group, and all groups fused to the larger social order. Ross referred to this function as the development of types that the individual would emulate. Each specialized group, he argued, would "develop for its members an invisible pressure subordinating them to the welfare or aims of the association."[81] These aims, naturally, were subordinate to the general welfare of the larger society of which the group was a functioning part.

Cooley's formulation was more explicit: "We need, then, a system of social groups, corresponding to the system of functions in society, each group having *esprit de corps*, emulation and standards

---

[77] Cooley, *Social Organization*, p. 118.

[78] Ross, *Principles of Sociology*, p. 389.

[79] Cooley, *Social Process*, p. 74.

[80] Ibid., p. 75.

[81] Ross, *Social Control*, p. 232.

within itself, and all animated with a spirit of loyalty and service to the whole. . . . Freedom, self-expression and competitive spirit would be cherished, but could not degenerate into irresponsible individualism."[82] These groups would include professions, unions, and social classes. Both argued that the individual could not be a useful member of society unless he was influenced by the constraints of beneficent group pressure. Cooley asserted: "Class loyalty in the pursuit of right ends is good. . . . If there is not class consciousness, men become isolated, degraded and ineffective; if there is too much, or the wrong kind, the group becomes separate and forgets the whole."[83] Ross concurred with this distinction between good and bad class consciousness. He argued that the wrong kind of class consciousness caused social control to degenerate into "class control" in which one class tried to dominate the others for its own selfish ends. Class control, he believed, destroyed the trust so requisite for an interdependent society.[84]

Social classes, and other social groups, were to control their individual members through *esprit de corps*. Ross and Cooley expressed special concern regarding the inherent potential for selfish class conflict which would destroy the desired social unity. One way to check this was to infuse each class with a spirit of service. "The feelings between classes will not be very bitter," Cooley believed, "so long as the ideal of service is present in all and mutually recognized."[85]

Moreover, it was necessary to convince each individual that he merited the assignment to render a particular social service. Exceptionally able and ambitious youth in the lower classes posed a potentially disruptive threat to social unity. Cooley pointed out that "no system can long endure that does not make a point of propitiating the formidable ambition of youth by at least an apparent freedom of opportunity."[86] Interclass mobility would continually funnel able men into the upper classes, and contribute to stability as the able would identify themselves with the class to which they aspire.[87]

[82] Cooley, *Social Process*, p. 143.

[83] Cooley, *Social Organization*, p. 242.

[84] Ross, *Social Control*, pp. 376–394.

[85] Cooley, *Social Organization*, p. 302.

[86] Ibid., p. 233.

[87] Ibid., p. 274; Ross, *Foundations of Sociology*, p. 288.

As representation from their ranks rose, the masses would be convinced their lot was in fact just.

When describing the difference in class antagonism displayed in Europe and America, Cooley observed that "a healthy, self-reliant tone, a disposition on the part of the masses of men to attribute their fortunes, good and bad, to something in themselves, is more general, I believe, in this country than in Europe, and may be ascribed largely to the comparatively free and open conditions that prevail here."[88] Although Ross disagreed with Cooley's assessment of the degree of mobility, he agreed with the principle. He said, "The poor do not generate a militant ethos of their own if their elite are able to escape upward."[89] Cooley's conservative social-class bias showed again when he said:

> When the way of ambition is opened to the most energetic individuals, the sharpest teeth of discontent are drawn, and the masses of men very willingly avoid trouble to themselves and to society by keeping on in the paternal road. . . .
>
> I am inclined to expect that, owing to somewhat more settled conditions of life, inheritance of function will be rather more common, and the tendency to see the individual as one of a stock rather greater, in the future than in the immediate past. On the other hand it is nearly certain that educational opportunities will become more open and varied, making it easier than now for special aptitude to find its place. These things are not inconsistent, and both will make for order and contentment.[90]

Cooley's affinity for the existing social order also surfaced when he cautioned union men against their "selfish use of power."[91] He further warned that working men "are not so badly off that they cannot be worse, and, unless they lose their heads, will always unite with other classes to preserve that state of order which is the guarantee of what they have. . . . All solid betterment of the workers must be based on and get its nourishment from the existing system

---

[88] Cooley, "Personal Competition," p. 210.

[89] Ross, Social Control, p. 402.

[90] Cooley, Social Organization, p. 237.

[91] Ibid., p. 288.

of production, which must only gradually be changed, however defective it may be."[92]

RATIONAL STANDARDS AND RESPONSIBLE DISSENT

Implicit in Cooley's and Ross's social recommendations was the necessity to bind the individual to a structure that defined the parameters of his possibilities. Order and continuity were essential aspects of the structure that would protect the larger social order. Cooley defined the "ethical aims of society" as "simply rational aims, representing the ideal of efficient total organization."[93] When the individual was forced to act outside this "higher sort of social organization," Cooley believed that "human nature, thrown back upon crude impulse, falls into sensualism and disorder."[94] Any radical social change, he argued, was destructive of this essential structure because "it is apt to break down established social relations and with them the moral order and discipline upon which the individual depends."[95]

Their analysis of the increased incidence of divorce provides an example of this belief that the individual was dependent upon structure. Ross charged that the "machine has captured most of the domestic processes," and destroyed the women's place in the economic structure of the family.[96] Men and women were, both argued, unable to cope with the resulting flux in family functions. Cooley maintained, moreover, that "personal affection is at best an inadequate foundation for marriage." Therefore, some new structure would be needed to salvage the family.[97] He believed that a new structure should be an ethical ideal—"both parties ought to be subject to some higher idea, in reverence for which they may raise above their own imperfections."[98] Ethical structure would replace economic structure as the basis for family, and both were considered superior to human affection in producing family stability. As

[92] Ibid., p. 277.

[93] Charles Horton Cooley, "Political Economy and Social Process," in *Sociological Theory and Social Research*, p. 258.

[94] Cooley, *Social Process*, p. 176.

[95] Ibid., p. 180.

[96] Ross, *Changing America*, p. 57. Cooley expressed similar sentiments in his *Social Organization*, p. 368.

[97] Cooley, *Social Organization*, p. 367.

[98] Ibid.

much as they desired stability, however, Cooley and Ross recognized that social change was an important fact of modern life. Their problem was to channel that change in ways to maintain the basic structures they believed necessary for civilized life. Cooley asserted: "The secret of a stable society is simple: give all forms of energy a chance to express themselves within the system."[99]

In order to do this the system would have to be relatively flexible. It would condone controlled conflict, useful kinds of nonconformity, and responsible free speech. In modern terminology, it would weclome "responsible nondivisive dissent," and Ross's distinction between constructive and destructive criticism of standards has a contemporary ring. He considered the destructive critic "dangerous" because he "dissected standards to death" and showed their arbitrary, inconsistent, and burdensome nature while not maintaining his sense of responsibility for the destruction he would thus cause.[100] Reflecting a similar sentiment, Cooley contended that "the system should be as tolerant and hospitable *as its institutional nature permits.*"[101] He further argued for institutions that "are not only tolerant but which, in a measure, *anticipate* and welcome *useful kinds* of nonconformity."[102]

One might question how much exceptionality, peculiarity, eccentricity, idiosyncrasy, originality, or individuality could be represented in the kind of nonconformity an institution might anticipate and welcome as useful. Cooley seemed certain that a responsible general will could be organized. Out of this general will he hoped would develop a "moral whole which prescribes rules, directs some agitation into healthy and moderate channels and takes away all rational grounds for violence or revolution."[103] In this context, Cooley encouraged individualism, for he believed "individuality, provided it be in harness, is the life of institutions, all vigor and adaptability depend upon it."[104] From this kind of individualism, he hoped, the good community could be constructed. He described

---

[99] Charles Horton Cooley, *Life and the Student* (New York: Scribner's, 1931), p. 39.

[100] Ross, *Principles of Sociology,* pp. 570–571.

[101] Cooley, *Social Process,* p. 324 (emphasis added).

[102] Ibid., p. 324 (emphasis added). For a contemporary statement of this position, see Donald Michael, *The Unprepared Society* (New York: Basic Books, 1968).

[103] Cooley, *Social Organization,* p. 308.

[104] Ibid., p. 324.

that community in these terms: "A well ordered community is like a ship in which each officer and seaman has confidence in his fellows and in the captain, and is well accustomed to do his duty with no more than ordinary grumbling."[105]

Self-discipline

The "harnessing of the individual" called for a new kind of discipline. Physical, coercive discipline of the past, Ross and Cooley charged, was dysfunctional in a complex urban society. Cooley felt that "self-discipline" had to replace "compulsory discipline."[106] Compulsory discipline was effective only in the village setting, where each individual was under constant community surveillance. Under modern urban conditions, Ross argued, "we cannot watch everybody all the time. As family and property are always exposed to the clandestine acts of trespassers, the need arises for something that will intimidate a man when he is alone."[107] Persuasion, he reasoned, was the way to bend "the stubborn individual will" to social purposes. And this persuasion was, according to Ross, "little else than the art of introducing into a man's mind unwelcome ideas so neatly as not to arouse the will to expel them."[108]

Cooley, resorting to his scheme of functional differentiation as the mechanism for self-discipline, opted for "a system of disciplinary groups corresponding to the chief aspects of human endeavor, each one surrounding the individual with an atmosphere of emulation and with ideals of a particular sort."[109] Both writers agreed that professions, occupational organizations, organized playgrounds, youth groups, schools, sports, and art were excellent means to inculcate the right kind of self-discipline. They described art as having a special power to stimulate the emotions and instill a feeling of social solidarity. Cooley said: "As music can melt us into a oneness of emotion, so drama and fiction can arouse and enlarge our social imaginations."[110] Ross suggested that a fictional type such as "Jean

[105] Ibid., p. 351.
[106] Cooley, *Social Process*, p. 346.
[107] Ross, *Social Control*, p. 126.
[108] Ibid., p. 147.
[109] Cooley, *Social Process*, p. 148.
[110] Ibid., p. 412.

Valjean will draw its imitators upward."[111] Obviously such a conception of art rejected as an "absurd phrase" the idea of "art for art's sake."[112] Indeed, it also rejected the notion that there was anything of intrinsic value in play, sports, or education.

The use of education to develop "self-discipline" illustrates the fact that self-discipline was not meant to imply that the individual was to be autonomous. The school, for Cooley, was a convenient manipulative device for the formation of the right self-discipline through group pressure. He stated: "Since the school environment is comparatively easy to control, here is the place to create an ideal formative group, or system of groups, which shall envelop the individual and mold his growth, a model society by assimilation to which he may become fit to leaven the rest of life. Here if anywhere we can insure his learning loyalty, discipline, service, personal address, and democratic co-operation, all by willing practice in the fellowship of his contemporaries."[113] The natural enthusiasm and idealism of youth were the raw material for the development of self-discipline, for "all we need to do . . . is to provide the right channels for it."[114]

Ross, with his usual flair for the colorful phrase, projected a similar stance: "To collect little plastic lumps of human dough from private households and shape them on the social kneedingboard, exhibits a faith in the power of suggestion which few peoples ever attain to. And so it happens that the role of the schoolmaster in the social economy is just beginning."[115] He believed that "the schooling of the young is a long–headed device to promote order.[116] Ross and Cooley could justify such a conception of education because they believed the individual must be defined in terms of a social group, and that his purpose in life was service to that group. Cooley argued: "It is a poor sort of an individual that does not feel the need to devote himself to the larger purposes of the group."[117] He

---

[111] Ross, *Social Control,* p. 268.

[112] Ibid., p. 273.

[113] Cooley, *Social Process,* p. 73.

[114] Ibid.

[115] Ross, *Social Control,* p. 168.

[116] Ibid.

[117] Cooley, *Social Organization,* p. 39.

believed that one way to insure that the individual be "ruled by emulation in service" was that he "be immersed in a group spirit and organization of which such emulation is a part."[118]

Freedom

Cooley's analysis of freedom summarized the idea that a series of functionally determined social groups dominate the individual. He emphatically rejected the notion of freedom as "the absence of constraint."[119] Such a concept was unacceptable because it was based on the twin beliefs that the individual could act apart from his social group and that all individuals could exercise choice. His rejection of the latter belief reflected his conviction that men were innately unequal and his fear of the irrationality of the masses. In rhetoric that would find increasing resonance in the twentieth century he declared that "an incontinent exercise of choice wears people out, so that many break down and yield even essentials to discipline and authority in some form. . . . Not so few so far exhaust the power of self-direction as to be left drifting at the mercy of undisciplined passions."[120] Free choice was seen as a burden too heavy for the many to bear. He even suggested that the burden of choice resulting from political enfranchisement of Negroes may have "caused an increase of insanity among them."[121]

Cooley's definition of the individual in terms of the social group led him to support a positive concept of freedom that further tied the individual to society. "Freedom can exist only in and through a social order," he argued.[122] His freedom allowed everyone a fair chance for assignment to his right place in his social order. It would, however, operate on a different level for different individuals and groups. Cooley said that "freedom is relative to the particular persons and states who are to enjoy it, some individuals within any society, and some societies as wholes, being capable of a higher response than others. . . . It is freedom to be disciplined in as rational a manner as you are fit for."[123] Since he had argued that the masses

---

[118] Cooley, *Social Process*, p. 137.

[119] Cooley, *Human Nature*, p. 422.

[120] Ibid., p. 70.

[121] Ibid., p. 433.

[122] Ibid., p. 427.

[123] Ibid., p. 426.

were ruled by sentiment, presumably when disciplined they would be free from appeals to their emotions. Freedom, for Cooley, was *"opportunity for right development."*[124] Freedom was to be qualitatively dissimilar for unequal groups and individuals. Nevertheless, for all people, right development was to be socially determined.

Frederick Wiseman's final scene in "Northeast High" portrays an elderly teacher reading a letter from a boy in Vietnam. After mentioning that he had made the school his life insurance beneficiary, the former student said he did not think of the war or his function in it because he was just a body doing a job. With tears in her eyes and a faltering voice, the teacher said, "When we get a letter like this, we know we are doing our job." This statement graphically displays the impact of a liberal ideology and its disfigured concept of freedom as opportunity to find the kind of service for which the individual is best fitted. The problems of Northeast High, as a microcosm of American society, seem less paradoxical, but hardly less frightening, when examined in the context of the progressive-liberal social philosophy of Charles Horton Cooley and Edward Alsworth Ross.

[124] Ibid., p. 423.

CHAPTER 4

JANE ADDAMS
AND THE NEW
LIBERALISM

Paul C. Violas

The concluding decades of the nineteenth century witnessed a number of significant changes in American society. Local isolation diminished as numerous inventions facilitated the development of rapid transit and instantaneous communications. Concurrently, immigration and urbanization brought sweeping demographic changes. At the same time, relationships between employers and employees underwent major modifications as new economic practices led to the rise of corporate industrialism. Intellectual trauma caused by the idea of evolution, studies in comparative theology, and higher criticism of the Bible contributed to social tensions. All these changes served to smash once-potent images and metaphors that had governed nineteenth-century thought. The values represented by these images and metaphors had been imposed upon Americans by the rural village. With a multitude of informal devices for social control, the village had provided American life with a powerful stabilizing influence. By the end of the century, as many intellectuals were aware, the American village as a source of social control was dead. Intellectuals became increasingly distressed by

This essay was originally presented as a paper at the American Educational Research Association meetings in Chicago, April 3–7, 1972.

the implications this passing held for the social cohesion of the nation.

Given existing conditions, the advent of a new century must have been a frightening experience for Americans nurtured on the folksy homilies of Scottish realism, or the doctrines of unity from transcendentalism, or on evangelical Protestantism's beatific faith in brotherhood and love. Protestant theology retained little of the intellectual vitality that had recommended it as a refuge in the past. For many it probably seemed that reality could no longer be adjusted to images and metaphors drawn from nineteenth-century sources. To view the world as simple and benign was increasingly difficult. Where men had imagined order, they now saw conflict. Hate and distrust were accepted as commonplace in the industrial world. Violence, with organized workers confronting capital's mercenaries at the Carnegie plant in Homestead and the police in Chicago, had become ordinary. Capitalists were even sabotaging competitors' factories and installations. Americans had always considered the city evil, yet the major demographic fact of the last quarter of the century was rapid urbanization.

THE THREAT OF IMMIGRATION

Compounding this perturbation was the ominous specter of immigration. By 1900, America was a land of strangers. Almost half the population was foreign-born or children of foreign-born. What seemed most threatening was the radical shift in the source of immigration from northern to southern and eastern Europe.[1] The new immigrant, representing a cultural background much different from the old, was seen not only as a threat to the mores of America but often as the cause of all problems in American society. Somehow this stranger in the land had to be changed if flux and chaos was to abate.[2]

---

[1] For example, during the following decades the percentage of the total immigrant population that came from southern and eastern Europe was as follows: 1861–1870 —1.4 percent; 1871–1880—7.2 percent; 1881–1890—18.3 percent; 1891–1900—51.9 percent; 1901–1910—70.8 percent. Samuel Eliot Morison and Henry Steele Commager, *The Growth of the American Republic*, vol. 2 (New York: Oxford University Press, 1956), p. 177.

[2] See Maldwyn Allen Jones, *American Immigration* (Chicago: University of Chicago Press, 1960), pp. 177–278; Thomas F. Gassett, *Race* (New York: Schocken Books, 1968), pp. 287–339; John Higham, *Strangers in the Land* (New York: Atheneum, 1969).

Within this milieu a new middle-class liberal ideology emerged. Considered humanitarian, this new liberalism developed in part as a response to the immense human suffering in urban America. Rejecting the classical liberal's concern for individual autonomy, the new liberals embraced community. They repeatedly expressed faith in the rational knowledge of the best minds and ridiculed the irrationalism of the unclean masses. The new liberals supported policies that moved the nation toward the acceptance of a compulsory corporate state in which the individual would be simply a part of the greater collective unity. The key concern became the development of more effective means of social control in order to eliminate conflict and to establish the harmonious organic community. Classical liberalism with its concern for individualism and negative liberty[3] gave way to a newer version that emphasized community and positive freedom —freedom that meant psychosociological control of the individual within a controlled community.

This change required a rationalization of both man and society. Although most of the new liberals were not in sympathy with the profit objectives of the corporate industrialists, their rationalization of society and manipulation of individuals was in harmony with the needs of these industrialists. Loren Baritz has shown the manipulative devices used by industry since the 1920s to rationalize the worker.[4] More recently, James Weinstein has demonstrated the identicalness of purpose between the progressives and corporate industry in their efforts to rationalize society since the turn of the century.[5] The new liberals were not at odds with these efforts. In fact, the new liberal ideology, developed earlier, not only lent intellectual credence to such endeavors, but, with its attendant metaphors, became the standard by which twentieth-century America determined its needs and measured its successes.

Jane Addams was a principal architect of this new liberalism, and any reappraisal of twentieth-century American liberalism would be incomplete without an analysis of her social philosophy. Born September 6, 1860, in the rural community of Cedarville, Illinois, her childhood was illuminated by the images and directed by the val-

---

[3] See Isaiah Berlin, *Four Essays on Liberty* (New York: Oxford University Press, 1969), p. 131.

[4] Loren Baritz, *The Servants of Power* (New York: Wiley, 1965).

[5] James Weinstein, *The Corporate Ideal in the Liberal State* (Boston: Beacon Press, 1968).

ues of the nineteenth-century American village. For Miss Addams, those values and images found their highest expression in the life of her father, John Addams, apparently the central figure in her early life. Certainly her recollections of this period indicated he was "so distinctly the dominant influence" that all of the important events of her childhood involved him.[6] The impact of this relationship can be seen in much of her adult work. As late as 1912, she found it necessary to justify to her dead father her role in the Progressive party convention that had allowed all-white delegations from the Southern states.[7]

Miss Addams' cherished memory of her father endowed him with the pious moral capital of nineteenth-century American evangelical Protestantism. John Addams was a devoutly religious and God-fearing man who did not suffer from the divisiveness of sectarian affiliation.[8] His personal honesty was of highest repute. One of his obituaries claimed that during his years in the Illinois legislature, he "had never been offered a bribe because bad men were instinctively afraid of him."[9] Moreover, the history of his economic life was a justification of the Protestant work ethic. From meager beginnings he rose to a position of economic and political leadership in his community, his hands bearing evidence of his devotion to the miller's trade.[10] In addition, John Addams was dedicated to the ideal of the brotherhood of all men. The two men he most admired because of their concern for a wider social unity were Abraham Lincoln and Joseph Mazzini.[11] Her father was the exemplar whom Jane Addams tried to emulate and the standard by which she measured all social philosophy.

Jane Addams first became aware of the contradiction between social ideal and social reality when, at age six, her father drove her through the poor quarter of Cedarville. Her response was both interesting and instructive. She first expressed shock that people should live "in such horrid little houses so close together." Then she voiced the conviction that "when I grow up, I should, of course, have a

[6] Jane Addams, *Twenty Years at Hull House* (New York: Macmillan, 1935), p. 1.

[7] Jane Addams, "The Progressive Party and the Negro," *Crisis* 5(November, 1912): 30–31.

[8] Addams, *Twenty Years at Hull House,* p. 16.

[9] Ibid., p. 33.

[10] Ibid., pp. 11–12.

[11] Ibid., p. 21.

large house, but it would not be built among the other large houses, but right in the midst of horrid little houses like these.''[12] The paternalism implicit in this response is reflected in much of her later work. To Jane Addams, the slum represented a failure of the nineteenth-century American village. This failure seemed responsible for much of the misery and pain that attended the life of the "other half." As the village declined, the social control it exercised over selfish individualism lessened. Barbarity and conflict characterized the new urbanized social and industrial order. Profoundly moved by sordid urban conditions, Jane Addams strove to ameliorate the attendant suffering. Her life work was an attempt to develop a new kind of community that would be relevant to twentieth-century conditions and yet preserve the values she felt her father had exemplified so well.

THE ORGANIC SOCIETY

At the heart of her effort was an attempt to replace the social control implicit in the village community with controls more suitable to an urban environment. The rural village community had collapsed under the pressures of rapid transit, improved communications, industrialization, urbanization, and immigration. Jane Addams proposed to use these very forces to erect a new community with more effective devices for social control. Like so many new liberals, she embraced the concept of an organic society as the superstructure for the new community. Achieving this new organic society required significant reforms, but they would transform the immigrant masses, the industrial order, and the style of urban life. Jane Addams, however, was not a radical. On the contrary, the intent of her proposed reforms was conservative. Her efforts were directed at conserving the older moral values under siege at the turn of the century.

Basic to most social philosophy resting on the concept of an organic society is the understanding that the individual must be subordinate to the larger social group. As the cell is insignificant when compared to the physical body, analogously, the individual has little importance when measured against the social body. The individual's value is assessed relative to his social value. The person, there-

[12] Ibid., pp. 4–5.

fore, is considered a means to social ends and not, as Kant argued, an end in himself.

So it was with Jane Addams' social philosophy. This view of society buttressed her understanding of contemporary events. A tenet of the new liberalism that she shared was the belief that the nation was moving from an era of individualism to one of collective association. She argued that "to attain individual morality in an age demanding social morality, to pride one's self on the results of personal effort when the time demands social adjustment, is utterly to fail to apprehend the situation."[13] The fundamental characteristic of democracy for Jane Addams was not individual freedom. It was, rather, the "identification with the common lot which is the essential idea of democracy."[14] The drive for a "deeper and more thorough-going unity" she believed to be the consuming trend of urban life. And this drive was based in the "essential likeness of the common human nature; for after all, the things that make men alike are stronger and more primitive than things that separate them."[15] The basis for "civic virtue" and the new "moral culture" would be the man "who thinks of himself, not as an isolated individual, but as a part in a social organism."[16] Miss Addams contended that the developing "fraternal relationship" would lead to "the discovery of a new vital relation—that of the individual to the races—which may lay the foundation for a new religious bond adequate to the modern situation."[17] She considered the motive power for the development of a collective social order to be the modern equivalent of the thirteenth-century social forces "which resulted in the building of the Gothic cathedrals."[18] If men could be made to understand their correct relationship to society, then the symbols of twentieth-century society would be able to move men as effectively as the cross and the Virgin moved thirteenth-century men.

Jane Addams had trouble identifying clearly the social unit that would provide the new locus of loyalty, commitment, and control.

[13] Jane Addams, *Democracy and Social Ethics* (New York: Macmillan, 1902), pp. 2–3.

[14] Ibid., p. 11.

[15] Jane Addams, *Newer Ideals of Peace* (New York: Macmillan, 1907), pp. 2–3.

[16] Addams, *Democracy and Social Ethics,* p. 269.

[17] Addams, *New Ideals of Peace,* pp. 19–20.

[18] Ibid., p. 22.

It is clear, however, that her new ideal community was quite similar to the Social Gospel concept of the Brotherhood of Man. She rejected the family as a primary object of loyalty. Filial loyalty was too narrow and selfish: "Our democracy is making in-roads upon the family, the oldest of human institutions, and a claim is being advanced which in a certain sense is larger than the family claim."[19] Family claims on its individuals' loyalty would have to be significantly altered in order to develop the ideal community.[20] For similar reasons, Miss Addams rejected social class,[21] ethnic groups,[22] geographic areas,[23] and even the nation-state[24] as the source of individual identification and validation. She asserted that men must devote themselves to the largest possible social unit and develop a sense of "cosmic patriotism." This "latent fellowship between man and man" would include "those emotions which stir the spirit to deeds of self-surrender and to highest enthusiasm."[25]

In one sense, urbanization and immigration presented a severe challenge to the development of the kind of community Jane Addams believed essential for the alleviation of human suffering. She understood that both movements had contributed to the destruction of the older community. In so doing, urbanization and industrialization became instrumental in the rise of unrestrained individualism, which she viewed as the root of modern human suffering. Nevertheless, she argued that both contained potential forces for the development of the new ideal. The city contained much evil that required understanding and reform: "Let us know the modern city in its weaknesses and wickedness, and then seek to rectify and purify it."[26] A substantial portion of that evil was the result of unrestrained, selfish individualism. The demand for unity, however, increased as cities continued to grow in size and diversity. "A deeper and more thoroughgoing unity is required in a community made up

---

[19] Addams, *Democracy and Social Ethics,* p. 77.

[20] Ibid., p. 100.

[21] Addams, *Twenty Years at Hull House,* p. 434.

[22] Jane Addams, *The Spirit of Youth and the City Streets* (New York: Macmillan, 1909), p. 141.

[23] Jane Addams, "A Function of the Social Settlement," *Annals of the American Academy of Political and Social Science* 13(May 1899):342–344.

[24] Addams, *Newer Ideals of Peace,* p. 231.

[25] Ibid., p. 236.

[26] Addams, *Spirit of Youth,* p. 14.

of highly differentiated peoples than in a more settled and stratified one, and it may be logical that we should find in this commingling of many peoples a certain balance and concord of opposing and contending forces; a gravitation toward the universal."[27] Like most new liberals, Jane Addams easily made the unwarranted leap from the knowledge that some restraint was necessary for communal living to the demand for "self-surrender" to the commonweal. The theme of unity provided the springboard. A longing for unity permeates most of her writings.

Like the city, the immigrant also presented both a threat and a hope. There is little doubt that Miss Addams held the southern European immigrant in rather low esteem. "Primitive," "illiterate," "unskilled," "clannish," "simple," "credulous" and "ignorant" are words she commonly used to describe those immigrants.[28] She complimented American workmen for their efforts in "the gigantic task of standardizing the successive nations of immigrants."[29] Nevertheless, the southern European immigrant could be particularly useful, she argued, because he was more malleable than older Americans: "The undeveloped peasant may be much more valuable to us here than the more highly developed, but also more highly specialized, town dweller, who may much less readily acquire the characteristics which the new environment demands."[30] Such immigrants were more easily controlled, she argued, because in the process of severing the old world ties they "are reduced to the fundamental equalities and universal necessities of human life itself, and they inevitably develop the power of association which comes from daily contact with those who are unlike each other in all save the universal characteristics of man."[31] The immigrant, for Jane Addams, presented a threat because his different ethnic background disrupted American cultural unity. The relative ease, however, with which he could be stripped of his cultural foundations and reduced to the simplest common elements of humanity enhanced his value as a building block for her new community.

[27] Addams, *Newer Ideals of Peace*, p. 16.

[28] See especially *Democracy and Social Ethics*, pp. 182, 184, 229; *Twenty Years at Hull House*, pp. 200, 209, 299; "Why the Ward Boss Rules," *Outlook* 58:879; "A Function of the Social Settlement," *Annals of the American Academy of Political and Social Science* 13(May 1899):337.

[29] Addams, *Newer Ideals of Peace*, p. 93.

[30] Ibid., p. 62.

[31] Ibid., p. 14.

The Expanded School

Jane Addams considered this building process one of education. She wanted the individual's educational experiences to promote social unity, arguing that the school should provide the child with experiences that have "a social value" and "teach him to direct his own activities and adjust them to those of other people."[32] For the immigrant child, the school had particular significance. His family, she asserted, "has no social life in any structured form and can supply none to the child. He ought to get it in school and give it to his family, the school thus becoming the connector with the organized society about them."[33] The schools were to play an integral role in the reshaping of the immigrant to facilitate his usefulness to the community.

In concert with many other new liberals, Miss Addams' conception of education was not limited to what took place in the schools, but included all of the social institutions and forces that impinged upon the individual. It was essential that these forces provide the individual with a store of common memories and shared experiences that would act as cement for the new organic society. She argued: "The nation can be saved only by patriots who are possessed of a contemporaneous knowledge."[34] Much of the conflict that had severed the fabric of the older community resulted from a lack of understanding among protagonists. Even families had disintegrated, Miss Addams believed, "because our experiences have been so unalike that we cannot comprehend each other. The old difficulties incident to the clash of two codes of morals must drop away, as the experiences of various members of the family become larger and more identical."[35] The formula for unity required shared experiences which were the result of group activity rather than individual enterprise. She asserted: "We must demand that the individual be willing to lose the sense of personal achievement, and shall be content to realize his activity only in connection with the activity of the many."[36]

---

[32] Addams, *Democracy and Social Ethics*, p. 180.

[33] Ibid., p. 184.

[34] Addams, *Newer Ideals of Peace*, p. 113.

[35] Addams, *Democracy and Social Ethics*, p. 93.

[36] Ibid.

The potential for social control through "cooperative" activity implicit in this statement became explicit when Miss Addams extolled the forces the factory system could exact through such activity: "There is no doubt that it would bring a new power into modern industry if the factory could avail itself of the *esprit de corps,* that triumphant bouyance which the child experiences when he feels his complete identification with a social group."[37] She further argued that simply having people do the same tasks was not, in itself, sufficient. "We naturally associate a factory with orderly productive action; but similarity of action, without identical thought and cooperative intelligence, is coercion, and not order."[38] Mere compliance with the goals of the group was not adequate; the individual had to make group norms his own. This would require one to surrender his individual identity for a collective group identity in the interest of harmony and unity.

The rejection of coercion and forms of physical force as a method of social control formed a significant aspect of the new liberalism Jane Addams espoused. She laid the blame for "much of the maladministration of our cities" on the fact that American governmental theory "depended upon penalties, coercion, compulsion, remnants of military codes to hold the community together."[39] Such methods were survivals of a more primitive past; for the present, she argued, "There would seem to be but one path open to us in America. That path implies freedom for the young people, made safe only through their own self-control."[40] Thus Miss Addams, like many other twentieth-century liberals, defined freedom as control. Freedom depended on "self-control." The independent, autonomous, individual self was to be submerged in the collectivity of the group as an interdependent cell of the organic society. Only when he desired what the group desired would the most effective kind of social control, the internalization of group norms, be effected.

The vital task, for Jane Addams, was to develop methods to facilitate this internalization process. She viewed art, history, the play impulse, and recreation as possessing irresistible unifying power.

[37] Addams, *Newer Ideals of Peace,* p. 172.

[38] Ibid., p. 173.

[39] Ibid., p. 34.

[40] Addams, *Spirit of Youth,* p. 45.

Art was defined as "that which causes the spectator to lose his sense of isolation."[41] Miss Addams always feared isolation because isolation might allow the individual to think selfish or antisocial thoughts. Aware that the conditions of life for most of her clients at Hull House could foster "antisocial" responses to their hardships, she expressed hope that art might blunt these responses if it could function as a mechanism to escape present conditions and, at the same time, connect the individual with the historic progress of the race.

> After all, what is the function of art but to preserve in permanent and beautiful form, those emotions and solaces which cheer life and make it kinder, more heroic and easier to comprehend; which lift the mind of the worker, from the harshness and loneliness of his task, and, by connecting him with what has gone before, free him from a sense of isolation and hardship?[42]

The study of literature at Hull House had a dual function. It was to provide an opiate and at the same time promote social unity. Reflecting on the impact of the Shakespeare Club, Miss Addams stated:

> I recall that one of its earliest members said that her mind was peopled with Shakespeare's characters during her long hours of sewing in a shop, that she couldn't remember what she thought about before she joined the club, and concluded that she hadn't thought anything at all. To feed the mind of the worker, to lift it above the monotony of his task, and to connect it with the larger world, outside of his immediate surroundings, has always been the object of art, perhaps never more nobly fulfilled than by the great English bard.[43]

Jane Addams strenuously directed the effort to channel the worker's thoughts away from the dehumanizing aspects of his industrial situation. Her goal was to eliminate any potential for class conflict that

---

[41] Addams, *Democracy and Social Ethics,* p. 57.

[42] Addams, *Spirit of Youth,* p. 57.

[43] Addams, *Twenty Years at Hull House,* p. 435.

might disrupt the desired social unity. Although her analysis of the alienation process in modern industrialism was remarkably similar to that of Marx, she proposed, as a first step, to change the individual worker rather than change the institutional structure of the factory system. The primary purpose of art, therefore, was to provide an opiate for the masses that would modify the divisiveness wrought by their protest movements. The positive force flowing from art was its ability to channel a person's impulses into a larger conception of his function in the organic society.

History, too, played an important role in Jane Addams' effort to produce self-disciplined, organically related units for her new community. When properly used, she believed, history would unite the individual to his society by demonstrating both the importance of his particular role and its historic development. She saw history as documenting the orderly evolutionary progress of humanity, making personal suffering and hardships simply a temporary part of the transition to a better future. She stated that the worker, "more than other men, needs the conception of historic continuity in order to reveal to him the purpose and utility of his work; he can only be stimulated and dignified as he obtains a conception of his proper relation to society."[44] The conservative impact of this kind of history was clearly reflected in her discussion of the Hull House Labor Museum. Miss Addams, after "many talks with Dr. Dewey," devised an exhibit of seven spinning wheels arranged in historic sequence.[45] Although one might question the relevance of sweatshop inmates' studying spinning wheels, the objective was quite clear: this exhibit "enabled even the most casual observer to see that there is no break in orderly evolution if we look at history from the industrial standpoint; that industry develops similarly and *peacefully* year by year among the workers of each nation."[46]

It is significant that Jane Addams, living in Chicago during the Pullman strike and the Haymarket riots, wanted the workers to learn from history that industry develops "peacefully" with no break in "orderly evolution." She proposed to teach the worker that even when his situation was desperate, industrial conflict was not necessary. Should not the worker, she asked, be "comforted by knowing

[44] Addams, *Democracy and Social Ethics,* p. 206.
[45] Addams, *Twenty Years at Hull House,* p. 237.
[46] Ibid. (emphasis added).

that other historical periods have existed similar to the one in which he finds himself, and that readjustment may be shortened and alleviated by judicious action; and is he not entitled to the solaces which an artistic portrayal of the situation might give him?"[47] When the individual understood the historic progress of evolution and his role in the present transition stage, she believed that he would be receptive to the internalization process that would produce a self-disciplined member of the community.

Diffusing Conflict

A serious problem resulting from modern industrial organization was the overspecialization of work that divorced the worker from the finished product and produced a sense of alienation among the production workers. Jane Addams' desire to diffuse conflict because conflict might produce divisiveness and, thereby, threaten social unity dictated her response to this problem. The worker needed, she believed, to have a sense of his own personal value and importance in the total process that would engender a feeling of belonging. She asserted: "If a working man is to have a conception of his value at all, he must see industry in its unity and entirety; he must have a conception that will include not only himself and his immediate family and community, but the industrial organization as a whole."[48] Such a conception would kindle the joy and solace she believed inherent in "collective labors."[49] These understandings and emotions would produce both better products and happier workers. Participation in this collective act would more than replace the older spirit of the individual craftsman. "A man who makes year after year, but one small wheel in a modern watch factory, may, if his education has properly prepared him, have a fuller life than did the old watchmaker who made a watch from beginning to end."[50] Only when the worker understood the big picture of which he was a small but integral part, could he really belong to the community. This sense of belonging would facilitate the internalization process by which the individual derived his identity from the group identity.

[47] Ibid., p. 240.

[48] Addams, *Democracy and Social Ethics,* p. 213.

[49] Ibid., p. 219.

[50] Addams, *Spirit of Youth,* p. 127.

Thus self-direction became community direction, eliminating much of the need for external coercion.

Jane Addams recommended properly directed children's play as another device to help graft the individual into an organic relationship with his community. The basis of her argument against child labor was that it denied society the opportunity to impose mature, self-disciplined workmanship in the child's play. "A modern state," she contended, "might rightly concern itself with the effect of child labor upon industry itself."[51] What American industry most sorely needed, Miss Addams believed, was the "instinct of workmanship," a quality she so ardently admired in German society.[52] She believed this quality could develop in a modern machine economy only if the worker were self-directed, self-disciplined, and motivated by a spirit of cooperation. She said: "As the foremen of factories testify again and again, factory discipline is valuable only up to a certain point, after which something else must be depended on if the best results are to be achieved."[53]

Children's play could provide the training ground for self-disciplined cooperation. "Play," she asserted, "is the great social stimulus, and it is the proven motive which unites children and draws them into comradeship."[54] Play in Miss Addams' community would be an important substitute for police action, self-discipline replacing police discipline. The play impulse, however, had to be carefully supervised and channeled or, "irregular expressions" of it such as gambling would result.[55] She argued that it was "only in the protected playgrounds that gangs can be merged into baseball nines and similar organizations, governed by well-recognized rules."[56] Jane Addams was certain that the city which properly educated the play impulse of its children could expect the most fruitful results: "an enlightened city government would regard these groups of boys as the natural soil in which to sow the seeds of self-government. As every European city has its parade ground, where the mimics of war

[51] Addams, Newer Ideals of Peace, p. 162.

[52] Ibid., p. 165; Addams, Spirit of Youth, p. 134.

[53] Addams, Newer Ideals of Peace, p. 164.

[54] Ibid., p. 171.

[55] Ibid., p. 176.

[56] Ibid., p. 178.

are faithfully rehearsed, in order that the country may be saved in times of danger, so, if modern government were as really concerned in developing its citizens as it is in defending them, we would look upon every playing field as the training place and parade ground of mature citizenship."[57] Such a course of action, she believed, could have facilitated the fusing to the community of the factory producer who previously worked without any inner coherence or sense of comradeship.

Miss Addams was convinced that socialized education would help the collective group identity necessary for her organic society. Throughout her discussion of the recreational activities at Hull House, one finds rationale for social control through the manipulation of subconscious and nonrational impulses.[58] Her enthusiastic description of the effects of baseball is suggestive of the kind of manipulation she desired:

> The enormous crowd of cheering men and boys are talkative, good-natured, full of holiday spirit, and absolutely released from the grind of life. They are lifted out of their individual affairs and so fused together that a man cannot tell whether it is his own shout or another's that fills his ears; whether it is his own coat or another's that he is wildly waving to celebrate a victory. He does not call the stranger who sits next to him his "brother," but he unconsciously embraces him in an overwhelming outburst of kindly feeling when the favorite player makes a home run.[59]

That she fully comprehended the rather wide implications for social control through "mass psychology" was evident when she pointed out several significant ways this psychology could be implemented:

> We are only beginning to understand what might be done through the festival, the street procession, the band of marching musicians, orchestrated music in public squares or parks, with the magic power they all possess to formulate the sense of companionship and solidarity. The experiments which are being

[57] Ibid., pp. 178–179.
[58] Addams, *Twenty Years at Hull House,* pp. 442–448.
[59] Addams, *Spirit of Youth,* p. 96.

made in public schools to celebrate the national holidays, the changing seasons, the birthdays of heroes, the planting of trees, are slowly developing little ceremonials which may in time work out into pageants of genuine beauty and significance. No other nation has so unparallelled an opportunity to do this through its schools as we have, for no other nation has so wide-spreading a school system, while the enthusiasm of children and their natural ability to express their emotions through symbols, gives the securest possible foundation to this growing effort.[60]

This echo of enormous crowds of cheering men, martial music, parades, the celebration of national heroes, the expression of emotions through symbols, and the fusion of individual voices into a collective expression of solidarity reverberates through the charred corridors of the twentieth century with deafening resonance. A resonance which, of course, Miss Addams could not have anticipated.

Manipulating the Masses

The concept of social control through mass psychology carried inherent implications for manipulation of the masses. Exponents of social control usually contend that this manipulation should be managed by men who clearly understand the requirements for salvation. Elitism was a logical and important aspect of the organic community projected by Jane Addams. The masses did generate substantial emotional force that provided the community with vitality.[61] The problem, however, was to organize and direct that force into socially acceptable channels. In harmony with the new liberalism she helped construct, Miss Addams believed the benevolent direction of the masses should be controlled by the more intelligent and morally superior individuals.[62] She asserted:

Progress must always come through the individual who varies from the type and has sufficient energy to express this variation. He first holds a higher conception than that held by the mass of his fellows of what is righteous under given conditions, and ex-

[60] Ibid., pp. 98–99.
[61] Addams, *Democracy and Social Ethics*, p. 275.
[62] Addams, *Newer Ideals of Peace*, p. 118.

presses this conviction in conduct, in many instances formulating a certain scruple which the others share, but have not yet
defined even to themselves. Progress, however, is not secure
until the mass has conformed to this new righteousness.[63]

The elite's task was to formulate, interpret, and gain mass conformity
to the general or corporate will, because "the public lacks the imagination, and also the power of formulating their wants."[64] To facilitate mass conformity to what the benevolent elite had determined
were mass wants, Miss Addams unblushingly proposed the use of
propaganda. She argued: "Ideas only operate upon the popular
mind through will and character and must be dramatized before
they reach the mass of men, even as the biography of the saints have
been after all 'the main guide to the stumbling feet of thousands of
Christians to whom the credo has been but mysterious words.' "[65]
Although the elite might profit through an open marketplace for the
free flow of competing ideas, Jane Addams was certain that the
masses must be molded by propaganda.

> Ethics as well as political opinions may be discussed and dis-
> seminated among the sophisticated by lectures and printed
> pages, but to the common people, they can only come through
> example—through a personality which seizes the popular imag-
> ination. The advantage of an unsophisticated neighborhood is,
> that the inhabitants do not keep their ideas as treasures.[66]

Jane Addams not only believed that the masses could not be motivated except through propaganda, but she also felt that their inabil-
ity to deal with ideas represented a positive gain for the community.
They would not be committed to ideas that did not fit the best interests of the community. The masses, like the immigrants, were
valuable for her new society because they were easily molded.

Lawrence Cremin has argued: "Progressivism implied the radical
faith that culture could be democratized without being vulgarized."
He has said that "the spiritual nub of progressive education" was
contained in a statement by "that noble lady who founded Hull
House," which he quoted from *Democracy and Social Ethics:* " 'We

---

[63] Addams, *Democracy and Social Ethics*, p. 159.
[64] Ibid.
[65] Ibid., p. 227.
[66] Ibid., p. 228.

have learned to say that the good must be extended to all of society before it can be held secure by any one person or any one class; but we have not yet learned to add to that statement: that unless all men and all classes contribute to a good, we cannot even be sure that it is worth having.' "[67]

Cremin is probably correct in locating the "spiritual nub" of progressive education in the works of Jane Addams. It is important, however, to recognize that she, along with other new liberals, redefined democracy and freedom in a particular twentieth-century context. Overwhelmed by the suffering and misery of urban industrialism, she found the genesis of modern problems in the demise of the rural village with its effective social controls over the individual. Miss Addams' attempt to ameliorate these problems depended on the construction of a universal village that would obtain an organic control over the individual. For all men to contribute to a common good did not mean, in Jane Addams' social philosophy, that there would be a democratization of culture. It did mean, however, that the purposes, goals, and kind of contribution each individual made would be determined according to the needs of the organic social order. The opportunity to contribute to a common good is not the same as the freedom to determine what is good. Such freedom would have been counterproductive to the interdependency she felt requisite for social unity.

Jane Addams' response to the inhuman conditions of life in urban industrial America was an integral part of the new liberal ideology that has dominated twentieth-century American social thought. In some measure it can be seen as a humanitarian response, but more significantly it was a middle-class response. Perhaps because of the middle-class orientation, Miss Addams and other new liberals generally conceived of remedies in terms of adjustments to the social order. For these adjustments to be effective, it was necessary to redefine many of the basic symbols used in social thought. Freedom became synonymous with control. Liberty and order were used interchangeably. Self-fulfillment was indistinguishable from self-sacrifice. And the individual was reduced to a means for the achievement of social goals. All this was sanctified in the name of community, for Jane Addams and other new liberals concluded that individualism was incompatible with twentieth-century America.

---

[67] Lawrence Cremin, *The Transformation of the School* (New York: Vintage Books, 1961), p. 14.

CHAPTER 5

LIBERAL IDEOLOGY
AND THE QUEST
FOR ORDERLY CHANGE

Clarence J. Karier

As conflict in American culture increases and the idea of revolution is no longer dismissed as some absurd anarchist dream, but increasingly entertained by men of more moderate persuasion, more and more voices can be heard echoing a common warning. The warning is this: The new left must either temper its attacks on the military, corporate, and educational establishment in this country, or we will all experience a fascist nightmare. In other words, the new left will be responsible for the advent of fascism in America. This notion follows from the premise that an attack on the liberal center from both the right and left weakens and eventually destroys democratic institutions. The process begins with the left questioning the mythologies that sustain bourgeois society, thus threatening the security of those in power, and ends with a repressive fascist order. The more the left agitates, the more the fascist right can be expected to grow. Few political and social analysts in this country seriously doubt the possibility that, given an open confrontation between left and right, fascism would result. Virtually every observer seems to predict that

From Clarence J. Karier, "Liberalism and the Quest for Orderly Change," *History of Education Quarterly* 12(Spring 1972): 57–80. Reprinted by permission of the publisher.

a socialism of the right, not of the left, would emerge. It is interesting that in times of severe crisis, most liberals can be relied on to move to the right rather than to the left of the political spectrum.

There are, of course, a number of problems with the above analysis. It is clear that it was created by liberals who see themselves as the guardians of a kind of middle-class democracy, abhorring conflict and violence, and taking pride in endorsing reasoned intelligent change. Espousing the moderate humanitarian views of the Enlightenment, these liberals see themselves as possible victims of extremist thought and action on both the left and right. Such an analysis, in effect, justifies the liberals' capitulation to fascist power. It was, after all, the agitation of the left that forced the liberals to support the fascist solution for law and order in the streets and the universities in the 1960s and early 1970s. Liberals are quick to point out that responsibility for the destruction of democratic institutions lies with their intemperate brothers on the left and not with any failure or perhaps fatal flaw in liberal philosophy. Although such an analysis is heavy on justification, it is relatively light on explanation. It does not, for example, explain how, despite the strong pragmatic liberal influence in American social, political, economic, and educational institutions for the past half century, the problems of race, poverty, and militarism have been exacerbated rather than alleviated. Such an analysis, furthermore, does not help us to understand just why it is that when the chips are down, liberals can be expected to move to support a fascist order rather than an equalitarian revolution.

Without suggesting a scapegoat view of the past, it might be fruitful to reexamine critically some of the key tenets of the twentieth-century liberal's faith. A more critical view of that faith might reveal some of its sources of weakness as well as develop a more realistic assessment of its strengths. Such an analysis might also shed some light on current problems. If, for example, we had fully appreciated the liberal's commitment to expert knowledge over populist opinion, or the elevation of his desire for unity, order, and universalism over respect for idiosyncratic needs of individuals and groups, we might have more realistically anticipated or at least understood his stand on such confrontations as Ocean Hill-Brownsville.

THE ROOTS OF CRISIS

The roots of the current crisis in American culture lie deep in both the social and intellectual history of the past one hundred years. Actually, the crisis is a result of both the success and the failure of the philosophy of enlightened progress. The collective side of that philosophy, with its scientifically organized technology and computer-managed bureaucracy, has become a reality; on the other side, however, individual freedom, dignity, and well-being have not fared so well. Caught up in collective institutional progress, the individual has become a means rather than an end to social order. Both the philosopher of nineteenth-century classical liberalism, John Stuart Mill, and the philosopher of twentieth-century liberalism, John Dewey, were concerned with this issue. Both agreed, in principle, that the enlightened society must strive to achieve the greater happiness of the greater number.[1] They disagreed, however, on how this was to be achieved. While Mill retained a mistrust of state power and discussed freedom in terms of freedom *from* government interference, the new liberals reversed this process and saw individual freedom tied to a positive use of state power. Positive liberalism means more than just the opposite of negative liberalism. The use of unchecked state power to control the future through shaping the thought, action and character of its citizens could ultimately lead to a totalitarian state. Isaiah Berlin succinctly stated the basic assumptions of many who espoused the philosophy of positive liberalism in his *Four Essays on Liberty:*

> First, that all men have one true purpose, and one only, that of rational self-direction; second, that the ends of all rational beings must of necessity fit into a single universal, harmonious pattern, which some men may be able to discern more clearly than others; third, that all conflict, and consequently all tragedy, is due solely to the clash of reason with the irrational or the insufficiently rational—the immature and undeveloped elements in life—whether individual or communal, and that such clashes are, in principle, avoidable, and for wholly rational beings impossible; finally, that when all men have been made rational, they will obey the rational laws of their own natures, which are one and the same in them all, and so be at once wholly law-abiding and wholly free.[2]

---

[1] See Robert Paul Wolff, *The Poverty of Liberalism* (Boston: Beacon Press, 1968), p. 31.

[2] Isaiah Berlin, *Four Essays on Liberty* (New York: Oxford University Press, 1969), p. 154.

To be sure, not all positive liberals held all these assumptions. They were, however, implicit in the thought and action of most.

Whether it was the negative freedom of Mill or the positive freedom of Dewey, each, in his own way, offered philosophic justification for the dominant economic organization of the period. By the time John Dewey assumed the role of philosophic leader in America, the *laissez-faire* idea that characterized much of the nineteenth-century economic rhetoric was being replaced by that of a managed corporate economy, more characteristic of the twentieth century. As capital began to be organized at the end of the century in new and unique ways, the corporate state of the twentieth century was born.[3] Classical liberalism, with its philosophic justification of a competitive economy, private property, individualism, and freedom from state interference, gave way to the new liberalism that espoused a controlled economy, state planning, group thought, and managed change.

Rise of the Corporate State

Behind this ideological change from a *laissez-faire* liberalism to a state-welfare liberalism existed social, political, and economic conflict of a violent nature. Violence was not new to frontier-minded America, nor was it new to the immigrant worker desperately trying to survive in a competitive industrial society. What was new, however, was the emergence of the corporate mass technological society, and with it, the rise of a middle-class liberalism that eschewed violence, conflict, and rugged individualism. The new liberals criticized the ends (private profit) but not the means (scientifically organized technology) of the emerging corporate society. They repeatedly expressed their faith in the rational knowledge of the expert and rejected the irrationalism of the masses. Fearing the potential for violence and chaos implicit in the uncontrolled immigrant masses of urban ghettoes, the new liberal turned increasingly

---

[3] For example, Charles Forcey in *The Crossroads of Liberalism* (New York: Oxford University Press, 1961), p. xiv, points out that "in 1897 the total capitalization of all corporations individually valued at a million dollars or more came to only 170 millions. Three years later the same figure for total capitalization stood at five billions, and in 1904 at over twenty billions." For the conservative effect of liberal reform, see Gabriel Kolko, *The Triumph of Conservatism: A Reinterpretation of American History, 1900–1916* (New York: Free Press of Glencoe, 1963), and James Weinstein, *The Corporate Ideal in the Liberal State, 1900–1918* (Boston: Beacon Press, 1968).

toward the development of nonviolent but coercive means of social control.

The new liberals directed the nation's social thought and action toward an acceptance of a compulsory state in which the individual would be "scientifically" shaped and controlled so as to fulfill the nation's destiny.[4] Such a compulsory state would as easily require compulsory schooling as it would military service. Rejecting both the classical liberal's rhetoric concerning individual autonomy as well as his justification of "robber baron" practices, many new liberals turned to some form of state socialism. In the process they turned to the social science expert for knowledge that would control and shape that state. The rhetoric of the new liberalism, whether in politics or education, reflected a key concern for more effective and efficient means of social control in order to eliminate conflict and to establish the harmonious organic community. Some of these men looked to a highly romanticized version of the nineteenth-century American village as a source of community. Others opted for a future in which scientific intelligence might rule out bloody conflicts and overt coercion as a means of social control. The new "science" of psychology, applied to the schooling of the masses, could be used to prevent revolution by committing the children of the disinherited to the larger and more universal social order through a process of internalizing the shared goals and ideals of the controlling middle class.

The immigrant was often viewed as a threat to social order, although by the closing decades of the nineteenth century the northern European immigrant was considered by the white Anglo-Saxon Protestant community to be relatively safe; southern Europeans, however, whose numbers increased considerably beginning in the 1880s,[5] were seen as an acute threat to the mores of America. These immigrants in particular had to be Americanized so as to protect the "American way."

Traditional Protestant theology offered little solace to those who viewed immigrants as a threat to social order. After Darwin and the

[4] See Herbert Croly, *The Promise of American Life* (New York: Dutton, 1963).

[5] For example, during the following decades, the percent of the total immigrant population that came from southern Europe increased as follows: 1881–1890—18.3 percent; 1891–1900—51.9 percent; 1901–1910—70.8 percent. See Samuel Eliot Morison and Henry Steel Commager, *The Growth of the American Republic*, vol. 2 (New York: Oxford University Press, 1956), p. 177.

higher criticism of the Bible, little intellectual vitality remained to support the credibility of theological and doctrinal disputes. What did remain, however, was the moral capital of a pious Protestant past and a missionary zeal to convert the heathen in our own midst. Missionary work was needed, not only in Africa and the Far East but in Hell's Kitchen in New York City and on Halsted Street in Chicago. The new immigrants had to be made safe for the streets of New York and Chicago, so that a better, more efficient American might emerge. The Social Gospel was the same whether preached by Walter Rauschenbusch in Hell's Kitchen or by Jane Addams at Hull House. The immigrant had to be educated for his own "good" and that good was defined by the mores of the new liberal.

The religion of the settlement houses and the urban ministries reflected the collapse of theological Protestantism and the rise of a secularized socially conscious Protestant Christianity made relevant to a rising middle class. Those men and women, reared in the earlier faith, and who, in the twilight of their youth, found themselves searching for more creditable meaning to their lives, usually turned to a secularized Protestant moral value system as the basis for their new progressive, reformist faith. Jane Addams, speaking before the Ethical Culture Society's summer session at Plymouth, Massachusetts,[6] proclaimed that the Settlement House Movement embodied the true spirit of Christ in the world. Similarly, John Dewey expressed his belief that the teacher in his concern for the "formation of the *proper* social life," and the "maintenance of *proper* social order," and the "securing of the *right* social growth: is the prophet of the true God and the usherer in of the true kingdom of God."[7] Both were translating their personal values into a new religion of humanity. Most spokesmen for progressive education in America were fundamentally moralists, working in the interest of an emerging middle class. To Dewey, as to many who followed him, science and technology was the new theology. All humanity was tied to a quest for "The Great Community" where men would ultimately learn, as Dewey put it, to "use their scientific knowledge to control their social relations."

[6] See Jane Addams, *Twenty Years at Hull House* (New York: Macmillan, 1935), pp. 113–127.

[7] Martin S. Dworkin, *Dewey on Education* (New York: Columbia University Press, 1959), p. 32 (emphasis added)

Political progressivism aimed not to destroy capitalism, but rather to rationalize and stabilize the system. Stability, predictability, and security were expected consequences of a controlled rational process of social change.[8] Federal control and regulation of labor, management, and the consumer market became the political progressive movement's trademark. The efforts of such liberals as Jane Addams, John R. Commons, Charles W. Eliot, Samuel Gompers, and others in the National Civic Federation brought labor, management, and government together into a cooperative working relationship.[9] The triumph of political progressivism meant the rise of the new managerial class to positions of power in the newer reform-type city governments, as well as in the growing bureaucratic structures at both state and federal levels.[10]

By World War I, the corporate state, embodying many of the values of both the political and educational progressives, had emerged.[11] The war itself brought political and educational progressives even closer together in common cause. Although most twentieth-century liberals believed that one could best serve the interest of the individual through involvement in a larger corporate society,[12] it is not at all clear that liberal thought and action has always served the interest of the individual except when that interest happened to coincide with the needs of the corporate society. John Dewey set the problem for the twentieth-century liberal fairly succinctly when, in discussing "What America Will Fight For," he said:

> Politics means getting certain things done. Some body of persons, elected or self-constituted, take charge, deciding and executing. In the degree in which a society is democratic this governing group has to get the assent and support of large masses of people. In the degree in which the things to be done run counter to the inertia, bias and apparent interests of the masses, certain devices of manipulation have to be resorted to. The political psychology of the older school, that of Bentham

---

[8] See Kolko, *Triumph of Conservatism*.

[9] See Weinstein, *Corporate Ideal in the Liberal State*.

[10] See Samuel P. Hayes, "The Politics of Reform in Municipal Government in the Progressive Era," *Pacific Northwest Quarterly* 55(October 1964):157–169.

[11] For the relationship between the schools and the political reformist groups, see Joel Spring, *Education and the Rise of the Corporate State* (Boston: Beacon Press, 1972).

[12] See John Dewey, *Individualism Old and New* (New York: Minton, Balch, 1930).

and Mill, taught that in a democratic state the governing body would never want to do anything except what was in the interests of the governed. But experience has shown that this view was over-naive. Practical political psychology consists largely in the technique of the expert manipulation of men in masses for ends not clearly seen by them, but which they are led to believe are of great importance for them.[13]

Rejecting this "practical political psychology" as both inefficient and ineffective in achieving broader social aims, Dewey went on to call for a more "businesslike psychology," which would consist of "intelligent perception of ends . . . and effective selection and orderly arrangement of means for their execution." The road could then be kept open for the possibilities of "world organization and the beginnings of a public control which crosses nationalistic boundaries and interests." In the closing days of the war, Dewey pointed with pride to the intelligent mobilization and management of the nation in crisis. He then looked to the future with hope that the same intelligence might be applied in developing a new social science that would help shape the new order in the future along similar lines.[14]

The Efficiency Goal

The major impetus of progressive reform, whether political or educational, was to make the system work efficiently and effectively, and progressives would use the compulsory power of the state to achieve that end. Progressive reform was, without question, conservative.[15] Many socialists were also, in effect, conservative in their quest for efficiency and orderly change and in their desire to maintain the system. For example, John Dewey in his *Confidential Report* to the War Department during World War I, was mainly concerned with the manipulation of Polish affairs so that we would not lose our cheap immigrant labor supply after the war. Said Dewey:

> The great industrial importance of Polish labor in this country must be borne in mind and the fact that there will be a shortage of labor after the war and that there is already a movement

---

[13] John Dewey, "What America Will Fight For," *New Republic*, Aug. 18, 1917.

[14] See John Dewey, "A New Social Science," *New Republic*, Apr. 6, 1918.

[15] See Kolko, *Triumph of Conservatism*.

under foot (which should be carefully looked into) to stimulate the return of Poles and others of foreign birth in Southeastern Europe to their native lands after the war. With the sharp commercial competition that will necessarily take place after the war, any tendencies which on the one hand de-Americanize and on the other hand strengthen the allegiance of those of foreign birth to the United States deserve careful attention.[16]

Although Dewey considered himself a socialist, his were not the concerns of a radical socialist but rather those of a management–welfare state socialist interested in developing and maintaining the system. To be sure, Dewey's values did not coincide with those values expressed by the National Association of Manufacturers, which represented the smaller entrepreneurs, but his values respecting order, conflict, and social change were close to those held by members of the National Civic Federation, who supported progressive social legislation in the interest of the new emerging corporate society.[17] Dewey was committed to the economic growth and progress of that society, even though such progress might require manipulating Polish workers. From this perspective one can account for his intense dislike and distrust of Papal Catholics as opposed to Protestant (Old) Catholics, as well as for his condescending attitude toward ethnic differences that appears throughout the report. Dewey viewed ethnic and religious differences as a threat to the survival of society, to be overcome through assimilation.[18] Dewey,

---

[16] John Dewey, "Conditions Among the Poles in the United States," in *Confidential Report* (Washington, D.C.: U.S. Government Printing Office, 1918), p. 73.

[17] See Weinstein, *Corporate Ideal in the Liberal State.*

[18] In his confidential report to the Military Intelligence Bureau of the War Department, Dewey was highly critical of those Poles who maintained strong loyalties to the Papacy. This report grew out of his seminar which he held in the Polish ghetto of Philadelphia. As Dewey saw it, the object of the seminar was to "ascertain forces and conditions which operate against the development of a free and democratic life among the members of this group, to discover the influences which kept them under external oppression and control," and to further develop a workable plan based on practical knowledge "to eliminate forces alien to democratic internationalism and to promote American ideals in accordance with the principles announced by President Wilson in his various public communications" (*Confidential Report,* p. 2). Brand Blanshard, a student in that seminar, has reported that during this time Dewey viewed the Poles as a "cyst" on the American community. For this documentation and for a further elaboration of Dewey's seminar, see Walter Feinberg, "Progressive Educators and Social Planning." *Teachers College Record* 73 (May 1972):485–505.

as well as other liberal reformers, was committed to flexible, experimentally managed, orderly social change that included a high degree of manipulation.

The war brought out numerous strengths and weaknesses of the new pragmatic liberalism. The central weakness, as Randolph S. Bourne so aptly put it, was that, in times of crisis, survival was the really fundamental value on which the pragmatist rested his case. Pragmatism, he argued, is a philosophy for those inclined to calculate consequences so as to survive. Faced with what appears as insurmountable opposition, the pragmatic liberal can be expected to compromise his values in the name of survival and effectiveness. Thus Dewey argued that the "pacifists wasted rather than investing their potentialities when they turned so vigorously to opposing entrance into the war. . . ." Later Dewey also criticized those Russians who resisted the politicizing of their schools along communist lines as the "more unhappy and futile class on earth."[19] The good pragmatist, he thought, should not waste his "influence" on lost causes. And Dewey was a good pragmatist. He never seriously challenged the power sources within American society; his nonviolent socialist views threatened few in power. In fact, much of his philosophy of nonviolent, reasoned, and orderly change (albeit toward a kind of welfare-state socialism) was adopted by those who directed and managed the corporate industrial state. His work in such organized efforts as the NAACP, the AAUP, and in teachers' unions was symptomatic of his pragmatic quest for limited objectives within the established system.

As Bourne saw it, pragmatism was not a philosophy for all seasons, but rather one more appropriate for "peaceful times," when critical decisions did not have to be made and compromises were easy. The tendency of the pragmatist confronted by power was to compromise from a base line of survival. In other words, expediency governed. If the self was never to be sacrificed, then only a philosophy of accommodation to the most powerful remained. Bourne's stinging analysis of John Dewey's pragmatism still remains a serious critique of the progressive liberal tradition in America. If, during times of crisis and in times of confrontation with power, the liberal can be expected to opt for the more powerful side in order to sur-

---

[19] John Dewey, *Impressions of Soviet Russia* (New York: New Republic, Inc., 1929), p. 66. For Bourne's criticism, see Lillian Schlissel, ed., *The World of Randolph Bourne* (New York: Dutton, 1965), p. 119.

vive, then one thing is clear—given a confrontation of left and right in which the political right is stronger, the liberal will often support the right. Crisis and power may be the twin Achilles' heels of pragmatic liberal philosophy in America.

Liberals are not fascists or communists. But their quest for orderly change within a managed society led some of them at times to become enthusiastic about certain characteristics of emerging totalitarian societies. Just as Dewey became enthusiastic about the role the Soviet schools were playing in the creation of a new Russia, other liberals were impressed with Italian corporate fascism as a grand experiment in social engineering. Herbert Croly, for example, warned critics of fascism to ". . . beware of outlawing a political experiment which aroused in a whole nation an increased moral energy and dignified its activities by subordinating them to a deeply felt common purpose."[20] Italian fascism was warmly received among such other well-known American liberals as Charles Beard, Horace Kallen, and Lincoln Steffens. This reception was prompted by more than a simple desire to have the "trains run on time." While the flexibility of the fascist state and its freedom from "consistent scheme" impressed Beard, the ability of that state to act decisively by subordinating outworn "principles to method" and law to order impressed other liberals. Corporate fascism seemed to satisfy the need of the corporate society for unity, order, efficiency, collective meaning, social engineering, and experimentation as well as to insure freedom from the older rationalistic liberal philosophies that tended to value individual liberty over state authority. Not until the early 1930s did these liberals begin to see the consequences of the fascist experiment in terms of political refugees. At that point they reversed their opinion about fascism.

We have tended to treat this sympathetic treatment of fascism by pragmatic liberals as an "accidental flirtation,"[21] or perhaps as an aberration in which normally rational men got carried away with

---

[20] Herbert Croly, "An Apology for Fascism," New Republic, Jan. 12, 1929, pp. 207–209.

[21] For example, see John P. Diggins, "Flirtation with Fascism: American Pragmatic Liberals and Mussolini's Italy," American Historical Review 71 (January 1966):487–506. Although Diggins does an excellent job of reviewing the literature of the period, he fails to consider seriously the possibility that there may be significant characteristics of liberal thought that can lead to enthusiastic support of a fascist regime.

the Zeitgeist of the time. If we had critically analyzed pragmatic liberal thought within the context of the corporate state, however, we might have understood the fascist flirtation as a logical and reasonable outcome of certain characteristics of liberal thought. If we considered the liberal's need for social experiment and reconciliation of opposites, we might further have understood why Charles A. Beard looked upon Benito Mussolini's fascist Italy as working out "new democratic direction," and why he might conclude that:

> Beyond question an amazing experiment is being made here, an experiment in reconciling individualism and socialism, politics and technology. It would be a mistake to allow feelings aroused by contemplating the harsh deeds and extravagant assertions that have accompanied the fascist process (as all other immense historical changes) to obscure the potentialities and the lessons of the adventure—no, not adventure, but destiny riding without saddle and bridle across the historical peninsula that bridges the world of antiquity and our modern world.[22]

CONSERVATIVE LIBERALISM AND JOHN DEWEY

The liberal role in American society was essentially that of the knowledgeable expert dedicated to the survival of the system through growth. The liberal educational reformer, like the liberal political reformer, was in effect a flexible conservative. To be sure, Dewey sharply disagreed with the mechanistic conservatism of men like David Snedden, Edward L. Thorndike, and Charles A. Prosser. His own commitment to flexible experimental change, however, would contribute to the system's survival. Consequently Dewey's experimentation in education, along with most of twentieth-century progressive educational thought, can be viewed as conservative.

The liberal philosophy that Dewey put together during his Chicago years (1894–1904) was really the ideological center for much of the progressive tradition in American education. At Chicago, working closely with Jane Addams, Ella Flagg Young, and Francis W. Parker, Dewey put his ideas to a practical educational test. By the time he opened his Laboratory School in Chicago, certain ideas were well fixed in his mind. Abstract theology held little meaning.

[22] Charles Beard, "Making the Fascist State," New Republic, Jan. 23, 1929, p. 278.

To Dewey, the spirit of God was in man and only through a more authentic community could that truth be set free.[23] The community was the sacrament through which the divine in man could be allowed to grow. For Dewey the end of education was "growth." The concept "growth" itself is an organic concept implying man's continuity with nature and his dependence on environment. Dewey searched—at Michigan, Chicago, and at Columbia—for organic unity and community. To him, the good community was more than a rural face-to-face model taken from a Vermont village.[24] His community would include the experimental, the scientific, and the technical, and it would necessitate a new man who realized his individualism in the emerging corporate community.[25] The older individualism, which saw the self as the center of the universe, was passing away. Collective, cooperative intelligence was the key to understanding the new technology as well as the new individualism.

Drawing on both his Hegelian and Herbartian past, Dewey saw history as a crucial factor in understanding the present and shaping the future. As Dewey later put it: "The past is of logical necessity the past-of-the-present, and the present is the past-of-a-future-living present."[26] The past was "a lever for moving the present into a certain kind of future." It is significant that Charles Sanders Peirce criticized Dewey and his Chicago school for confusing logic with history.[27] If, for example, one were to delete all of Dewey's discussion of the history of various problems in *Democracy and Education*, little would remain for the serious student of experimental philosophy to tackle. Man's destiny, of course, is not predetermined by his history, but rather by the way he uses his history. Dewey was using history with a particular "end in view." In addressing parents and teachers in his Laboratory School in 1897, Dewey explained why history was so important a subject in his school.

---

[23] See John Dewey, "Christianity and Democracy," in *Religious Thought at the University of Michigan* (Ann Arbor, Mich.: Inland Press, 1893), pp. 60–69.

[24] S. T. Kimball and J. E. McClellan in *Education and the New America* (New York: Random House, 1962) tend to overestimate Dewey's agrarian roots and underestimate his awareness of twentieth-century forces.

[25] See Dewey, *Individualism Old and New*.

[26] John Dewey, *Logic: The Theory of Inquiry* (New York: Holt, 1938).

[27] See *The Nation*, Sept. 15, 1904, p. 220. For confirmation of the authorship of this review of Dewey's *Studies in Logical Theory*, see Charles Sanders Peirce, *Collected Papers*, vol. 8, ed. by Walter Burks (Cambridge: Harvard University Press, 1958), p. 145.

History is introduced at a very early period and is conducted on the principle that it is a means of affording the child insight into social life. It is treated, therefore, not as a record of something which is past and gone, but as a way of realizing what enters into the make-up of society and of how society has grown to be what it is. Treated thus, as a mode of insight into social life, great emphasis is laid upon the typical relations of humanity to nature, as summed up in the development of food, shelter, habitation, clothing and industrial occupations. This affords insight into the fundamental processes and instruments which have controlled the development of civilization and also affords natural and frequent opportunities for adjusting the work in history to that in manual training on the one side and to science on the other.[28]

In Herbartian fashion, Dewey constructed his Laboratory School history course so as to help the child "gradually to shape his expression to social ends, and thus make them, through his growing control, more and more effective in the corporate life of the group."[29] The enrollment of Dewey's school consisted primarily of middle-class and upper-middle-class children.[30] Following his historical perspective, the social studies curriculum emphasized social unity, cooperative living, and the rational, orderly, progressive development of technology from the spinning wheel to the modern, industrial, corporate society. The violent, bloody history of Indians, blacks, and immigrants, as well as the labor conflicts of the previous decades, were peculiarly missing in the school's history of the progressive evolution of American technology. Thirty years later, while reflecting on his "Chicago Experiment," Dewey stated that "historical material was subordinated to the maintenance of community or cooperative group in which each child was to participate."[31]

Although Dewey in 1936 said that historical materials in his "Chicago Experiment" were designed to maintain community, during

---

[28] As quoted in Katherine Camp Mayhew and Anna Camp Edwards, *The Dewey School* (New York: Appleton Century, 1936), pp. 29–30.

[29] Ibid., p. 22.

[30] Tuition charges in 1901–1902 were from $75 to $105 per year.

[31] Mayhew and Edwards, *The Dewey School*, p. 473. This appears in the afterword of the Mayhew-Edwards book written some thirty years after the Chicago experiment.

the same decade he also advocated the use of historical materials to change community. However, what Dewey seemed to generate earlier at Chicago was a kind of middle-class history that eschewed conflict and violence and supported the organizational thinking of the new managerial class. Even though Dewey vacillated and at times called for a more critical use of the past, it was unfortunately his earlier kind of uncritical history that generally came to dominate much of the public schools' social studies curriculum.

The schoolroom was to be a miniature community, and just what kind of community was important. Dewey's school had to be an idealized abstraction. As long as the larger community contained some unworthy aspects, the schoolroom would be selective with regard to enhancing those social values Dewey prized. Although he found fault with Plato's limited conception of individual potentialities, his own reconciliation of individuality and social coherency was largely Platonic. "True" individualism and "true" community were for Dewey, as for Plato, one. In Plato's *Republic*, all men were to be educated according to their natural talents so as to maintain order and virtue. In Dewey's *Democracy and Education*, all men were to be educated in order to realize their individual talents and yet develop "a personal interest in social relationships and control, and the habits of mind which secure changes without introducing disorder."[32]

While all might participate in Dewey's conception of democracy and education, knowledge and the expert were powerful determiners of social policy. Like most liberals in the twentieth century, Dewey turned to the specialist rather than to the masses for social guidance. In 1897 he said, "The school, accordingly, is endeavoring to put the various lines of work in charge of experts who maintain agreement and harmony through continued consultation and cooperation."[33] Thirty years later, he consistently argued: "It is more than probable that the only genuine solution of the question of the place of social guidance and indoctrination in education will be found in giving a central place to scientific method as the key to social betterment."[34] Plato had his logic, Dewey his scientific method. Dewey, in accordance with the new liberal ideology he helped construct,

---

[32] John Dewey, *Democracy and Education* (New York: Macmillan, 1916), p. 99.

[33] Mayhew and Edwards, *The Dewey School*, p. 36.

[34] Ibid., p. 473.

turned not to the masses for social guidance, but to the expert. This ultimately led to the rise of a kind of bureaucratic meritocracy whose members talked about democracy and education without seriously threatening the power elite that controlled the system.

The problem of relating a progressive school to the main currents of the emerging technological society was a continuous problem for Dewey. If the school was relevant and at the same time experimental, then only in an experimental society could educational reform occur. Only in such a society could one get an "organic" relationship between school and society. As for democracy: "A society which makes provision for participation in its good of all its members on equal terms and which secures flexible readjustment of its institutions through interaction of the different forms of associated life is in so far democratic."[35] What was meant by "on equal terms" remained ambiguous enough to allow Dewey to see democracy wherever he saw an involved social experimental group.[36] When he visited Russian schools, he found:

> . . . the children much more democratically organized than are our own; and to note that they are receiving through the system of school administration a training that fits them much more systematically than is attempted in our professedly democratic country, for later active participation in the self-direction of both local communities and industries.[37]

Dewey's inadequate conception of political democracy led him to look at a totalitarian society organizing its population educationally to participate in the bureaucratic system at various institutional levels and call that society democratic. What impressed him most about the Russian system was that in it, unlike in his Chicago Lab-

---

[35] Dewey, *Democracy and Education*, p. 99.

[36] It is significant that the political progressives reshaped political organizations so as to disenfranchise the masses to as large an extent as possible and to heighten the political influence of the better classes. Similarly, the educational progressives moved to take politics out of the school (nonpartisan school board), and progressive education theorists, like Dewey, used the term *democracy* to mean little more than participatory democracy, without facing the political power issue. "Rule by the people" gave way to rule by the "scientific expert." See Elinor Mondale Gersman, "Progressive Reform of the St. Louis School Board, 1897," *History of Education Quarterly* 10(Spring 1970):3–21.

[37] Dewey, *Impressions of Soviet Russia*, p. 105.

oratory School, the progressive educator could be true to himself and teach in unison with the shaping forces of the larger community. As he put it, "The Russian educational situation is enough to convert one to the idea that only in a society based upon the co-operative principle can the ideals of educational reformers be adequately carried into operation."[38] He was impressed by the organic unity that existed between the school and Soviet society, as well as by the social behaviorism employed in using the school as a vehicle for entering and shaping family life. In viewing Russian education, Dewey had some difficulty distinguishing propaganda from education. He said:

> The present age is, of course, everywhere one in which propaganda has assumed the role of a governing power. But nowhere else in the world is employment of it as a tool of control so constant, consistent and systematic as in Russia at present. Indeed, it has taken on such importance and social dignity that the word propaganda hardly carries, in another social medium, the correct meaning. For we instinctively associate propaganda with the accomplishment of some special ends, more or less private to a particular class or group, and correspondingly concealed from others. But in Russia the propaganda is in behalf of a burning public faith. One may believe that the leaders are wholly mistaken in the object of their faith: but their sincerity is beyond question. To them the end for which propaganda is employed is not a private or even a class gain, but is the universal good of universal humanity. In consequence propaganda is education and education is propaganda. They are more than confounded; they are identified.[39]

Propaganda became education when it served a universal good. Dewey later suggested that certain kinds of propaganda were "obnoxious" to him personally, but then went on to say: "The broad effort to employ the education of the young as a means of realizing certain social purposes cannot be dismissed as propaganda without relegating to that category all endeavor at deliberate social control."[40] Dewey's impressions of the Soviet schools are revealing, not

[38] Ibid., p. 86.
[39] Ibid., pp. 53–54.
[40] Ibid., pp. 81–82.

so much with respect to what they tell us about the schools themselves, but with respect to the light they shed on what Dewey, the philosopher of American liberalism, meant by democracy, freedom, and the organic unity between school and society.

Scientific Socialism

Dewey had long ago rejected the classical conception of individualism and its political corollary of a free marketplace of conflicting ideas. According to Dewey, the traditional notion of democracy, dependent on conflict of parties and public discussion, had passed. In *Liberalism and Social Action,* he discussed the collapse of both the capitalistic system and *laissez-faire* democracy, neither of which had much in common with scientific method. He said:

> The idea that the conflict of parties will, by means of public discussion, bring out necessary public truths is a kind of political watered-down version of the Hegelian dialectic, with its synthesis arrived at by a union of antithetical conceptions. The method has nothing in common with the procedure of organized cooperative inquiry which has won the triumphs of science in the field of physical nature.[41]

Rejecting confrontation politics, Dewey turned to science and what he termed a method of intelligence. His ideal was the new *scientific* socialism, not democratic socialism (*democratic* in the older sense of the term). The new theology, for Dewey, had become science and technology, which in a way, had become a creator of new values and ends. As he put it, "Take science (including its application to the machine) for what it is, and we shall begin to envisage it as a potential creator of new values and ends."[42]

The older theology had called for a new Adam. Dewey's unbounded faith in science and technology led him to call for a new man.[43] Such a man must work well within the corporate system where, almost in Orwellian fashion, positive freedom would mean control. Freedom for Dewey meant rational control over future pos-

---

[41] John Dewey, *Liberalism and Social Action* (New York: Capricorn Books, 1935), p. 71.

[42] Dewey, *Individualism Old and New,* pp. 160–161.

[43] Ibid.

sibilities. As he put it, "Control is the crux of our freedom."[44] This kind of freedom over future possibilities would be maximized when the "great society" would become the "great community." Only then would a true public exercising a maximum degree of freedom and control come into being. Such a public would, in Rousseauian fashion, assert its "general will" in situations in which "force is not eliminated but is transformed in use and direction by ideas and sentiments made possible by means of symbols."[45] Ideas, sentiments, and words become the force vehicles of social control in Dewey's great community.[46]

One aspect of his search for the great community had its precursors in Rousseau, Emerson, Royce, and Walt Whitman; another was rooted in Lester Frank Ward, Albion Small, and Herbert Croly. As Dewey put it, "Democracy will come into its own, for democracy is a name for a life of free and enriching communion. It had its seer in Walt Whitman. It will have its consummation when free social inquiry is indissolubly wedded to the art of full and moving communication."[47] The age-old problem of educating the man or the citizen would be resolved when the great society became the great community, and the new man, indeed the one-dimensional man, would become a living reality. This new community was one in which men would ". . . systematically use scientific procedures for the control of human relationships and the direction of the social effects of our vast technological machinery."[48] The solution to social conflict, for Dewey, remained the intelligent use of education for social control. The direction such control should take, he believed, could be determined by scientific method.

Dewey's benign faith in the scientific method and technology remained undaunted. Perennially optimistic, he believed there was a way of humanizing American social institutions, industrial or educational. He saw one possibility in the progress of science and technology toward what he called a "humane age." The experimental method, he believed, was "the foe of every belief that permits habit and wont to dominate invention and discovery, and ready-made

---

[44] John Dewey, *Human Nature and Conduct* (New York: Holt, 1922), p. 311.

[45] John Dewey, *The Public and Its Problems* (New York: Holt, 1927), p. 153.

[46] Ibid.

[47] Ibid., p. 184.

[48] Quoted in Nelson Blake, *A History of American Life and Thought* (New York: McGraw-Hill, 1963), p. 408.

system to override verifiable fact."[49] Influenced by a somewhat romantic view of the scientific community, he went on to suggest that
not only are science and technology revolutionizing our society, but
that science carries with it the germ of a more open society. He said:

> No scientific inquirer can keep what he finds to himself or turn
> it to merely private account without losing his scientific stand-
> ing. Everything discovered belongs to the community of work-
> ers. Every new idea and theory has to be submitted to this
> community for confirmation and test. There is an expanding
> community of cooperative effort and of truth. . . . Suppose
> that what now happens in limited circles were extended and
> generalized.[50]

There is a problem here. Although theoretical science may be
open-ended, technology concerned with serving particular social
institutions may not be so dedicated to truth or an open community
of discourse. On the contrary, a social institution dedicated to survival may find it expedient to sacrifice truth.[51] The new liberalism
of Dewey and others failed at this critical juncture. Perhaps in some
ideal world where all men were governed by "rational self-direction," Dewey's idea of science might be applicable. In the world of
twentieth-century power politics, however, most scientists and technologists became hired men of the industrial militarized society. It
is significant that neither Dewey nor the many educators who followed him in preaching the gospel of science in education paid
much attention to the social environment in which modern science
and technology was born and bred, that is, Prussianized Germany.
Instead, the rhetoric of American educators simply abounds with
the association of freedom and democracy with scientific method
and technology.[52] Dewey made a significant contribution to this

[49] Dewey, *Individualism Old and New*, p. 156.

[50] Ibid., pp. 154–155.

[51] This may account in part for the fact that the Nazi movement received stronger
support from those who worked in the applied sciences, and more resistance from
those who worked in the theoretical sciences. The conservative characteristics of
technologists may be as much a function of the role they play in serving the interests of the established institutions as it is their own social-class origins or personal idiosyncrasies.

[52] The term *science* in American educational rhetoric has been part of one of the
more controlling, yet unexplored, myths in American twentieth-century education.

mythology. Repeatedly he treated technology as either a positive or a neutral tool and seldom ever seemed to sense or show serious concern with the negative and limiting consequences of the technological system itself.[53] More fundamentally, however, he failed to realize that neither democracy nor individual freedom had any inherent connection with science and technology.

The relationship Dewey saw between democracy and science could, however, have an intimate connection with his passion for unity and order and for systematic, rational change, as well as with his high regard for the expert. This passion characterized Dewey's new liberal ideology and, moreover, remained fairly constant from his Chicago Laboratory School days until late in life, when he favorably reviewed Karl Mannheim's book, *Man and Society* (1940), in which Mannheim called for elites to plan the new social order.[54] Even then, Dewey's faith in science, knowledgeable elites, and scientific social planning remained firm. By 1943, R. Bruce Raup, George E. Axtelle, Kenneth D. Benne, and B. Othanel Smith published *The Improvement of Practical Intelligence,* which attempted to create a method of social dialogue through which collective planning might occur. Dewey called this work too subjectivistic and insisted that values for social planning could be arrived at through an objective science. Two decades later, Daniel Bell, following in the footsteps of John Dewey, published *The End of Ideology,* in which he asserted that the new social order will be planned by an ideology-free social scientist, charting the course of a future civilization.

END OF IDEOLOGY

Just a century after Comte had prophesied the emergence of a positive objective science of man and values, liberals such as Dewey[55] and Bell heralded the development of an objective science of human values. Bell had correctly surmised that this was, indeed, the end of ideology. It was also the culmination of one of the sig-

---

[53] See, for example, Jacques Ellul, *The Technological Society* (New York: Vintage Books, 1964).

[54] See John Dewey, "The Techniques of Reconstruction," *Saturday Review,* Aug. 31, 1940, p. 10. It is significant that Karl Popper and others consider Mannheim an enemy of the open society. For these and other insights, I am indebted to the research of Joseph Hamilton, University of Illinois.

[55] See John Dewey, "Theory of Valuation" in *The International Encyclopaedia of Unified Sciences,* vol. 2, ed. by Otto Neurath (Chicago: University of Chicago Press, 1939).

nificant ideologies in the first half of the twentieth century—liberalism itself. If human values could be objectively determined and predictably controlled by the social science expert using systems analysis in the cybernated world of the future, then there was little need for that once burning faith that called for rational progressive change. To be sure, the "games" that engaged the think-tank experts seemed a pallid substitute for the philosophic discourse in which the liberals had engaged for the past century; nevertheless, games were still a logical extension of liberal thought and action. Just as many nineteenth-century liberals found themselves justifying "robber baron" capitalism, so many twentieth-century liberals found themselves justifying the military-industrial establishment. This, however, could be expected. The twentieth-century liberal was in many ways the articulate spokesman for that managerial middle class that participated in creating the militarized society of the post-World War II period.

Perhaps, if we had fully appreciated the liberal's commitment to the survival of the system through evolutionary, orderly change, we might have understood why so many of them were impressed by early fascist and communist experiments in human engineering. It might also have been easier to understand why the "liberal"-dominated Committee for Cultural Freedom in 1939 opted for McCarthy-like solutions to the problems of communist teachers in the schools fully a decade before the McCarthy era.[56] Nor would it seem unusual that Sidney Hook would be one of the founders in 1951 of the American Committee for Cultural Freedom, an offspring of the C.I.A.-supported Congress for Cultural Freedom.[57] Finally, if we had an accurate historical analysis of the role the liberal has played in the development and maintenance of the corporate state, we would not have been so repeatedly surprised along the road from Berkeley to Attica to find a liberal mind behind the hand on the policeman's club or the finger on the trigger.

With respect to education, the liberal supported the creation of a mass system of schooling dedicated to filling society's need for citizens capable of adjusting to an industrial system. Society required

---

[56] See Paul Violas, "Fear and Constraints in Academic Freedom of Public School Teachers, 1930–1960," *Educational Theory* 21(Winter 1971):70–81.

[57] See Christopher Lasch, "The Cultural Cold War: A Short History of the Congress for Cultural Freedom," in *Towards A New Past: Dissenting Essays in American History*, ed. by Barton J. Bernstein (New York: Pantheon Books, 1968), pp. 322–359.

citizens who respected the authority of the expert and who accepted the mythologies sustaining bourgeois culture. Despite equalitarian rhetoric, educational liberals most often, in practice, supported an education directed from the top. They repeatedly supported the professionalization of the expert-teacher and the use of improved technique to enlighten the ignorant masses. "Enlightenment," for most, implied education for social control.

Words such as freedom, democracy, and individualism took on new and different meanings to Dewey and other liberals. The philosophy of John Dewey, and that of most liberals who attacked ancient dualisms, could readily lead to a one-dimensional view of reality that blurred opposites. Freedom, for example, became control. Dewey's conception of *Democracy and Education* bypassed politically potent power questions, moving toward a cultural participatory perspective that assumed an increasing acceptance on the part of the masses of the scientific method as the "key to social betterment."

Cultural participation, however, was no substitute for political and economic power. In spite of the fact that Dewey in *Liberalism and Social Action* called for greater militancy, the behavior of liberals in the past decades has been best characterized as acquiescence in the face of political, economic, and military power. Perhaps Isaiah Berlin put his finger on the problem when he suggested that "virtue is not knowledge, nor freedom identical with either."[58] Liberals tended to confuse all three. They sought social change without conflict and violence, placing their faith in science and technology as "creators of human values," and turning to a mass system of education that would impart those values to the children of the immigrant. In the process, education of the individual was sacrificed to the greater need for social control and security. As a consequence, large numbers of people were ultimately not educated to be critical, individual citizens, but trained to seek security and comfort in the symbols and mythologies manipulated by Madison Avenue social science experts. Political office came to be as merchandizable as soap, and the people simply pawns of "expert policy decision-makers." Neither science nor technology was effectively employed to enhance democracy (rule by the people). Rather, science and technology became effective tools with which the powerful con-

---

[58] Berlin, *Four Essays on Liberty,* p. 154.

trolled the social system. Perhaps the liberal faith in science and technology is not an adequate substitute for a philosophy of man.

Weaknesses in the liberal ideology are exposed during times of crisis. Whether it was Dewey calling for a more effective manipulation of the Polish immigrant during World War I, or President Johnson manipulating public opinion while he escalated the Vietnam war, liberals in crisis directly or indirectly have usually supported the existing power structure. They were, in fact, *Servants of Power*.[59] If, indeed, the unfortunate time shall come when the left meets the right in open battle, little doubt should remain where many liberals will stand.

[59] See Loren Baritz, *The Servants of Power* (New York: Wiley, 1960).

CHAPTER 6

TESTING FOR ORDER AND CONTROL IN THE CORPORATE LIBERAL STATE

Clarence J. Karier

In 1897, total capitalization of all corporations individually valued at a $1 million or more came to only $170 million. Just three years later, total capitalization stood at $5 billion and, in 1904, at over $20 billion.[1] With this rapid consolidation of corporate capital, mass production industries with their own needs for standardized producers and consumers emerged.[2] During this same short period, the last great wave of immigrants flooded into the burgeoning urban centers to fill the need for workers in rapidly expanding mass production industries. Large corporate interests eventually faced the complex problems resulting from urbanization, industrialization, and immigration and, in utilizing the state to ameliorate social, economic, and political problems, followed the lead of Germany. Unlike those in Germany, however, American social-service institutions at city, state, and federal levels were not as responsive to efficient management. Neither the populist nor the immigrant in the urban

Reprinted from *Educational Theory* 22(Spring 1972):159–180, by permission of the publisher.
[1] Charles Forcey, *The Crossroads of Liberalism* (New York: Oxford University Press, 1961), p. xiv.
[2] Robert H. Wiebe, *The Search for Order* (New York: Hill & Wang, 1967).

ghetto was easily controlled.[3] Progressive reformers, working at the city and state, and eventually at the national level, sought to reorganize a pluralistic America in the interest of efficient, orderly production and consumption of goods and services.

Whether it was John R. Commons, Edward A. Ross, and Richard T. Ely at the University of Wisconsin; or Samuel Gompers and Andrew Carnegie in the National Civic Federation; or perhaps Jane Addams and Walter Rauschenbusch in the settlement houses of Chicago and New York—all envisioned and worked toward a larger, more orderly corporate state, utilizing experts to ameliorate the state's many and varied problems. On the one hand, public institutions had to be reorganized to increase administrative and bureaucratic effectiveness at each level of government.[4] On the other hand, in the private sector, new organizations were created to channel corporate wealth toward the support of liberal progressive reform. Philanthropic foundations became a major stimulus for political as well as educational reform. For example, many municipal research bureaus that conducted urban studies provided the evidence that led to progressive reform of city governments (which indirectly but effectively disenfranchised many immigrant groups) were originally funded by large foundations and later taken over by city councils.[5] Initiating various kinds of activity and then allowing the public sector to assume control became common practice among major foundations dealing with policy formation in America. Foundations could flexibly employ large blocks of wealth for research, initiate new activities, and facilitate existing programs. This made them profoundly influential.[6] As Fred M. Hechinger aptly put it:

[3] See Norman Pollack, *The Populist Response to Industrial America* (New York: Norton, 1962). Also see William Appleman Williams, *The Roots of the Modern American Empire* (New York: Random House, 1969).

[4] Increased efficiency in city, state, and federal government often meant a corresponding decrease in political influence on the part of the poor and the disinherited. See Samuel P. Hays, "The Politics of Reform in Municipal Government in the Progressive Era," in *American Urban History,* ed. by Alexander B. Callon (New York: Oxford University Press, 1969).

[5] See Norman N. Gill, *Municipal Research Bureaus* (Washington, D.C.: American Council on Public Affairs, 1944), pp. 15–17.

[6] See David W. Eakins, "The Development of Corporate Liberal Policy Research in the United States, 1885–1965" (Ph.D. diss., University of Wisconsin, 1966). Also see James Weinstein, *The Corporate Ideal in the Liberal State, 1900–1918* (Boston: Beacon Press, 1968).

The ideal foundation-sponsored enterprise is one that blazes a new trail, thrives for a while on sponsored dollars, gathers momentum, and is quickly taken over as a permanent program by the local school board, the state education authority, or a university's own budget.[7]

A FOURTH BRANCH OF GOVERNMENT

In effect, the rise of foundations to key positions in policy formation amounted to the development of a fourth branch of government, one that effectively represented the interest of American corporate wealth. To be sure, America has had a long history of philanthropy. The development and creation of large corporate foundations, however, was very much a twentieth-century phenomenon. Foundations grew rapidly in numbers from 21 in 1900 to a total of 4,685 in 1959.[8] To the chagrin of many congressmen and taxpayers, the number of tax-exempt foundations of all kinds in the United States increased from 12,295 at the close of 1952 to 42,124 by the end of 1960.[9]

From the very beginning of the century, corporate wealth directed its new philanthropic endeavors at influencing educational policy. John D. Rockefeller's General Education Board, which received its national charter in 1903, greatly influenced and shaped educational policy for blacks in the South, while the Carnegie Institution of Washington (1904) and the Carnegie Foundation for the Advancement of Teaching (1906) came to play a major role in shaping educational policy in both South and North.

By 1912 Congress had become hostile toward foundation activity, while many state legislatures remained sympathetic. Consequently, the incorporation of philanthropic foundations proceeded along lines of least resistance, that is, at the state rather than the national level. In 1913, a concerned Sixty-second Congress created the Industrial Relations Commission to investigate the role of foundations, before which Charles W. Eliot testified as to their noble purposes and activities. Said he:

---

[7] Warren Weaver, *U.S. Philanthropic Foundations* (New York: Harper and Row, 1967), p. 245.

[8] John Lankford, *Congress and the Foundations in the Twentieth Century* (River Falls, Wis.: Wisconsin State University, 1964), pp. 6, 92.

[9] Ibid., p. 92.

I have never known a charitable or educational corporation to do anything which threatened the welfare or the liberties of the American people. I have had no observation of any such corporation—of any such attempts. And I have, on the other hand, seen a great deal of the activity and intelligent promotion of the public welfare by such corporations. There is in them, so far as my experience teaches me, not only no menace, but a very great hope for the Republic.[10]

Nevertheless, after a year of testimony, the majority of the commission concluded: "The domination of men in whose hands the final control of a large part of American industry rests is not limited to their employees, but is being rapidly extended to control the education and social service of the nation."[11] The majority report went on to point out that foundation policies would inevitably reflect those of the corporations sponsoring them. While some members of the commission called for the confiscation of the foundations, liberals such as John R. Commons and Florence Harriman cautioned against such precipitous action. Even though the findings of the commission cut close to the heart of the problem of power in the corporate liberal state, its findings were ignored as the attention of the Congress and the nation shifted to the war then developing in Europe.

America's entry into the war brought certain progressive trends together. Radical populists and socialists were jailed in the name of national unity, demoralizing the native American left, while large corporations found more ways to profitably work with government, and a large cadre of social science experts had opportunities to try out newfound techniques for the management of the new corporate state. John Dewey, for example, now saw the great possibility for "intelligent administration" based eventually on a solid social science. The corporate liberal state emerged from the war stronger than ever. Progressive liberal reform did not come to an end with the war; rather, it became institutionalized. Henceforth, most social change would be institutionally controlled and the interests of government, corporate wealth, and labor more securely managed. The

---

[10] Quoted in ibid., p. 29.
[11] Quoted in ibid., p. 31.

state that emerged included a mass system of public schools that would serve its manpower needs. And one of the more important ways in which that system served those needs was to rationalize and standardize manpower for both production and consumption of goods and services. The testing movement, financed by corporate foundations, played a vital role in fashioning a peculiar American meritocracy.

BACKGROUND TO TESTING

Historians generally mark the beginning of the testing movement with the mass testing of 1.7 million men for classification in the armed forces during World War I. The roots of the American testing movement, however, are deeply imbedded in the American progressive temper, which combined a belief in progress, certain racial attitudes, and faith in the scientific expert working through state authority to ameliorate and control the evolutionary progress of the race.

A key leader of the eugenics movement in America was Charles Benedict Davenport who, having studied Galton and Pearson, sought to persuade the new Carnegie Institution of Washington to support a biological experiment station with himself as director. In 1904, he became director of such a station at Cold Spring Harbor on Long Island. As his interest in experiments in animal breeding began to wane, Davenport used his position as secretary of the Committee on Eugenics of the American Breeders Association to solicit aid for the study of human heredity. Supported by donations from Mrs. E. H. Harriman, Davenport founded the Eugenics Record Office in 1910. Eight years later the Carnegie Institution of Washington assumed control of it. The endeavors of the Record Office were facilitated by the work of various committees. The Committee on Inheritance of Mental Traits included among its members Robert M. Yerkes and Edward L. Thorndike. The Committee on Heredity of Deafmutism included Alexander Graham Bell. H. H. Laughlin was on the Committee on Sterilization, and the Committee on the Heredity of the Feeble Minded included, among others, Henry Herbert Goddard.

Race Betterment

These committees took the lead in identifying persons who carried defective germ-plasm and disseminating the propaganda that became necessary to pass sterilization laws. It was Laughlin's Committee to Study and Report on the Best Practical Means of Cutting off the Defective Germ-Plasm in the American Population, for example, that reported that "society must look upon germ-plasm as belonging to society and not solely to the individual who carries it."[12] Laughlin found that approximately 10 percent of the American population carried bad seed, and he wished to sterilize the group. He defined these people as "feebleminded, insane, criminalistic (including the delinquent and wayward), epileptic, inebriate, diseased, blind, deaf, deformed and dependent (including orphans, ne'er-do-wells, the homeless, tramps and paupers)."[13] Social character, from murder to prostitution, was associated with intelligence and the nature of one's germ-plasm. Indiana passed the first sterilization law in 1907, followed in quick succession by fifteen other states. In Wisconsin, such progressives as Edward A. Ross and Charles R. Van Hise, president of the University of Wisconsin, took strong public stands supporting sterilization laws. Fully twenty years ahead of other nations, America pioneered in the sterilization of mental and social defectives.

Between 1907 and 1928, twenty-one states practiced eugenic sterilization involving over 8,500 people. California under the influence of the Human Betterment Foundation, which counted Lewis M. Terman and David Starr Jordan as its leading members, accounted for 6,200 sterilizations. California's sterilization law was based on concepts of race purity as well as those having to do with criminology. Persons "morally and sexually depraved" could be sterilized. Throughout the sterilization movement in America ran a *Zeitgeist* reflecting the temper of pious reformers calling for clean living, temperance, and fresh-air schools as well as for sterilization (see figure 6.1). The use of sterilization for punishment reached the point where laws were introduced calling for sterilization for chicken stealing and car theft, as well as for prostitution.[14]

---

[12] Quoted in Mark H. Haller, *Eugenics: Hereditarian Attitudes in American Thought* (New Brunswick, N.J.: Rutgers University Press, 1963), p. 133.

[13] Ibid.

[14] On March 4, 1971, a bill was introduced into the Illinois legislature that required sterilization of a mother who had two or more children while on welfare roles before that mother could draw further support. The argument, however, is no longer based on racial purity or punishment, but rather more on the economic burden to society. The federal government also carries on voluntary sterilization programs for the poor. By the spring of 1972, the Office of Economic Opportunity

FIGURE 6.1 PROGRESS THROUGH RACE BETTERMENT

The Race Betterment Movement Aims

To Create a New and Superior Race thru EUTHENICS, or Personal and Public Hygiene and EUGENICS, or Race Hygiene.

A thoroughgoing application of PUBLIC AND PERSONAL HYGIENE will save our nation annually:

1,000,000 premature deaths.

2,000,000 lives rendered perpetually useless by sickness.

200,000 infant lives (two-thirds of the baby crop)

The science of EUGENICS intelligently and universally applied would in a few centuries practically

WIPE OUT

Idiocy   Insanity   Imbecility   Epilepsy

and a score of other hereditary disorders, and create a race of HUMAN THOROUGHBREDS such as the world has never seen.

Evidences of Race Degeneracy

Increase of Degenerative Diseases - - -
$\begin{cases} \text{Cancer} \\ \text{Insanity} \\ \text{Diseases of Heart and} \\ \quad\text{Blood Vessels} \\ \text{Diseases of Kidneys} \\ \text{Most Chronic Diseases} \\ \text{Diabetes} \end{cases}$

Increase of Defectives
$\begin{cases} \text{Idiots} \\ \text{Imbeciles} \\ \text{Morons} \\ \text{Criminals} \\ \text{Inebriates} \\ \text{Paupers} \end{cases}$

Diminishing Individual Longevity

Diminished Birth Rate

Disappearance, Complete or Partial, of Various Bodily Organs - - -
$\begin{cases} \text{According to Wie-} \\ \text{dersheim there are} \\ \text{more than two hun-} \\ \text{dred such changes in} \\ \text{the structures of the} \\ \text{body} \end{cases}$

Methods of Race Betterment

Simple and Natural Habits of Life.

Out-of-Door Life Day and Night, Fresh-Air Schools, Playgrounds, Out-of-Door Gymnasiums, etc.

Total Abstinence from the Use of Alcohol and Other Drugs.

Eugenic Marriages.

Medical Certificates before Marriage.

Health Inspection of Schools.

Periodical Medical Examinations.

Vigorous Campaign of Education in Health and Eugenics.

Eugenic Registry.

Sterilization or Isolation of Defectives.

Source: *Official Proceedings of the Second National Conference on Race Betterment*, August 4–8, 1915, Battle Creek, Michigan (Battle Creek, Mich.: Race Betterment Foundation, 1917), pp. 147, 150, 160.

Henry Herbert Goddard, fresh from G. Stanley Hall's seminars at Clark University, translated the Binet-Simon scale in 1908 and used the test to identify feebleminded at the training school at Vineland, New Jersey. Various scales and tests freely used and patterned after the original scale were later proven to lack reliability to the extent that, according to some testers, upwards of half the population was feebleminded. From the Binet scale, Goddard went on to publish *The Kallikak Family*, which showed the family history of Martin Kallikak as having both a good and a bad side. The bad side, which began with Martin's involvement with a feebleminded girl, contributed such "social pests" as "paupers, criminals, prostitutes and drunkards." Goddard's next book, *Feeble-mindedness: Its Causes and Consequences*, gave further "scientific" support to the notion that feeblemindedness and moral character were related.

Interestingly enough, the American liberal tradition from Jefferson on usually assumed a positive relationship between "talent and virtue." So it is not surprising to find people assuming that a person low in talent will also lack virtue, a relationship assumed in most sterilization laws. Society would rid itself of not only the genetic defective but, more importantly, the socially undesirable. Laughlin, Goddard, Terman, and Thorndike all made similar assumptions. Terman argued that the feebleminded were incapable of moral judgments and, therefore, could be viewed only as potential criminals. He said:

> All feebleminded are at least potential criminals. That every feebleminded woman is a potential prostitute would hardly be disputed by anyone. Moral judgements, like business judgement, social judgement or any other kind of higher thought process, is a function of intelligence.[15]

The same thinking that guided Terman to find a lower morality among people of lesser intelligence had its mirror image in the work

---

was deeply involved in trying to persuade the poor people of Appalachia to submit to sterilization. See *New York Times,* May 28, 1972, p. 40.

While the constitutionality of pauper sterilization might be questionable, the right of the state to sterilize for eugenic purposes was settled in *Buck v. Bell,* when Justice Holmes argued: "The principle that sustains compulsory vaccination is broad enough to cover the cutting of the Fallopian tubes . . . three generations of imbeciles is enough" (quoted in Haller, *Eugenics,* p. 129).

[15] L. M. Terman, *The Measurement of Intelligence* (Boston: Houghton Mifflin, 1916), p. 11.

of Edward L. Thorndike, who found a higher morality among those with greater intelligence. Thorndike was convinced that "To him that hath a superior intellect is given also on the average a superior character."[16] Both Thorndike and his pupils continued to advocate the sterilization solution to moral behavior problems and the improvement of intelligence. By 1940, in his last major work, he concluded that

> By selective breeding supported by a suitable environment we can have a world in which all men will equal the top ten per cent of present men. One sure service of the *able* and *good* is to beget and rear offspring. One sure service (about the only one) which the inferior and vicious can perform is to prevent their genes from survival.[17]

The association of inferiority with viciousness and intelligence with goodness continued to appear in the psychology textbooks. Henry E. Garrett, who was a former student and colleague of Thorndike and who won a "reputation for eminence,"[18] continued to project the story of Martin Kallikak in terms of goods and bads in his textbook on *General Psychology* as late as 1961. Just in case someone might miss the point, the children of the feebleminded tavern girl were pictured with horns, while the offspring of the "worthy Quakeress" wife were described as the "highest types of human beings" and portrayed as solid Puritan types (see figure 6.2).[19]

This view of the Kallikaks was no accident. As chairman of Columbia's department of psychology for sixteen years and as past president of the American Psychological Association as well as a former member of the National Research Council, Garret sympathized with Thorndike's views on the place of the "inferior and vicious" in American life. By 1966, as a professor emeritus from Co-

[16] Edward L. Thorndike, "Intelligence and Its Uses," *Harper's*, January 1920, p. 233.

[17] Edward L. Thorndike, *Human Nature and the Social Order* (New York: Macmillan, 1940), p. 957 (emphasis added).

[18] Geraldine Jonich, *The Sane Positivist* (Middleton, Conn.: Wesleyan University Press, 1968), p. 443.

[19] For much of the research in this essay I am indebted to the research assistance of Russell Marks, University of Illinois. See also Russell Marks, "Testing for Social Control" (Paper delivered at the A.E.R.A. meetings, New York City, February 4–7, 1971).

FIGURE 6.2 THE GOOD AND BAD OF MARTIN KALLIKAK

MARTIN KALLIKAK

He dallied with
a feeble-minded
tavern girl

He married a
worthy Quakeress

She bore a son
known as "Old Horror"
who had ten children

She bore
seven upright
worthy children

From "Old Horror's"
ten children came hundreds
of the lowest types of
human beings

From these seven worthy
children came hundreds
of the highest types
of human beings

FIGURE 28 *The influence of heredity is demonstrated by the "good" and the "bad"*
Kallikaks.

Source: Henry E. Garrett, *General Psychology* (New York: American Book Co., 1955),
p. 65. The illustration was retained in the second edition published in 1961, p. 56.

lumbia, in the midst of the civil rights movement, he produced a series of pamphlets that proclaimed what he believed to be the implications of sixty years of testing in America. Published by the Patrick Henry Press, over 500,000 copies of his pamphlets were distributed free of charge to American teachers. In *How Classroom Desegregation Will Work, Children Black and White,* and especially in *Breeding Down,* Garrett justified American racism on "scientific" grounds. Returning to Davenport and the Eugenics Record Office as well as to Terman's work and others, Garrett argued:

> You can no more mix the two races and maintain the standards of White civilization than you can add 80 (the average I.Q. of Negroes) and 100 (average I.Q. of Whites), divide by two and get 100. What you would get would be a race of 90s, and it is that 10 per cent differential that spells the difference between a spire and a mud hut; 10 per cent—or less—is the margin of civilization's "profit"; it is the difference between a cultured society and savagery.
>
> Therefore, it follows, if miscegenation would be bad for White people, it would be bad for Negroes as well. For, if leadership is destroyed, all is destroyed.[20]

Going on to point out that the black man is at least two hundred thousand years behind the white, he asserted that intermarriage, as well as desegregation, would destroy the genetic lead the white man had achieved through "hard won struggle" and "fortitudinous evolution." The state, he argued, ". . . can and should prohibit miscegenation, just as they ban marriage of the feeble-minded, the insane and various undesirables. Just as they outlaw incest."[21]

"Scientific" Justification

The style and content of Garrett's arguments were but echoes of similar ones developed earlier by Davenport, Laughlin, Terman, Brigham, Yerkes, and Thorndike. C. C. Brigham, for example, praised the superior Nordic draftees of World War I and worried about the inferior germ-plasm of the Alpine, Mediterranean, and Negro races

---

[20] Henry E. Garrett, *Breeding Down* (Richmond: Patrick Henry Press, n.d.), p. 10.
[21] Ibid., p. 17.

in *A Study of American Intelligence.*[22] What disturbed Brigham, and the U.S. Congress as well, was, of course, the fact that 70 percent of the total immigration in the early 1920s was coming from Mediterranean racial stock. H. H. Laughlin of the Carnegie Foundation of Washington provided the scientific evidence on this problem to the Congress in his report, "An Analysis of America's Melting Pot." Using information from the army tests and from his Eugenics Record Office dealing with the insane and feebleminded, Laughlin built his case—the numbers of southern Europeans appearing as wards of the state proved that those immigrants were of inferior racial stock.[23]

Supported by the Commonwealth Fund, Lewis M. Terman reported similar evidence from his study. Addressing the National Education Association at Oakland, California, on July 2, 1923, he expressed concern about the fecundity of the superior races. As he put it:

> The racial stocks most prolific of gifted children are those from northern and western Europe, and the Jewish. The least prolific are the Mediterranean races, the Mexicans and the Negroes. The fecundity of the family stocks from which our gifted children come appears to be definitely on the wane. . . . It has been figured that if the present differential birth rate continues, 1,000 Harvard graduates will at the end of 200 years have but 50 descendants, while in the same period 1,000 South Italians will have multiplied to 100,000.[24]

This kind of hard "scientific" data derived from the testing and eugenics movements entered the dialogue that led to the restrictive immigration quota of 1924, which clearly discriminated against southern Europeans.

America had moved definitely toward a more restrictive immigration policy after World War I. While small manufacturers, rep-

---

[22] C. C. Brigham, *A Study of American Intelligence* (Princeton, N.J.: Princeton University Press, 1923), pp. 159, 207, 210. It should be noted that during the thirties, however, Brigham went to considerable effort to refute his former work.

[23] See House Committee on Immigration and Naturalization, *Europe as an Emigrant-Exporting Continent and the United States as an Immigrant-Receiving Nation,* by H. H. Laughlin, 68th Congress, 1st sess., Mar. 8, 1924, p. 1311.

[24] Lewis M. Terman, "The Conservation of Talent," *School and Society* 19(Mar. 29, 1924):363.

resented by the National Association of Manufacturers and the Chamber of Commerce, tended to favor a sliding-door policy that would open and close according to the labor needs of small manufacturers, most larger manufacturers and labor unions, represented by the National Civic Federation, favored restrictive immigration. The motivation, one suspects, was best stated by Bostonian Edward A. Filene, a pioneer in employee management, when he said:

> Employers do not need an increased labor supply, since increased use of labor saving machinery and elimination of waste in production and distribution will for many years reduce costs more rapidly than wages increase, and so prevent undue domination of labor.[25]

The Carnegie money that Laughlin used in his campaign for greater restrictions ultimately became money well spent in the interest of the larger manufacturer. Generally, though, the rhetoric of the times and the testers was, perhaps, best symbolized by President Coolidge, who proclaimed, "America must be kept American."

RISE OF THE MERITOCRACY

Nativism, racism, elitism, and social-class bias, so much a part of the testing and the eugenics movement in America, were in a broader sense part of the *Zeitgeist* that was America. This was the land of the Ku Klux Klan, the Red Scare, the Sacco-Vanzetti and Scopes trials. It was also the land where the corporate liberal state took firm root, fostering the development of a kind of meritocracy that even Plato could not have envisioned. Just as Plato ascribed certain virtues to certain occupational classes, so Lewis Terman assigned numbers standing for virtue to certain occupational classes. Terman clearly saw America as the land of opportunity, where the best excelled and where the inferior found themselves on the lower rungs of the occupational order. Designing the Stanford-Binet intelligence test, Terman developed questions that were based on presumed progressive difficulty in performing tasks he believed necessary for achievement in ascending the hierarchical occupational structure. He then proceeded to find that, according to the results of his tests, the intelligence of different occupational classes fit his

---

[25] Quoted by Robert DeC. Ward, "Our New Immigration Policy," *Foreign Affairs* 3(September 1924):104.

ascending hierarchy. Little wonder the intelligence quotient reflected social-class bias! It was *based* on the social-class order. Terman believed that, for the most part, people were at a certain level
because of heredity and not social environment:

> Preliminary investigations indicate that an I.Q. below 70 rarely
> permits anything better than unskilled labor; that the range
> from 70 to 80 is preeminently that of semi-skilled labor, from
> 80 to 100 that of the skilled or ordinary clerical labor, from 100
> to 110 or 115 that of the semi-professional pursuits; and that
> above all these are the grades of intelligence which permit one
> to enter the professions or the larger fields of business. Intel-
> ligence tests can tell us whether a child's native brightness cor-
> responds more nearly to the median of (1) the professional
> classes, (2) those in the semi-professional pursuits, (3) ordinary
> skilled workers, (4) semi-skilled workers, or (5) unskilled la-
> borers. This information will be of great value in planning the
> education of a particular child and also in planning the differ-
> entiated curriculum here recommended.[26]

Plato had three classes, Terman had five. Both maintained the "myth
of the metal." And both advocated a differentiated curriculum to
meet the needs of the individuals involved. Terman so completely
accepted the assumption of the social-class meritocracy and the
tests that were based on that meritocracy that he never seemed to
even wonder why, in his own study of the gifted, "The professional
and semi-professional classes together account for more than 80
percent. The unskilled labor classes furnish but a paltry 1 percent
or 2 percent."[27]

Social class was not the only problem with the tests. Whether one
reads Terman's Stanford-Binet or his Group Test of Mental Ability
or the Stanford Achievement Tests, the army tests, or the National
Intelligence Tests,[28] certain characteristics emerge. They all reflect
the euphemisms, the homilies, and the morals that were, indeed,
the stock and trade of *Poor Richard's Almanac,* Noah Webster's

---

[26] Lewis M. Terman, *Intelligence Tests and School Reorganization* (New York:
World Book Co., 1923), pp. 27–28.

[27] Terman, "Conservation of Talent," p. 363.

[28] The National Intelligence Test, interestingly enough, was standardized on army
officers and used in the schools after World War I.

Blue-back Speller, and *McGuffey's Readers.* The child who grew up in a home and attended a school where these books were in common usage had a distinct advantage over the newly arrived immigrant child. At a time when over half the children in American schools were either immigrants or children of immigrants, the testing movement represented massive discrimination.

In 1922, Walter Lippmann, in a series of six articles for *The New Republic,* questioned whether intelligence is fixed by heredity and whether the tests actually measured intelligence.[29] Although Lippmann seemed to have the better of the argument, Terman fell back to the high ground of the condescending professional expert who saw little need to debate proven "scientific" principles.[30]

Conscious of the social implications of their work, Goddard, Terman, and Thorndike viewed themselves as great benefactors of society. Concern for social order and rule by the intelligent elite was ever present in their writings. Goddard put it bluntly when he argued: "The disturbing fear is that the masses—the seventy or even eighty-six million—will take matters into their own hands."[31] The "four million" of "superior intelligence" must direct them. The definition of democracy had changed. It no longer meant rule by the people. It meant rule by the intelligent. As Thorndike put it, "The argument for democracy is not that it gives power to men without distinction, but that it gives greater freedom for ability and character to attain power."[32] Meritocracy had replaced democracy.

Luckily, mankind's wealth, power, ability, and character were all positively correlated. This, indeed, was not only Plato's ideal, but also the testers' view of the meritocracy they in fact were fashioning. Reflective late in life, Thorndike said:

> It is the great good fortune of mankind that there is a substantial positive correlation between intelligence and morality, including good will toward one's fellows. Consequently our

[29] See Walter Lippmann, "A Future for the Tests," *New Republic,* Nov. 29, 1922. See also "The Mental Age of Americans," *New Republic,* Oct. 25, 1922; "The Mystery of the 'A' Men," *New Republic,* Nov. 1, 1922; "The Reliability of Intelligence Tests," *New Republic,* Nov. 8, 1922; "The Abuse of Tests," *New Republic,* Nov. 15, 1922; "Tests of Hereditary Intelligence," *New Republic,* Nov. 22, 1922.

[30] See Lewis M. Terman, "The Great Conspiracy," *New Republic,* Dec. 27, 1922, p. 117.

[31] H. H. Goddard, *Human Efficiency and Levels of Intelligence* (Princeton, N.J.: Princeton University Press, 1920), p. 97.

[32] Thorndike, "Intelligence and Its Uses," p. 235.

superiors in ability are on the average our benefactors, and it is often safer to trust our interests to them than to ourselves. No group of men can be expected to act one hundred per cent in the interest of mankind, but this group of the ablest men will come nearest to the ideal.[33]

To be sure, there have been and still are inequities between men of intelligence and of wealth, Thorndike argued, but through the "beneficence of such men as Carnegie and Rockefeller," this discrepancy had been somewhat overcome.[34]

Although Thorndike was directly involved in army classification testing during World War I and the creation of the National Intelligence Test after the war—all of which skyrocketed the testing movement in American schools—perhaps he influenced American schools most profoundly through his work in organizing the curriculum. His name appears on approximately 50 books and 450 monographs and articles, including the much used Thorndike *Dictionary*. He wrote many textbooks, tests, achievement scales, and teacher's manuals. In short, he told teachers what to teach and how to teach and, finally, how to evaluate what they had done. Much of his work was, indeed, made possible through the beneficence of Carnegie. The Carnegie Foundation from 1922 to 1938 had made grants supporting his work totaling approximately $325,000.[35] It was men like Thorndike, Terman, and Goddard, supported by corporate wealth,[36] who successfully persuaded teachers, administrators, and school boards to classify and standardize the school's curriculum with a differentiated track system based on ability and values of the corporate liberal society. The structure of that society was based, then, on an assumed meritocracy, a meritocracy of white middle-class, management-oriented professionals.

Tests discriminated against members of the lower class—southern Europeans and blacks—indirectly by what they seemed to leave out, but more directly by what they included. For example: on a Stan-

---

[33] Edward L. Thorndike, "How May We Improve the Selection, Training and Life-Work of Leaders?" in *Addresses Delivered Before the Fifth Conference on Educational Policies* (New York: Teachers College, Columbia University Press, 1939), p. 32.

[34] Ibid., p. 31.

[35] U.S. House of Representatives, *Special Committee to Investigate Tax Exempt Foundations, Summary of Activities,* June 9, 1954, p. 20.

[36] It should be noted here that up to 1954 the Carnegie Foundation alone had invested approximately $6.5 million in testing. Ibid., p. 78.

ford-Binet (1960 revision), a six-year-old child is asked the question, "Which is prettier?"[37] He must select the Nordic Anglo-Saxon type to be correct. If, however, the child happens to be Mexican-American or of southern European descent, has looked at himself in a mirror, and has a reasonably healthy respect for himself, he will pick the wrong answer. Worse off yet is the child who recognizes what a "repressive society" calls the "right" answer and has been socialized enough to sacrifice himself for a higher score (see figure 6.3). The same holds true for the black six-year-old (see figure 6.4). Neither blacks nor southern Europeans were beautiful according to the authors of the Stanford-Binet, but then, there was no beauty in these people when Goddard, Laughlin, Terman, Thorndike, and Garrett called for the sterilization of the "socially inadequate," the discriminatory closing of immigration, the tracking organization of the American school or, for that matter, when they defined these peoples' place in the meritocracy.[38]

Tests, then, discriminated in content against particular groups in the very questions that were used as well as in the questions that were not used with respect to particular minority experiences. While some educational psychologists sought to eliminate bias from the content of the tests, as well as introduce a broader cultural basis for them, others sought the impossible: a culturally free I.Q. test. Still other educational psychologists, hard pressed to define intelligence, fell back on the assertion that intelligence was simply that which the tests measured. Although many gave up their concern about intelligence, others argued that the various intelligence tests were achievement tests that could also be good predictors of success within both the corporate society and the bureaucratic school system serving that society. At this point, the testers ended up where Terman started.

---

[37] It should be noted here that this is the latest revision of the Stanford-Binet Intelligence Test. For calling my attention to the racial bias on this Stanford-Binet Test, I am indebted to Lamont Wyche.

[38] Of this group, only Terman wavered from the original position. When he wrote his autobiography in 1932 he had stated as his belief that "the major differences between children of high and low I.Q. and the major differences in the intelligence test-scores of certain races, such as Negroes and whites, will never be fully accounted for on the environmental hypothesis." By 1951 he had penciled in around that statement, "I am less sure of this now"; in 1955 another note said, "I'm still less sure." See Ernest R. Hilgard, "Lewis Madison Terman," *American Journal of Psychology* 70(September 1957):472–479.

FIGURE 6.3   ETHNIC BIAS IN INTELLIGENCE TEST

Source: Stanford-Binet Intelligence Scale, 1960, L-M IV-6, 1 Card C.

FIGURE 6.4   RACIAL BIAS IN INTELLIGENCE TEST

Source: Stanford-Binet Intelligence Scale, 1960, L-M IV-6, 1 Card A.

The Occupational Hierarchy

Terman's tests were based on an occupational hierarchy that was, in fact, the social-class system of the corporate liberal state then emerging. Various tests, all the way from I.Q. to personality and scholastic achievement, periodically brought up-to-date, would play a vital role in rationalizing the social-class system. The tests also created the illusion of objectivity which, on the one side, served the needs of the "professional" educators to be "scientific," and on the other, served the system's need for a myth that could convince the lower classes that their station in life was part of the natural order of things. For many, the myth had apparently worked. In 1965, the Russell Sage Foundation issued a report entitled *Experiences and Attitudes of American Adults Concerning Standardized Intelligence Tests*.[39] The major findings of that report indicated that the effects of the tests on social classes were "strong and consistent" and that while "the upper class respondent is more likely to favor the use of tests than the lower class respondent," the "lower class respondent is more likely to see intelligence tests measuring inborn intelligence."[40]

The lower-class American adult was, indeed, a product of fifty years of testing. He had been channeled through an intricate bureaucratic educational system which, in the name of meeting his individual needs, classified and tracked him into an occupation appropriate to his socioeconomic status. The tragic character of this phenomenon was not only that the lower class learned to believe in the system, but worse, through internalizing that set of beliefs, the lower class made it work. It worked because the lowered self-image that the school and society reinforced[41] on the lower-class child did result in lower achievement. A normal child objectified as subnormal and treated by the teacher and the school as subnormal will almost surely behave as a subnormal child. Likewise, the lower-class child who is taught in many ways to doubt his own intelligence can be expected to exhibit a lower achievement level than those chil-

---

[39] Orville G. Brim, John Neulinger, David C. Glass, *Experiences and Attitudes of American Adults Concerning Standardized Intelligence Tests*. Russell Sage Foundation Technical Report No. 1 on the Social Consequences of Testing (New York: Russell Sage, 1965).

[40] Ibid., p. 89.

[41] Ibid. One of the findings was that a member of the lower class "estimates his intelligence as inferior to others."

dren who are repeatedly reminded that they are made of superior clay,[42] and therefore, are of superior worth.

Intelligence and achievement tests used throughout American society are a vital part of the infrastructure that serves to stabilize and order the values of the corporate liberal society.[43] Arthur R. Jensen put it well when he said: "Had the first I.Q. tests been devised in a hunting culture, 'general intelligence' might well have turned out to involve visual acuity and running speed, rather than vocabulary and symbol manipulation."[44] Jensen, as Terman and others, argued that,

> . . . what we now mean by intelligence is something like the probability of acceptable performance (given the opportunity) in occupations varying in social status. So we see that the prestige hierarchy of occupations is a reliable objective reality in our society. To this should be added the fact that there is undoubtedly some relationship between the levels of the hierarchy and the occupations' intrinsic desirability, or gratification to the individual engaged in them. Even if all occupations paid alike and received equal respect and acclaim, some occupations would still be viewed as more desirable than others, which would make for competition, selection, and again, a kind of prestige hierarchy.[45]

The hierarchy, Jensen argued, was inevitable: "Most persons would agree that painting pictures is more satisfying than painting barns, and conducting a symphony orchestra is more exciting than directing traffic."[46] While the hierarchy was culturally determined, it is clear that certain values that Jensen preferred appeared to him more intrinsic than others. Nevertheless, he admitted, "We have to face it: the assortment of persons into occupational roles simply is not

---

[42] For an analysis of the way the idea of self-fulfilling prophecy works, see R. Rosenthal and L. Jacobson, "Self-Fulfilling Prophecies in the Classroom: Teachers' Expectations as Unintended Determinants of Pupils' Intellectual Competence," in *Social Class, Race and Psychological Development*, ed. by Martin Deutsch et al. (New York: Holt, Rinehart and Winston, 1968).

[43] For an analysis of the role of psychologists in business, see Loren Baritz, *The Servants of Power* (New York: Wiley, 1965).

[44] Arthur R. Jensen, "How Much Can We Boost I.Q. and Scholastic Achievement?" *Harvard Educational Review* 39(Winter 1969):14.

[45] Ibid., pp. 14–15.

[46] Ibid., p. 15.

'fair' in any absolute sense. The best we can hope for is that true merit, given equality of opportunity, acts as the basis for the natural assorting process."[47] Herein lies the crucial weakness of the argument. Given the current racist, economic, and socially elitist society where wealth, power, and educational privilege are so unevenly distributed, what does it mean to assume "equality of opportunity," and "hope" that "true merit" will somehow result from a "natural assorting process"?

Jensen, like Thorndike and Terman before him, assumed an ideal liberal community where "equality of opportunity" balanced with lively competition produced a social system in which "true" merit was rewarded. Although the "Jefferson-Conant" ideal of the good community is in itself questionable, the problem was compounded when the ideal society was confused with the real society. In spite of Terman's, Thorndike's, and Jensen's idealized assumptions about "equal opportunity" and "natural assorting process," all based their objective data on the real world of economic and social privilege. Most testers refused to admit the possibility that they were, perhaps, servants of privilege, power, and status. They preferred instead to believe and "hope" that what they were measuring was, in fact, true "merit." This was an act of faith, a faith based on the belief that somehow the "prestige hierarchy of occupations" and the people in it who provided the objective standard upon which the tests were based, were there not because of privilege, wealth, power, status, and violence, but because of superior talent and virtue. This was a fundamental axiom in the liberal's faith in the meritocracy that emerged in twentieth-century American education.

Throughout this century, within this liberal faith, there emerged a series of doctrinal disputes engaging the attention of millions of people. The nature-nurture argument was one such continuous dispute from Galton to Jensen. The course of this dispute reflected little more than increasing refinement of statistical techniques and accumulation of data on both sides of the issue. Given the number of unprovable propositions on both sides, one finds the choice between heredity and environment more a matter of faith than of hard evidence. In many respects, the nature-nurture argument is misleading. One can accept a strong hereditarian position and still advocate political, economic, and social equality, just as one might accept a

---

[47] Ibid.

strong environmentalist position and still argue for political, economic, and social inequality. There is, in fact, no inherent logic either in the mind of man or in a universe that dictates that differences in intellectual ability necessarily should mean differences in social power. Why, for example, should a person be more favorably rewarded because, through no effort of his own, he happened to inherit a superior intelligence or because he happened to be born into a superior social environment. Repeatedly, from Terman to Hernstein, psychologists have attempted to link ability to the meritocracy without questioning the values inherent in the meritocratic principle itself.[48]

Most liberal environmentalists do not take their position to its logical conclusion. To do so would be to question not only the ideal assumption upon which the meritocracy rests (such as equal opportunity and the inherent value of competition), but to further question the hierarchy of values that undergird the work of the professional expert in the liberal society. The expert, with his esoteric knowledge, is a vital element in both the creation and maintenance of the corporate meritocracy. His economic and political self-interest as well as his very survival is at stake. Thus, it is understandable that so few in the professional middle class are disturbed by the presumed meritocracy, or are seriously inclined to question it. Those who have done well by the system can hardly be expected to be its severe critics. To be sure, some are willing to suggest that we ought to look at the social system from the bottom up, and out of humanitarian or perhaps survival motives allow more opportunity for those who have been cut out of the system, but few are willing to critically doubt the validity of the system itself.

Meritocracy and the Courts

It is also understandable that those who have been cut out of the system should provide the most vehement source of criticism. The unusual thing, however, is that in the past half century there have been so few real challenges. The meritocracy issue was bound to surface as the Supreme Court of the United States attacked segregation of children in the public schools in the 1954 Brown decision. Effects of segregation on the basis of race could be achieved in most communities through segregation on the basis of "tested" ability. If,

[48] For this insight, I am indebted to Russell Marks.

in fact, the tests were based on socioeconomic class, then the net result of segregation was possible.

In Bolling v. Sharpe (1954) the Court ordered the desegregation of the District of Columbia schools, and in 1956 the board of education adopted a tracking system for the Washington public schools based on so-called "ability grouping." In Hobson v. Hansen (District Court case, 1967) Skelly Wright, a U.S. circuit judge, wrote the opinion that challenged not only the use of ability tracking in the Washington public schools to circumvent desegregation, but went on to question the basis of tracking in the first place. While the school board insisted that the tracking system was based on meeting the needs of individuals through curricular adjustment according to their ability, it denied racial bias. The board did admit, though, that placement in the tracks was related to socioeconomic status of the students.

The Washington, D.C. school system was operating a four-track system—an honors track for the gifted, a college preparatory track, a general education track, and a special track for the "slow learners." Highly rationalized and objectified, the system was supported by empirical data derived from an extensive testing program. It was a fairly typical track system which, since the work of Terman and others, had come to be part of a standard curricular design of the American school. Terman's 1924 forecast had come true: "I predict that within a decade or two something like the three-track plan of Oakland, Berkeley and Detroit, supplemented by opportunity classes for defectives and for the very gifted, will become standard."[49] The track system had become standard, and interestingly enough, rested on Terman's argument that it represented a step toward "educational democracy." If a school recognizes individual differences and adjusts the curriculum according to individual needs, he argued, every child will have the "opportunity to make the most of whatever ability he possesses."[50] Terman went on to say that he had little patience with critics who condemn his tracking plan as undemocratic and labeled them as "educational sentimentalists." Forty-three years later, Skelly Wright, in reviewing the Washington, D.C. tracking system, which was similar to the system espoused by Terman, concluded:

---

[49] Terman, "Conservation of Talent," p. 364.
[50] Ibid.

Even in concept the track system is undemocratic and discriminatory. Its creator admits it is designed to prepare some children for white-collar, and other children for blue-collar jobs. Considering the tests used to determine which children should receive the blue-collar special, and which the white, the danger of children completing their education wearing the wrong collar is far too great for this democracy to tolerate.[51]

The court carefully considered the basis for ability grouping in both theory and practice. In theory, the tests were intended to measure ability while the tracks were designed to serve individual needs. In practice, however, the court found that the tests measured past socioeconomic advantage as much as presumed ability, and the curricular track served mainly to lock the child into the socioeconomic class from which he came. Few children ever crossed tracks. Once the child was objectified or tracked, a self-fulfilling prophecy seemed to follow:

The real tragedy of misjudgements about the disadvantaged student's abilities is, as described earlier, the likelihood that the student will act out that judgement and confirm it by achieving only at the expected level. Indeed it may be even worse than that, for there is strong evidence that performance in fact declines.[52]

The court went on to warn that,

. . . a system that presumes to tell a student what his ability is and what he can successfully learn incurs an obligation to take account of the psychological damage that can come from such an encounter between the student and the school; and to be certain that it is in a position to decide whether the student's deficiencies are true, or only apparent.[53]

After raising issues about "true" or "apparent" deficiencies, equal opportunity and the credibility of the tests, and further recognizing the fact that mental ability grouping corresponded to social class, the court proceeded to declare the tracking system as employed in the Washington schools a violation of the plaintiff's constitutional

[51] Hobson v. Hansen, Civil Action, No. 82–66, *Federal Supplement,* V. 269, p. 515.
[52] Ibid., p. 491.
[53] Ibid., p. 492.

rights.[54] Even though the court came close, it did not question the social basis of the meritocracy in the liberal state, nor did it contest the right of that state (using a Jeffersonian phrase) ". . . to rake from the rubbish annually."

Although the Hobson v. Hansen decision had little effect generally on the nation's schools, it did threaten the security of some testers, especially those who had come to believe in their own myths. Those who realized that the tests were based on a meritocracy which, in turn, was based on a socioeconomic hierarchy, remained secure. Clearly, it would take nothing short of a fundamental socioeconomic revolution to shake the position of testing in the corporate liberal state. To chip away at the tests was almost akin to chipping away at an iceberg. While the blacks in the ghetto schools might do away with standardized tests in outrage against the white middle-class bias and values they reflected, blacks still could not do away with the socioeconomic hierarchy that controlled entrance into virtually every occupation within the corporate liberal state. And that, after all, was what the tests represented. For the most part, the tests were not arbitrary. They rather validly represented the requirements of corporate America. And one of the central values reflected in that state's schools as well as in its social and political life was "efficiency."

Tests and Efficiency

Virtually all educational debate seemed to end with the efficiency criterion. The need to classify and standardize an entire nation so as to maximize productivity efficiently had become commonly accepted by 1970. There were problems, however, in both the way in which people were tested and classified and the way in which the classification system was used to restrict employment opportunities. As various institutions increasingly used tests and educational requirements, more as a vehicle for keeping people out of specific occupations than as a test of actual job performance, the credentialing system became strained and inflated to the point where employers could discriminate against minority groups with relative ease.[55] In

---

[54] Skelly Wright's decision was viewed by many in 1967 as the probable direction the Warren Court would take when it eventually faced the thorny problem of de facto segregation. Given the development of the new court, this prediction is questionable.

[55] For the questionable relationship between education and actual job performance, see Ivar E. Berg, *Education and Jobs: The Great Training Robbery* (New York: Praeger, 1970).

1971, the Supreme Court of the United States struck down the personnel policies of Duke Power Company's Dan River power station that required a high school diploma or acceptable performance on two standardized tests. The company had difficulty showing any clear relationship between these educational or test requirements and actual job performance. This decision sent a cold chill through those private companies profiting from the $55 million educational testing business, even though the Court attacked merely the test's relationships to actual job performance, not the testing procedure. The Court declared that the employer who uses personnel tests must show a "manifest relationship" of such tests to the "employment in question."

Tests, then, were used to discriminate against children in their schools and against adults in their occupations. While some might see in these events minor problems in Condorcet's dream of progress, others saw it as an Orwellian nightmare of "double think." Perhaps they were the same.

In 1965 the Carnegie Corporation, under the leadership of Francis Keppel, John Gardner, and James B. Conant, initiated the development of a national testing program called "A National Assessment of Educational Progress." Employing the same statistical-sampling techniques used to measure industrial productivity, these men suggested that eventually a "growth" national product index could be developed to measure the progress of American schools. Conant advocated national assessment, in part at least, because of the difficulty he had in obtaining hard data when he made his earlier reports on *The American High School Today, The Junior High School* and *Teacher Education*. This concern, coupled with his interest in the development of a commission that would serve as a vehicle to shape national educational policy, led him to propose, while financially supported by the Carnegie Corporation and Danforth Foundation, the development of the Compact of the States.[56] The compact provided the "quasi-public" vehicles through which national testing could proceed without too much public interference. Reflecting on his many and varied educational accomplishments, Conant in *My Several Lives* counted the compact as his "greatest" achievement.

---

[56] See James B. Conant, *Shaping Educational Policy* (New York: McGraw-Hill, 1964). The financial report of the Compact of the States (as of May 1966) showed that Carnegie and Danforth contributed $300,000 of a $318,000 budget. See Frederick Raubinger and Harold C. Hand, "It Is Later Than You Think" (unpublished paper, 1967), p. 29.

On the surface it might appear that American education is controlled by locally elected boards, and that at the national level a power vacuum exists owing to the American people's reluctance to create a national system of education. This is misleading. There does exist within the corporate liberal state a quasi-public bureaucracy of boards, compacts, councils, and commissions that serves to shape policy by giving and withholding both public and private funds at key points in the system. The American Council on Education is one such agency through which hundreds of philanthropic foundations, private businesses, and public colleges and universities work to establish nationwide educational policy.[57] In many ways the council has acted as both a meeting ground for what appear to be disparate interests, but it also has served as a conduit for channeling funds into selected areas of higher education, thereby effectively shaping practice as well as policy.

While World War I provided a strong stimulus for the testing movement, foundations like the Carnegie Corporation and the Carnegie Foundation for the Advancement of Teaching, the Commonwealth Fund, the Graduate Records Office of the Carnegie Foundation, and others, provided the funds that sustained and propelled the movement. World War II demonstrated the usefulness of systems analysis and the need, in the name of efficiency, for systematic overall manpower planning.[58] The idea of a centralized testing service was born.

In 1946–1947, the American Council on Education received reports from the Carnegie Foundation for the Advancement of Teaching recommending the consolidation of a number of testing units that had developed over the years, such as the College Entrance Examination Board and the Graduate Records Office.[59] Under a self-perpetuating board of trustees, which included people drawn from the American Council on Education, foundations, public and private colleges, as well as from business and government, the Educational

---

[57] For the membership in that council, see *A Brief Statement of the History and Activities of the American Council on Education* [1918–1959] (Washington, D.C.: American Council on Education). There is some similarity between the kind of makeup and function of the council and the earlier National Civic Federation, which also served disparate interests while at the same time working for the common good of the liberal state.

[58] It should be noted that it was Conant's concern for manpower planning that led him to recommend the G.I. Bill, which in essence used the school as a holding device that effectively checked severe economic dislocation resulting from the war.

[59] For the connection here, I am indebted to Professor Fred Raubinger.

Testing Service (ETS) began with a grant from the Carnegie Corporation. The rapid growth of ETS is reflected in its operating budget. Operational expenses for ETS increased from approximately $2 million in 1947 to $29.7 million by 1969.[60] By then ETS, a private nonprofit organization, provided the tests taken by millions of Americans to determine their eligibility for the service academies, the Peace Corps, colleges and universities, and the professions.[61] The doorway to virtually every profession in the corporate liberal state came under the influence and control of the new organization. It is interesting, but not unusual, that such power would be exercised by private rather than public boards. This is a key characteristic of the liberal corporate state.

Role of Foundations

That fourth branch of government born in the progressive era and representing liberal corporate interests—that is, the foundations—has flexibly and effectively served to maintain the interests of corporate wealth through the support and maintenance of the liberal state. Judging the shifting support policy of the foundations in the

---

[60] See *ETS Developments* 17(May 1970):2.

[61] The kinds of tests used included The Preliminary Scholastic Aptitude Test, the Advanced Placement Examinations, the College Placement Tests, the College-Level Examination Program, and the Comparative Guidance and Placement Program—the last two for two-year colleges.

ETS also administers other admissions tests: the Graduate Record Examinations for admission to graduate study; more specialized tests for admission to architectural schools and to the colleges of podiatry; and now a test for admission to grades seven through eleven of independent secondary schools. As one staff member remarked, "We have a test for admission to everything except heaven."

Achievement tests. In addition to the achievement tests of the College Board, there are the numerous Cooperative Tests (which now extend even to a Preschool Inventory), the Undergraduate Program (replacing the Graduate Record Examinations as formerly used by colleges for testing undergraduates), and the Graduate School Foreign Language Testing Program (to satisfy the language requirement for advanced degrees).

In a special category is the Test of English as a Foreign Language to measure the English proficiency of foreign students, government trainees, and others who apply for education in an English-speaking country.

Professional examinations. Among the many professional examinations offered by ETS are the National Teacher Examinations, the National Council of Architectural Registration Boards Examinations, the Chartered Life Underwriter Examinations, the American Board of Obstetrics and Gynecology Examination, and the Examination in Speech Pathology and in Audiology. Perhaps the stiffest of all examinations offered by ETS is called the Written Examination for Appointment as Foreign Service Officer (for Department of State and U.S. Information Agency assignments). From *ETS Developments,* 17(May 1970):2.

twentieth century, one need not conjure up a conspiracy theory in order to perceive some rather consistent practices that emerge. The key is enlightened self-interest. Foundation trustees and executives were intelligent men who recognized their own interests in what they viewed as a progressively developing society. In the interest of what its officers perceived as racial progress, the Carnegie Institution of Washington supported the Laughlin studies used to close immigration, and in the interest of educational progress, they supported the testing movement after the war and the standardization of American education along the values laid down by Thorndike. Whether it was Terman calling for special education for the gifted, or Conant calling for "national educational assessment," or ETS striving to develop, in the name of "accountability," performance-based teacher tests, all served as part of a broader efficiency movement to classify, standardize, and rationalize human beings to serve the productive interests of a society essentially controlled by wealth, privilege, and status.

The tests, and the meritocracy as well, served to mask power so well that any real revolutionary opposition was effectively immobilized. If a man truly believes that he has a marginal standard of living because he is inferior, he is less likely to take violent measures against the social system than if he believes his condition a product of social privilege. In the nineteenth century, Daniel Webster said: "Public education is a wise and liberal system of police, by which property, and life, and the peace of society are secured." In the twentieth century public education serves much the same purpose. The foundations' deep involvement in educational policy, whether it be the activities of the Ford Foundation in educational television, or of the Carnegie Corporation and Carnegie Foundation in testing, or of the Rockefeller Foundation in black education, all had an interest in an effective, efficiently managed system. Foundations' management of educational policy in the twentieth century has been clearly and intimately involved in every educational reform from the "Carnegie unit" to the "open classroom."

Even the rhetoric that engages the professional educators seems fairly well managed. Throughout the last four decades, the pendulum of educational rhetoric has swung from the child-centered discussion of the thirties to the society-determined needs of the fifties, then again, to the child-centered needs of the seventies. In the thirties, the Carnegie Corporation supported the Progressive Education Association with over $4 million, while in the fifties, Carnegie aided James Conant's study of American schools, as well as the project that culminated in Charles Silberman's *Crisis in the Classroom* in the 1970s.

It is useful to recall that during periods of labor surplus, our educational rhetoric tends to be child-centered, while in periods of shortage the rhetoric shifts to society-oriented needs. The ups and downs of the labor supply may be the propelling factor. It is interesting, however, to note one other thing. When the rhetoric became so heated that people could be heard suggesting that we do away with the system or radically change it, the Carnegie Corporation supported James Conant, who, in effect, said the system was basically sound but then co-opted the rhetoric of the attackers to recommend limited change. Conant, after all, had the survival of the system in mind when he spoke of social dynamite in the ghettoes. By the 1970s, when most manpower projections clearly indicated surplus of labor for the next decade, the educational reform rhetoric shifted from training scientists and engineers to open classrooms. Again, critics could be heard suggesting that the system be radically altered if not abolished and, once again, the Carnegie Corporation supported a study, this time by Silberman, which in effect said that the system was basically sound but needed some reforming. Again, the rhetoric of the attackers was co-opted for limited change. While the Carnegie Corporation and Foundation do not obviously control the pendulum, they have played a major role in managing the rhetoric at critical points when the system has been in acute danger.[62]

It is this function of governor of the educational machinery to prevent destructive unmanaged revolution that the foundations have performed so well. One, then, is left to ponder the question of whether Charles W. Eliot was right in 1913 when he testified before Congress that he had "never known a charitable or educational corporation to do anything which threatened the welfare or the liberties of the American people." Or perhaps the majority of the committee that heard his testimony was more correct when it concluded that the foundation policies would inevitably be those of the corporations sponsoring them, and that the "domination of men in whose hands the final control of a large part of American industry rests is not limited to their employees, but is being extended to control the education and social services of the nation."

---

[62] This seems to occur more as a condition of whom the foundations support rather than any overt attempt to control the rhetoric directly.

CHAPTER 7

DESCHOOLING
AS A FORM OF
SOCIAL REVOLUTION

Joel Spring

The Center for Intercultural Documentation (CIDOC) in Cuernavaca, Mexico, is both a language school and a gathering place for students from all over the world who want to study and lecture on a variety of topics. CIDOC offers a continuous lecture cycle in which anyone can participate as lecturer or listener. The school is operated on a supply and demand basis, a fee being paid to a lecturer only if more than ten students sign up for his course. The spring 1970 lecture cycle, with its theme "Alternatives to Schooling," attracted both the famous, like Paul Goodman and John Holt, and others simply interested in educational change within their own institutions, such as a sheep farmer, a psychiatrist, teachers, latterday socialists, and present-day black nationalists.

Deschooling as a form of social revolution is probably the most unique and important argument emerging from the educational dialogue taking place at CIDOC. In stating this I must stress the fact that I am giving my interpretation of events in Cuernavaca. Others who have attended the center might emphasize the concern there with learning centers, educational credit cards, and computermatching techniques. To me these are neither as original nor as important as the discussion of the social role of the school. For deschooling does not mean reforming the schools, it means getting rid of them.

I want to make it clear at the outset that social revolution as used here does not refer to the immediate destruction of A.T.& T. and General Motors. It refers rather to the release of the creative potential of the poor to effect important social changes. Deschooling as a form of social revolution means destroying the poor's faith in and acceptance of schooling. Schools cause the worst form of social slavery because the slaves they hold believe in the goodness of the institution that condemns them. Deschooling of society should end the poor's acceptance of enslavement.

THE ORIGIN OF DESCHOOLING

The deschooling idea originated with the two leaders of the educational seminar at CIDOC, Ivan Illich and Everett Reimer, both concerned with educational development in Latin America. Illich and Reimer first met in Puerto Rico in 1956. At the time Reimer, then Executive Secretary of the Committee on Human Resources of the Commonwealth, was outlining an educational program to meet Puerto Rico's manpower needs. Illich was Vice-Chancellor of the Catholic University and member of the Commonwealth Board of Higher Education. Reimer's Manpower Report recommended the reduction of dropouts from all levels of the school system, and results were obtained at the expense of grade standards. It was later found that more childern were staying in school but they were not learning more. Reimer joined the Alliance for Progress in 1962 as an advisor on the social aspects of development and found that other Latin American countries suffered from the same educational problems as did Puerto Rico. Cost estimates of what would be needed to upgrade Latin American schools convinced Reimer of one important fact: expanded schooling was beyond the present economic resources of Latin America.

Meanwhile, Illich went to Mexico in 1961 to train missionaries and volunteers for service in Latin America. He quickly became aware that his students were not reaching the mass of Latin Americans. In fact, he found that they were actually strengthening the power of a privileged minority by operating school systems that would never reach the masses. Illich's concern for the development of effective leadership in Latin America resulted in the organization of the Center for Intercultural Documentation in Cuernavaca as an independent institutional base for Latin America studies, research, and publication. And during the summers of 1967 and 1968 Reimer and Illich began at CIDOC a systematic analysis of schooling and school systems.

Their analysis is based on two important lessons taken from their work in Latin America. First, underdeveloped countries could not economically support universal schooling; second, schooling tended to reinforce and support the position of the upper class. Illich and Reimer quickly realized their analysis had important implications throughout the Western world. The attempt to export schooling from developed to underdeveloped countries had resulted in highlighting the underlying meaning of educational systems. Noting that past eras have been characterized as the "Feudal Age" or the "Christian Era," Illich labeled the modern period the "Age of Schooling." And in Latin America, the meaning of the Age of Schooling became quite clear.

Illusions and Myths

Schooling as defined within the Reimer-Illich analysis refers to an institutional structure that exercises obligatory custodial control for the purposes of teaching within the framework of a graded curriculum. A graded curriculum creates the illusion that educational progress is the result of moving from one grade level to another. Of equal importance is the myth that all education results from schooling. Schooling has the important functions of instilling in the young society's basic beliefs and of providing for ritual certification. Educational achievement is measured by the number of years of schooling, diplomas being awarded after persons pass through a certain number of grades. The important thing about the certification process is this: if people believe in schooling, they accept the level of certification the school gives them. Schooling not only creates and perpetuates the myth that all education is schooling, but also the myth that schooling constitutes the only fair means of determining social position.

The key to the Age of Schooling is faith, the same type of faith that supported the medieval Church as a place for all men. The Church promised equality in heaven while supporting a highly stratified and economically exploitative life here on earth. The school promises educational equality while insuring the economic exploitation of the lower classes and assuring the continued existence of social inequalities. Everyone believes in schooling; only a few benefit.

For instance, it is not the poor who reap the full benefits of the state monies spent on education. One must go through the whole process of schooling from the early grades through the universities to obtain a full return on the educational dollar. Nowhere is this more clearly shown than in Latin America. No government in that region spends less than 18 percent of its budget on schools and some spend more than 30 percent. But despite the expenditure of a large percentage of state monies only a small percentage of the population is fully aided. Nowhere in Latin America does more than 27 percent of the population get beyond the sixth grade, or more than 1 percent graduate from universities! Most university graduates are from upper-middle and upper-class families who could have afforded the education without state support. Illich stressed this point in a University of Puerto Rico commencement address, telling the graduates: "The graduation rite that we solemnly celebrate today confirms the prerogatives which Puerto Rican society, by means of a costly system of subsidized public schools, confers upon the sons and daughters of its most privileged citizens." He emphasized that they represented the privileged 10 percent of their generation in Puerto Rico that was able to complete university studies. "Public investment," Illich told them, "in each of you is fifteen times the educational investment in the average member of the poorest 10 percent of the population, who drops out of school before completing the fifth grade."[1]

The Fiction of Equality

In the United States the same form of economic inequality rests on a universal belief in the fiction of equality of educational opportunity. In a study of higher education in California, Wisconsin, and Florida, W. Lee Hansen and Burton A. Weisbrod concluded that there existed a "perverse redistribution of higher education subsidies from low-income to high-income families. . . ." In California, for instance, Hansen and Weisbrod found that 40 percent of the families with college-age children received no public subsidy for higher education, a public subsidy referring to the amount of state money required to educate a college student in a state institution. Forty percent—meaning, in general, the poor—received no public subsidy because they did not attend college. Of those who attended state institutions, the public subsidy was distributed on an unequal basis. The highest subsidy, $5,000 a year, went to those who attended the University of California, while only $3,000 was spent on a California state college student, and $1,000 on a junior college

[1] See Ivan Illich, "The Futility of Schooling in Latin America," *Saturday Review*, Apr. 20, 1968, pp. 57–59+.

student. Average family income of students attending these state institutions varies with the amount of the subsidy, the wealthiest families receiving the largest subsidy. Average family income for students at the University of California is $12,000, at state colleges $10,000, and at junior colleges $8,800. The fact that the wealthier families receive a larger share of state subsidization is not reflected in the distribution of the tax burden. Low-income families pay a larger percentage of their incomes in taxes than high-income taxpayers. Weisbrod and Hansen concluded that the "result is lower-income families not only do not receive significant amounts of public higher-education subsidies but actually pay a larger fraction of their income in taxes to support higher education than do more affluent families."[2] The state taxes the poor to school the rich.

Illich and Reimer perceptively saw that belief in educational equality led not only to exploitive forms of taxation but also to submissiveness among the poor and their acceptance of a low social position. When the poor believe that the schools will provide them with opportunity for social advancement, they are willing to support education economically. This leads to economic exploitation founded on the mythology of schooling. When the poor believe the school will provide them social advancement, that advancement becomes measured by the number of years in school. Since the rich will always have more years of schooling than the poor, schooling becomes just another way to measure established social distance. It becomes an extremely powerful means of social division because the poor believe and accept the rightness of the school standard.

Once the mythology of schooling is accepted, the poor believe they are poor because they did not make it through school. This belief is reinforced by the fact that they believe and are told they were given the opportunity for advancement. Social position is translated by schooling into achievement and underachievement. Within the school, the social and economic advantages of the rich become educational achievement. The social and economic disadvantages of the poor become underachievement. The school creates dropouts. Dropouts do not exist without the school.

The school therefore acts as a powerful instrument of social condemnation and acceptance because everyone believes in the insti-

---

[2] W. Lee Hansen and Burton A. Weisbrod, "The Equality Fiction," *New Republic*, Sept. 13, 1969, pp. 23–24.

tution. If one assumes that an adequate self-concept depends on acceptance and on ability to function in a social context, one understands the school's psychological power. A most helpful and democratic institution, the school, tells the dropout in the ghetto essentially that he has been given all opportunities and he has failed. The dropout cannot help but feel this failure and rejection and conclude that there is little he can now do about getting ahead. Rejection by the schools leads to submission and apathy and in the end to complete helplessness and social stagnation.

SCHOOL AND THE CLASS STRUCTURE

The school strengthens the authority of one social class over another. The school teaches that those with more schooling are better, even though schooling and education are not necessarily the same thing! The poor learn in the school that they should now submit to the leadership of those who are more schooled, namely the upper classes. If the poor believe in the mythology of the school, they are led to believe that this submission is proper and just.

Schooling also tends to make social class structure rigid. One might think that this argument has little relevance for the United States because, compared to other countries, social class differences here appear relatively minor. This attitude was generated by the conditions of nineteenth-century America, when movement between social classes was relatively easy. It could be argued that the possibility of movement between social classes has steadily decreased in the United States in the twentieth century with the implementation of universal schooling. Schooling might well decrease the possibilities for unconventional social crossings, such as through entrepreneurial ability or inventiveness. It does not completely eliminate these possibilities, but it does curtail them by upholding the idea that advancement depends on schooling. In Latin American countries, of course, schooling adds the final stamp of approval to a well-established class structure.

In a well-schooled society people are daily schooled into their social places. If any feel frustrated by their status, they are referred to other forms of schooling, such as night or trade school. If such individuals do not take advantage of these opportunities, their continued exclusion from a higher social status becomes their own fault. If they do, they find that they make minor economic gains but that they cannot go much further because they did not take full advantage of school while young. In either case these individuals are forced to accept what they are as the result of their own failure.

One might think that this analysis of the effects of schooling applies more to underdeveloped countries than to highly developed industrial countries with a large middle class. Certainly the middle class in countries like the United States would not agree that this was a fair assessment of schooling. And little wonder! The schools have supported and improved their middle-class social position. The analysis is most relevant for the large numbers of poor who still exist in industrially advanced countries. It is the poor who are unequally taxed to support a school system that translates their poverty into underachievement. Accepting schooling myths, the poor demand better schools to solve problems rooted in social and economic conditions. The mythology of the school thus drains off what little capital there might exist among the poor, and creates institutional condemnation and frustration.

The middle class, of course, has not gone unharmed by the mythology of schooling. Middle-class youth today believe that education and schooling are the same thing, which leads to inevitable discontent with college courses that can transmit knowledge but not necessarily wisdom. Professors and students alike fall back on the belief that problems can be solved by reforming teaching techniques. Certainly the content and unfair procedures in many courses can be changed to better facilitate the flow of important and relevant knowledge. But one can never achieve in a college classroom a full comprehension and understanding of the meaning of one's life and self and the relationship of that self to others. Self-knowledge most often results from life's less structured experiences. It could quite possibly occur within the context of the social life of the university, and quite often does, but not frequently within the planned atmosphere of the classroom.

Reforming the schools is like adding another lane to a freeway. This eases the traffic problem for a short time but another jam will inevitably occur. Yet for those trapped in the mythology of schooling, deschooling as a solution to pressing social and economic problems is sacrilegious. As Illich suggests in rather colorful language, "Once the child becomes viscerally aware that he has been socially conceived in the school-womb, he demands to suck at the breasts of mother school forever. He perceives the unity of mankind as the result of common gestation by Alma Mater. He can no longer imagine a society without one organ, one institution, which monopolizes the social reproduction called education." Only, too often, discontent with schooling leads people to seek better ways of being or of training teachers, a solution to education that has been tried over and over, without much success, during the past hundred years. And only too often student discontent degenerates into a quest for more schooling. Illich, I think, quite rightly argues, "University and high school rebels reject the motherly care of Alma Mater. But the student radical who dreams of the day when he, too, will be a teacher only sets out to make his mother."[3]

BENEFITS OF DESCHOOLING

Deschooling means getting rid of an obligatory, custodial institution that exercises monopolistic control over education. It means getting rid of the mythology of equal educational opportunity. As long as there are rich and poor, educational opportunities will remain unequal because of the social conditions of the learner. Deschooling means abandoning the myth that education is a fair and just method of determining social position. Social selection through the school simply acts as an insidious method of branding the student with the mark of his social class. The school changes the poor into dropouts.

Deschooling represents an important social revolution in a society that has increasingly poured countless dollars into schooling. President Lyndon B. Johnson's great war on poverty was waged through the school, and it proved that the school can probably utilize more money to accomplish less than any other institution in our society. The failure of Head Start led educators to search for reasons, a search that produced Jensen's argument that the poor are poor because of low I.Q.'s and nothing can be done about it. Ironically, the fruit of the war on poverty was the condemnation of the poor as being too stupid to be anything but poor. One wonders what would have happened if all the money spent on educational administrators, teachers, educational materials, and testing had just been given to the poor. This, of course, would never have happened. After all, one has to be schooled to know how to use money properly.

One thing that has constantly hindered the meaningful expression of social discontent has been the general acceptance of the school. In accepting the mythology of the school, the poor learn to see their poverty as a result of a lack of schooling and the only

---

[3] Quoted from unpublished lectures given by Ivan Illich at Yale University, Feb. 18 and 19, 1970.

escape from poverty through the school. The few among the poor and among minority groups who do make it through the school to a higher social status generally abandon their social-class origins. The school does not train leadership for the poor, only escapees.

Stripped of the mythology of the school, the poor might see their position as a consequence of specific economic and social conditions. Once this is realized, they might abandon the futile attempt to escape through the school and redirect their energies toward changing those conditions. The poor might eventually realize that there is something they can do about their poverty. The school tells the poor that they have been given a chance and they failed to utilize it. History tells the poor they have been the victims of social and economic conditions. Rather than accept that fate, they should do something about changing the direction of history.

School, like the medieval Church, has been a source of social stability. When universal systems of education emerged in the nineteenth century their primary purpose was to assure social order by training the citizen for the state. In the United States the schools reflected a basic fear that freedom would lead to social chaos unless the character of the citizen was molded in the proper direction. But the search for social stability through the school has led to social stagnation and a feeling that one is constantly trapped within the womb of the school. Last year I met a young Russian Orthodox priest in Alaska who had awakened one morning at Columbia University during his eighteenth consecutive year of having attended schools with the realization, "My God, I have never lived except within the institution of the school." He quit.

Schooling provides an orderly transition from cradle to school to job and finally to death. But the joy of life is not in orderly transitions but in the unexpected and unplanned. There is joy in planning only if it is by oneself for oneself, and schooling has decreased the flexibility of society to allow for the development of individual lifestyles. How can one do what one wants if first he must go through high school, then if he does not go to college, be drafted or face the prospect of a dreary, low-status job? In previous times eighteen- and nineteen-year-olds were captains of sailing ships. Today they are all kept in a state of infantile dependency. Deschooling, therefore provides a means for releasing the creative energies of the poor and the young and thus for increasing the flexibility of society.

A deschooled society would rest on the basic faith that when a man wants to learn something he will find some way of learning it.

There would also be a recognition that all things are not of equal value for all men. One individual might find beauty in the workings of a machine while another in the imaginative reconstruction of history. But, one might argue, the school can facilitate these possibilities by providing wide contacts and organized learning. In the end, however, wide contacts in the school means tuning out on all those courses one finds irrelevant to concentrate on the one that is important. Just because one is forced to be in a classroom does not mean that anything is learned. Moreover, modern society's potential to build awareness is underestimated when one assumes the school can do a better job of exposing the individual to possibilities than he himself can. We are no longer living in the isolated and self-contained world of the nineteenth century. Through mass media, transportation, and a highly mobile population, the individual is made aware of unlimited possibilities for self-development. The high school actually is a waste of time for the modern teen-ager. As Paul Goodman has suggested, the teen-ager should be given the money spent on his high school education and told to see the world.

A man will learn something faster and easier if it is related to his goal. In most cases, men can probably teach themselves, and people certainly do not have to be taught how to learn. Learning is a problem only within the school. The school creates learning difficulties.

True, some tasks require organized learning. If I want to learn how to fly an airplane without killing myself I will seek a qualified instructor with an organized method of instruction. The difference between this instruction and that found in the school, however, is vast. The pilot will teach me a particular task without attempting to socialize me, turn me into a good citizen, or help me to find a social role. Learning that requires complex equipment could be achieved through job training or working in research institutions.

Deschooling society will not be easy. Illich suggests that eliminating the school and school teachers will be as difficult as eliminating the practioners of the world's oldest profession. Yet, as he has stated, "Once the red bricks of the schoolhouse are seen in the red light of the whorehouse, laws will be passed to protect or at least tolerate the personal weaknesses of adult citizens, so long as the young and the weak are not forced to visit either professional teachers or professional prostitutes."[4]

4 Ibid.

CHAPTER 8

THE INDOCTRINATION DEBATE
AND THE
GREAT DEPRESSION

Paul C. Violas

In the midst of the severe economic and social dislocations brought on by the depression of the 1930s, the educational world was rocked with the great indoctrination debate. The central question of the controversy was how and what to teach about social, political, and economic issues. Educational journals of the time record a tripartite literary conversation. Some radicals demanded that teachers prepare their students to create a new social order. Conservatives insisted that teachers protect society's continuity by insuring that students accept the existing social order's dominant values. Both groups agreed that the teacher should attempt to direct the conclusions that students reached. They disagreed over context to be taught. A third group took issue with both positions. Its members argued that the student should have the right to construct and continually reconstruct his own social outlook without pressure or influence from the teacher. Interestingly enough, although the debate was heated and seemed important, no one knows whether it had any influence on practices in the schools. Educational historians have not explored the question to any great extent.

Reprinted from *The History Teacher* 4(May 1971):25–35, by permission of the publisher.

Considerable confusion entered the dialogue when charges were leveled at those who would use the schools to "build a new social order." Often without any careful definition of terms, critics charged these educators with "indoctrination," "imposition," "inculcation," and "propaganda." The terms were usually interchangeable. If by the word *indoctrination* one means a deliberate falsification of facts or a withholding of facts from the lesson to insure the acceptance of a particular conclusion by students, then indoctrination seems too strong a term to apply to the efforts of most of those who argued for the development of a "new social order" through education. Rather than suppress views, they seemed more concerned that the teacher stress certain facts that seemed to justify the proper conclusions. They did believe that the development of a new society depended on certain social outlooks. They also believed that it was the teacher's duty to persuade his students to adopt these outlooks.

COUNTS AND THE NEW SOCIAL ORDER

A storm of controversy greeted the three speeches George S. Counts published under the title *Dare the Schools Build a New Social Order?*[1] Counts argued that some imposition was inevitable in all education; the only issue, he said, was the kind of values to be imposed. Imposition, he contended, should be the result of a conscious effort by the teacher. The economic catastrophe of 1929 had proved to Counts that the old social order, based on individualism, nationalism, competition, and capitalism, was no longer viable. He believed that the teacher's duty was to be certain that his students developed a social outlook compatible with a new social order. Asserting that the development of this new order was inevitable, Counts believed that it would be based on cooperation, socialism, and internationalism.

There was a curious and interesting absolutism at work in Counts's argument. While he disapproved of truth's suppression, he seemed certain that his vision was the only valid and real one on which to build the American utopia. Counts seemed aware of the philosophical similarities between his position and that of the conservatives. In commenting on the efforts of patriotic societies to

---

[1] George S. Counts, *Dare the Schools Build a New Social Order?* (New York: John Day Co., 1932; reprinted by Arno Press, 1969).

force teachers to inculcate their vision of America, Counts said that "only when we have fashioned a finer and more authentic vision than they will we be fully justified in our opposition to their efforts."[2]

George S. Counts was not a lonely voice crying in the wilderness. Other writers echoed and reinforced his demands. Some carried them much farther than Counts had suggested. The striking feature of his followers was their belief that they possessed enough of the truth to be justified in their efforts to construct the conclusions students should accept. Franz Schneider graphically displayed the missionary zeal of those who have seen the vision and now possess the truth. While contending that teachers must have "a positive social philosophy," he said, "In the future every society will demand of its teachers the same spirituality and highminded leadership which the society of the nineteenth century demanded of its ministers of the Gospel."[3]

Haven Hubbard reemphasized Counts's argument that teachers should inculcate only those values that are true. Hubbard asserted, "When the naked facts admit of only one interpretation, I say that if we are men and women, and not slaves, then they *demand* that interpretation. What I advocate is a propaganda of the naked facts."[4] Such statements might not bother a person until he remembers that nearly every visionary has been certain that his vision was true because it was based on "naked facts." Elmer Ellis supported Counts's contention that since imposition was inevitable, the real question was, "which philosophy to substitute."[5] Nevertheless, he realized that imposition meant a restriction of choices. He argued, therefore, that imposition in the field of moral and ethical concepts be restricted to conclusions upon which scholars could agree.

Two editorials in *Social Frontier* classified and expanded Counts's views.[6] The first emphasized the dangers to academic freedom from

---

[2] Ibid., p. 17.

[3] Franz Schneider, "The Scholar and Society: Reactions and Reflections," *School and Society* 38(Aug. 5, 1933):177.

[4] Haven Hubbard, "Should We Hide?" *School and Society* 37(May 6, 1933):585.

[5] Elmer Ellis, "The Dilemma of the Social Studies Teacher," *Social Education* 2(February 1938):81.

[6] "Academic Freedom," *Social Frontier* 1(November 1934):4–6; "Academic Freedom and Responsibility," *Social Frontier* 2(March 1936):191–192. George Counts was editor of *Social Frontier*.

those who would have teachers indoctrinate students with values drawn from the inherited social order. The editor then stated, "Freedom within the academy may be important enough but freedom of the academy—in all its branches, the kindergarten, elementary, and secondary school and the university—to give direction to social change is far more important."[7] In the second editorial, the editor contended that academic freedom is based on the teachers' freedom to "discharge their social obligations."[8] Those obligations were to bring about a new social order. The editor also recognized that imposition would limit the available choices: "The function of intelligence in education, as in other fields of human endeavor, is not to choose a course from among an infinite number of possible courses. Intelligence emancipates education rather by discovering a socially necessary course."[9] Holding a vision of the new social order, the teacher would determine those values and social sentiments the student should adopt and then proceed to insure their acceptance by his students.

The Childs-Bode Debate

Later in the thirties, John Childs and Boyde Bode engaged in an extended debate in the pages of *Social Frontier*. Although the original debate found Childs defending and Bode attacking imposition, it eventually degenerated into a semantics game, with several contributors from Columbia supporting Childs and others from Ohio State allying themselves with Bode. This dialogue was interesting not only because it indicated the intense interest in the issue, but also because it seemed to force some supporters of the effort to build a new social order to examine their arguments more closely. In reaction to persistent probing by Bode, Childs's supporters subsequently qualified their position, attempting to make their position compatible with the ideals of free and open classroom discussion. The attempt was only partially successful.[10] It is difficult to reconcile the idea of truly free discussion of social ideals with the belief that such free discussion will result in the acceptance of a predeter-

---

[7] "Academic Freedom," p. 6.

[8] "Academic Freedom and Responsibility," p. 191.

[9] Ibid., p. 192.

[10] See especially Kenneth Benne and William Stanley, "The Ohio School of Democracy in Education," *Social Frontier* 5(May 1939):240–244.

mined conclusion. This would seem possible only in a social order where truth is singular.

In a large measure, these social reconstructionists represented the same paternalism adopted by many earlier political progressives. Both groups were unhappy with the social evils they faced and both were unwilling to gamble that the people would be able to make correct decisions. They wanted to invest the decision-making authority in an elite group, one supposedly possessing an adequate degree of expertise. Many of the progressives' earlier urban reforms, such as the commissioner and city manager form of urban governmental organization, were attempts to remove the decision-making process from politics, that is, to insure that the masses, particularly the immigrant groups, would not have the opportunity to make wrong decisions. Similarly, the social reconstructionists represented the paternalistic wing of progressive education—a radical form of elitism to be sure. They seemed certain that they possessed the correct vision of the truth and the proper prescription to cure the social ills they faced. Their problem was to assure that vision's acceptance in order to produce a new society.

THE CONSERVATIVE VIEW

Conservatives who believed that teachers should impose only the dominant values of the existing social order on their students were closely allied, methodologically, with the radicals. They were, however, more inclined to use the term *indoctrination* and seemed less concerned with preserving the ideal of free classroom discussion. Thomas H. Briggs, perhaps the best-known spokesman for this position, agreed with Counts that imposition was "inevitable." He, however, declared that "propaganda" should be used by society "in its most powerful agency, the schools, to achieve its own ends."[11] A major difference between Briggs and Counts was that Briggs agreed with Laurence Dennis that the schools follow, not initiate social change.[12] He stated: "Only with the approval from the adult public has the reformer, then, the right to use the powerful instrument of education to lead youth to an understanding and

---

[11] Thomas H. Briggs, "Propaganda and the Curriculum," *Teachers College Record* 34(March 1933):468–472.

[12] Thomas H. Briggs, "Should Education Indoctrinate?" *Educational Administration and Supervision* 22(November 1936):561–593, esp. pp. 570–571 where he quotes Dennis to support his position.

conviction of the righteousness of a proposed program."[13] A primary function of the teacher was to act as spokesman for society, "as a teacher he is a servant of society . . . and as such he must speak for that majority rather than for himself."[14] Briggs did not suggest, though, how anyone might determine the sentiment of the majority. Moreover, the problems associated with validating truth by counting noses did not seem significant enough for him to consider.

Briggs was not alone in his conservatism. Marvin L. Darsie believed that the teacher "is a public servant functioning in an agency maintained by society for the direct purpose of indoctrinating the youth with the established institutional patterns."[15] Even when the teacher becomes aware of the shortcomings of the social order, "he must at all times encourage discussion and experimental thinking within the limits of public toleration."[16] Edmund E. Day found a similar role for education in the maintenance of social order: "formally organized education is always regarded by the society which provides it as a means of transmitting and perpetuating the existing culture. . . . Incoming youths are to be given those skills, habits, interests, attitudes, and ideals which will assure later effective participation in adult life with no serious disturbance of the existing social organization."[17] Edward H. Reisner also seemed to support this concept of education. This statement of his may seem more ominous in retrospect than it did in 1935, but even then its implications must have been clear: "In the last analysis, the instruction in American schools is controlled by the accepted and dominant American culture, just as exactly as the schools of contemporary Russia, Germany, and Italy are controlled by the social purposes of the groups which find themselves in power."[18] Conservatives agreed that the

---

[13] Ibid., p. 586.

[14] Ibid., p. 588.

[15] Marvin L. Darsie, "An Enduring Dilemma of Education: Freedom or Indoctrination?" *School and Society* 41(Feb. 2, 1935):140.

[16] Ibid., p. 141.

[17] Edmund E. Day, "How Can Our Schools Contribute to a Better Social Order?" in *NEA Addresses and Proceedings*, vol. 75 (Washington, D.C.: National Education Association, 1937), p. 48.

[18] Edward H. Reisner, "Academic Freedom and Radical Propaganda," *Teachers College Record* 37(November 1935):90. Also see "Can the Schools Change the Social Order?" *Teachers College Record* 36(February 1935):388–396.

teacher should indoctrinate his students with those values and social commitments sanctioned by the existing society.

THE THIRD POSITION

A third group of writers attacked both the conservatives and those who wanted to use the school to build a new social order. This group tended to gloss over the differences between radicals and conservatives, frequently charging both groups with advocating indoctrination, imposition, inculcation, and propaganda. Generally, however, terms were not defined sufficiently to allow one to assess the validity of the charges. Moreover, critics frequently used the terms interchangeably. Most often, writers among the third group seemed to object to the idea that a teacher should attempt to determine the students' conclusions, especially their social ideals. They argued that each student should be free to construct and continually reconstruct his own social beliefs, and that the teacher's major contribution to this process should be the facilitation of truly open and free classroom discussions.

John Dewey clearly delineated the scope of the debate. He stated: "There are three choices that education can take. It can go on dwelling in the past; it can set up ideal pictures for the future and strive to educate on the basis of that picture; or we can strive through our schools to make pupils vividly and deeply aware of the kind of social world in which they are living."[19] He advocated the last course, rejecting the first because it based education on a "static, relatively fixed, social order,"[20] which did not measure up to present needs and realities. He also rejected the idea of indoctrinating for a new social order. Ideal pictures of the future were illusory because "nobody knows what the future is going to be."[21] Those who agreed with Dewey usually objected to what they considered indoctrination for at least some of the following reasons: it was inconsistent with the ideals of democracy; it was incompatible with the philosophy of education that placed highest priority on individual student growth; and it stressed fixed ends at the expense of the process of critical inquiry.

[19] John Dewey, "Education for a Changing Social Order," in *NEA Addresses and Proceedings*, vol. 72 (Washington, D.C.: National Education Association, 1934), p. 754.

[20] Ibid., p. 745.

[21] Ibid., p. 744.

Many writers cogently and forcefully argued that citizens in a democracy must develop abilities to critically analyze problems and then select the most reasonable solution. They claimed that the process of critical inquiry could best be developed in the laboratory situation of the classroom under conditions of free debate where students were allowed to draw their own conclusions. When teachers sought to short-circuit the investigatory process and impose "correct" solutions upon the students, they were undercutting the very democratic process itself. Samuel Engle Burr stated: "The pupil should not be taught what to think about the present situation or about proposed changes in it. They should be furnished with all the tools for thinking (facts, opinions, existing plans, and proposed panaceas) and then guaranteed freedom to come to a conclusion for themselves."[22] William H. Kilpatrick concurred with this assessment and contended that American schools, "need not, and of right must not, use the indoctrinating procedures naturally adopted by the dictatorship school systems."[23] He believed that "we must have in school, college and adult forums, full and free study and discussion. . . . it is study not indoctrination that is here sought."[24]

Similarly, Boyde Bode charged that John Childs and others who would require the student to accept the teacher's conclusion, even if that conclusion was necessary for the development of a new social order, had rejected "both the ideal and the method of democracy."[25] He believed that Childs's anger with the existing social problems had caused him to confuse his solutions with democracy itself. This resulted, according to Bode, in Childs's "bold demand for 'inculcation' and a crusade to win adherents."[26] Bode charged this was no less than a "process of emotional conditioning," even though Childs asserted that it was a process by which beliefs are "communicated in such a manner that an individual can make cre-

---

[22] Samuel Engle Burr, "The Teacher's Part in Social Reform," *NEA Journal* 24(January 1935):28.

[23] William H. Kilpatrick, "The School and the State in American Democracy," in *NEA Addresses and Proceedings,* vol. 77 (Washington, D.C.: National Education Association, 1939), p. 180.

[24] William H. Kilpatrick, "Watchman, What of the Night?" *Social Frontier* 5(February 1939): 135.

[25] Boyde H. Bode, "Dr. Childs and Education for Democracy," *Social Frontier* 5(November 1938):39.

[26] Ibid.

ative use of them."[27] What Bode objected to was a substitution of a solution for the creative process of problem-solving.[28]

Some writers believed that indoctrination posed a threat to democracy because it seriously restricted freedom of speech. They saw indoctrination as an attempt externally to impose ideals, sentiments, and social solutions on students rather than allowing them to make free choices following a full and open discussion. Erling M. Hunt said, "Propaganda, censorship, and appeals to emotion become at the same time, in their evasion of free and open discussion, a confession of weakness and a denial of the basic principles of democracy. Indoctrination for democracy is a contradiction in terms."[29] Speaking against indoctrination, William F. Russell voiced the traditional liberal confidence in free speech: "The defense against a bad idea is a better idea; the defense against a half truth is a truth; the defense against propaganda is education."[30] He asserted that the best solution to social problems would result from free discussion rather than from indoctrination. Bertrand Russell expressed supreme confidence in free discussion when he told the National Education Association: "I should like to see people exposed in schools to the most vehement and terrific argumentation on all sides of every question."[31] Russell saw such exposure to full articulation of every side of a question as necessary if the student

[27] Ibid.

[28] Other writers who supported this position are represented in *The Christian Science Monitor's* article "Free Schools" reprinted in *School and Society* 41(March 9, 1935):342. See also I. L. Kandel, "Academic Freedom for Teachers," *Teachers College Record* 37(December 1935):188–196; I. L. Kandel, "Factors Which Contribute Toward a Philosophy of Secondary Education," *Teachers College Record* 38(January 1937):273–285; I. L. Kandel, "Liberalism and Education," *The Educational Forum* 1(March 1937):261–270; William A. McCall, "My Philosophy of Life and Education," *Teachers College Record* 36(January 1935):303–316; J. W. Studebaker, "Education and Democracy," *School and Society* 44(Aug. 1, 1936):129–132; J. W. Studebaker, "Education for Democracy," *School and Society* 43(March 7, 1936): 305–311.

[29] Erling M. Hunt, "Educating Leaders for Democracy," *Social Education* 2(November 1938):542.

[30] William F. Russell, "Education for Free Men," *School and Society* 50(Aug. 19, 1939):226.

[31] Bertrand Russell, "Education for Democracy," in *NEA Addresses and Proceedings*, vol. 77 (Washington, D.C.: National Education Association, 1939), p. 528.

was to become immune to the siren of propaganda while formulating his own opinions.[32]

Joseph Wood Krutch also leveled the charge of indoctrination against those who would use the schools to insure the development of the social ideals necessary for a new social order. Krutch fired perhaps the most devastating salvo aimed at them. He asserted that the battle for academic freedom had entered a new phase when educators asked for freedom to indoctrinate. The "liberals" who had once demanded the free competition of ideas in the schools, Krutch charged, had deserted their posts. This "liberal," he stated, "begins to think less of the importance of free discussion and insist more and more upon his duty to indoctrinate youth with his new convictions."[33] He compared this liberal with the old conservative —both demanded "correct opinions." Krutch saw the battle as "not over the right either to be impartial, or to teach what he believes, but primarily over what is and what is not a 'correct' opinion."[34] He continued, "the question of academic freedom is only a special case of the question of free speech which is, in turn, only a special case of the general question of civil rights. And the liberal turned radical has, of course, taken up a new position in regard to this final question."[35] Although Krutch directed his wrath at those who wanted to use the schools to develop a new social order, it was obvious that he had a similar opinion of the conservatives.

OBJECTIONS TO INDOCTRINATION

Thomas B. Stroup made the most appropriate summary of the ideas of those who opposed indoctrination because they believed it did violence to democracy. Education, he argued, could not become a prop for any social system, present or future, without becoming propaganda. He said:

> To educate for a democracy is paradoxical, self-contradictory. Such a phrase indicates an alien meaning of the term, if

---

[32] Bertrand Russell, "Education for Democracy," *NEA Journal* 28(April 1939):528.

[33] Joseph Wood Krutch, "On Academic Freedom," *The Nation,* April 17, 1935, p. 449.

[34] Ibid.

[35] Ibid.

it has not already peradventure lost all meaning. For if *democracy* retains any meaning at all, that meaning has to do with the right of a person to develop himself as an individual human being, not as a cog in the political wheel; with the notion that the wisdom of man, not his mere indoctrination, is a dependable source for the guidance of governments; with the idea that governments are for men, not men for governments.

Now, *education for a democracy* must be distinguished from *the necessity for education in a democracy.* . . . The development of the man as a human being is enough. He should be looked to and he alone. Out of his wisdom will come the social order. At the moment we begin to educate for citizenship, for the prevailing social order, for democracy or for the New Deal, at that moment we begin to educate for something opposed to democracy.[36]

A second objection to indoctrination was that it stunted the student's intellect. Writers voicing this objection could closely identify with Stroup's statements. They defended the integrity of the individual student and his right to freely construct his own values and social outlook after an open discussion that considered all the available facts. M. M. Chambers defined the function of education "to be the liberation and development of the capacities of each individual, without any attempt to impress upon him from above any ready-made opinions or cut-and-dried solutions of the social problems which he as a citizen must help to solve. . . . It will be noticed that this entirely excludes and repudiates the concept of education as indoctrination."[37] Henry W. Holmes agreed with this, stating, "An education that deliberately purposes to prejudge the issues of life and prevent the individual from coming to his own convictions and establishing his own loyalties is untrue to itself because it leads away from the best that can be and towards the worst."[38] This sentiment led Joseph Jablonower to conclude that teachers who indoctrinated, either for the status quo or for a new social order,

[36] Thomas B. Stroup, "For Democracy: Current Educational Shibboleth," *School and Society* 48(Feb. 25, 1939):249.

[37] M. M. Chambers, "A Theory of Educational-Administrative Organization," *School and Society* 38(Aug. 12, 1933):215.

[38] Henry W. Holmes, "Teaching as Prophecy: The Duty of the University in Education of Teachers," *Harvard Teachers Record* 6(June 1936):135.

should forfeit the rights of academic freedom because they had violated the personality of the student.[39]

Some critics argued that the student's right to self-determination was not only more significant than any contemporary social crisis but essential to the intelligent solutions of these and future crises. James K. Skipper struck this chord when he said, "The educative right of the individual to participate in the reconstruction of his beliefs should have priority over the demands of any particular social program for immediate action."[40] He concluded that "education should be concerned with a method of acquiring beliefs that will guarantee their continued flexibility rather than a method which substitutes new rigidities for outmoded old ones, however appropriate the new ones may appear in the light of the current crisis. To use Bridgman's brilliant phrase, 'We must not exact hostages of future experience.' "[41]

These writers contended that indoctrination was not compatible with the optimal development of individual students. To them, indoctrination meant restricting the right of each student to determine the content of his own beliefs and his world outlook. They asserted that indoctrination decreased the student's capacity for critical analysis and intelligent decision-making by presenting solutions to be accepted rather than issues to be resolved.[42] Unfortunately,

---

[39] Joseph Jablonower, "Basic Factors in Academic Freedom," *The American Teacher* 18(June 1934):20–21.

[40] James K. Skipper, "Anent Bode, Childs and Democracy," *Social Frontier* 5(April 1939):210.

[41] Ibid., p. 211.

[42] See Charles A. Beard, "The Scholar in an Age of Conflicts," *School and Society* 43(Feb. 29, 1936):278–283; Boyde H. Bode, "Democratic Education and Conflicting Cultural Values," *Social Frontier* 5(January 1939):104–107; Roger P. Bristol, "Dynamic Economics Teacher," *School and Society* 36(July 16, 1932):84–86; Lotus D. Coffman, "The Challenge to Education," *School and Society* 45(Feb. 27, 1937):276–281; Milton C. Cummings, "How Can the Schools Build a New Social Order," *School and Society* 36(Dec. 9, 1932):756–758; Henry W. Holmes, "Indoctrination, the Teacher in Politics and the Social Aim of Education," *Harvard Teachers Record* 3(June 1933):157–160; J. Cayce Morrison, "Liberal Education and the Elementary School," *School and Society* 36(July 20, 1932):129–134; D. A. Prescott, "Educational Policy and International Justice," *School and Society* 36(Nov. 12, 1932):604–617; H. L. Smith, "Academic Freedom," in *NEA Addresses and Proceedings*, vol. 77 (Washington, D.C.: National Education Association, 1939), p. 872; J. W. Studebaker, "Freedom of Thought and Instruction," *School Life* 21(December 1935):89–90; A. L. Threlkeld, "Current Issues Relating to the Curriculum and Instructional Materials," in *NEA Addresses and Proceedings*, vol. 71 (Washington, D.C.: National Educational Association, 1933), pp. 609–616.

like the others, these writers did not submit the term *indoctrination* to careful or analytic definition, nor did they fail to use the terms *indoctrination, inculcation,* and *propaganda* interchangeably.

IMPACT OF THE DEBATE

The tripartite dialogue we have discussed did not burst full bloom upon the American educational scene for the first time in the 1930s. All three positions resounded throughout the pages of American educational history. The conservatives could recount a long history for their position, ranging from John Winthrop to Horace Mann through William T. Harris to Thomas Briggs. All these men believed that teachers should indoctrinate those values accepted by contemporary society. Conservatives have always believed the greatest threat to American democracy was rapid social change. During the depression era they were especially fearful that "radicals" would destroy a system that really needed only minor adjustments. Their strongest support came from those who tended to equate the American business establishment with American democracy.

George S. Counts similarly could trace the lineage for his assertion that the teacher should develop in his students the social outlook necessary for a new and higher social order. His intellectual ancestors included Robert Dale Owen, Lester Frank Ward, and Albion Small. The characteristic most common to this group was the belief that extensive and radical changes in the social order were necessary. These men argued that necessary changes could be accomplished only if the schools guaranteed the development of correct student attitudes. This idea incurred the resistance of both the conservatives and those who opposed any indoctrination. Thus, it is not surprising that this group's influence seemed confined to a rather small number of radicals, a conclusion that seems consonant with the rather ineffective impact of radicalism in America during this period.

Those who opposed all forms of indoctrination could also recount their progenitors. They included William Maclure, who was Owen's protagonist at New Harmony, Thomas Jefferson, Ralph Waldo Emerson, and Henry David Thoreau. The antiindoctrination position seemed to dominate the debate in the journals during the thirties. This was the case probably because the position's logic was more attuned to ideas about the special role of the school and the resulting function of the teacher that stemmed from the societal fears of this era. Of the three, only this position would advance the development of "critical intelligence" deemed so necessary to protect democracy from its special enemies.

Although the sociological and historical data showing teachers' actual classroom practices during the depression era have yet to be catalogued, there is, nevertheless, some evidence on which to base a tentative hypothesis regarding the relationship of the debate to the real world of the schools. This evidence indicates that the conservative position best described what teachers were actually doing in their classes. At least two conditions had to obtain if either of the other positions were to be implemented in teaching practices. First, it was necessary for the schools to be relatively secure against conservative demands of the community or pressure groups. Second, teachers had to be convinced that either radical reform of the social order or critical analyses of the social structure was necessary. The evidence suggests that neither of these conditions were present during this era.

The studies of Bessie Pierce[43] and William Gellerman[44] clearly indicate the successful influence of conservative pressure groups on school curriculum.[45] The demands of conservative community attitudes further restricted the teachers. Several studies of specific communities describe an effective impact of conservative demands on the school.[46] Combined conservative forces stood as a guardian against the radical teacher who would indoctrinate for a new social order or the liberal teacher whose attempts to develop "critical intelligence" conflicted with the goal of developing "an appreciation and understanding of the superiority of the American way of life." The assumption that there were significant numbers of radical or liberal teachers whose classroom practices would conflict with the

---

[43] Bessie Pierce, *Citizens Organizations and the Civic Training of Youth* (New York: Scribner's, 1933).

[44] William Gellerman, *The American Legion as Educator* (New York: Bureau of Publication, Teachers College, Columbia University, 1938).

[45] More recent studies demonstrate the continued effectiveness of this pressure in the Cold War era. See Neal Gross, *Who Runs Our Schools* (New York: Wiley, 1958); Jack Nelson and Gene Roberts, Jr., *The Censors and the Schools* (Boston: Little, Brown, 1963); and Mary Anne Raywid, *The Ax Grinders* (New York: Macmillan, 1962).

[46] See Granville Hicks, *Smalltown* (New York: Macmillan, 1947); Robert Lynd, *Middletown in Transition* (New York: Harcourt, Brace, 1937); and Arthur J. Vidich and Joseph Bensman, *Smalltown in Mass Society* (New York: Macmillan, 1947).

conservative position also seems without substantiation. Howard K. Beale[47] and Willard Waller[48] present rather persuasive evidence that few liberal and even fewer radical teachers could be found in the public schools during the thirties.[49] Thus, while the liberal position rejecting both conservative and radical indoctrination swept the debate in the journals, it is doubtful whether this position was practiced in the nation's classroom.

[47] Howard K. Beale, *Are American Teachers Free?* (New York: Scribner's, 1936).

[48] Willard Waller, *The Sociology of Teaching* (New York: Wiley, 1932).

[49] Harmond Ziegler in *The Political Life of American Teachers* (Englewood Cliffs, N.J.: Prentice-Hall, 1967) contends that the conservative persuasion is still the most dominant among teachers.

CHAPTER 9

ACADEMIC FREEDOM AND THE PUBLIC SCHOOL TEACHER, 1930–1960

Paul C. Violas

Freedom and fear are strange bedfellows. A study of the history of the idea of academic freedom for public school teachers from 1930 to 1960, though, reveals an intimate relationship between the two. During this period, over twelve hundred articles dealing with various aspects of the idea of public school teachers' academic freedom appeared in educational, legal, and popular journals. An analysis of these articles reveals that, all too often, the rationale supporting teachers' freedoms was based on a sacrifice of the freedom of students. One explanation of this incongruous phenomenon suggests that the academic freedom dialogue reflected the fears emerging from successive crises in American society.

The period 1930–1960 was visited by three traumatic events: the Great Depression, World War II, and the Cold War. During each era, the trauma that dominated it gave rise to a peculiar set of social fears. These fears had an important impact on the academic freedom dialogue because, first, the objectives of the school were constructed as responses to society's fears; and, second, the justification

Reprinted from *Educational Theory* 21(Winter 1971):70–80, by permission of the publisher.

of academic freedom rested on the teachers' function in implementing those objectives.

This relationship, however, was complicated. The crescendo of fear did not necessarily mean closure on teachers' freedom. On the contrary, fear often stimulated the development of rationale that enhanced certain aspects of academic freedom. Because of the limitations of space, all of the dialogue cannot be examined here. Rather, this chapter will more modestly analyze the dialogue surrounding one academic freedom issue during each of the three eras to illustrate the impact of the relationship of fear and freedom.

THE GREAT DEPRESSION AND LOYALTY OATHS

Fears arising from social issues stemming from the economic dislocations caused by the Great Depression strongly colored the academic freedom dialogue during the 1930s. The feelings of fear and frustrations one can sense in the literature of the era, however, were not directed toward the entire economic or social system. While the overwhelming majority of Americans had not lost faith in the system, it was obvious, nevertheless, that all was not right. Some evil had penetrated the American Garden of Eden and blocked the cornucopia. It was necessary to dislodge the evil without destroying the Garden. When the evil had been expelled, America would again be all right. Within the Garden lurked two satanic enemies: the selfish businessmen who had caused the system to break down; and those who would overthrow the system—the revolutionaries who wanted a new game rather than just a new deal after the deck had been reshuffled. The national mood, however, was for reform rather than revolution, and the support accorded to Franklin Roosevelt and his New Deal indicated that most Americans favored a patchwork approach to reform—reform that amounted to little more than a minor reshuffling of the deck.

The school, as often in the past, was viewed as a vehicle to alleviate social problems. Now an important objective for the schools was to create safeguards against the dual threat to the Garden. To fulfill this objective, the schools must produce a special kind of citizen—a citizen who possessed what was termed *critical intelligence*. This kind of intelligence would help the citizen understand that both the selfish businessman and the revolutionaries would contaminate America, and many writers were able to utilize this objective to develop a persuasive rationale for increased teacher freedom. An analysis of the dialogue concerning the question of loyalty oaths provides a typical example of this process.

During the thirties, considerable effort was directed toward the passage of laws requiring loyalty oaths for teachers. By 1935, over twenty states had passed such legislation.[1] The main idea was to eliminate radical teachers. Most of the support for loyalty oaths stemmed from the belief that there existed a real danger to the republic in the person of teachers who were imposing un-American and subversive doctrines on the nation's school children. The 1934 American Legion National Convention passed a resolution demanding that schools hire only teachers who were "citizens of unquestioned patriotism and advocates of American ideals."[2] William Kelty of the YMCA contended, "There are forces at work in the schools, as elsewhere, that are insidiously undermining the confidence of children in their government. Teachers have been guilty of subversive indoctrination of their classes . . . the truly American forces are taking steps to eradicate the un-American ones. One of the most important moves in this campaign has been the loyalty pledge."[3] The president of the New York City Board of Education wrote to the Board of Examiners instructing it to go beyond the mere requirement of the loyalty oath and "make personality and character your first consideration, and that under the head of character you consider loyalty and love of country."[4] These statements represented attitudes typical of people who feared the radical as the greatest threat to the American system and believed the loyalty oath the best weapon to expunge evil from the Garden of Eden.

The conservative position, however, conflicted with that assumed by liberal reformers who were certain that selfish business interests posed the greater threat to the nation. They argued that loyalty oaths hindered the development of the critical intelligence necessary to cleanse the Garden of Eden and redirect America toward its promise. One approach suggested that the oaths were neither needed nor effective. In 1936 the National Education Association

---

[1] "Loyalty Oaths," *Social Frontier* 2(October 1935):23; "Loyalty Oaths for Teachers," *School and Society* 42(Aug. 24, 1935):267–269.

[2] Quoted in "Educational Resolutions by the American Legion," *School and Society* 40(Dec. 22, 1943):839.

[3] William Kelty, "Is It 'Misguided Patriotism'?" *School and Society* 41(June 1, 1935): 735. See also Glenn W. Moon, "Club Activity as Training for Democracy," *Social Education* 3(January 1939):103–107.

[4] Quoted in "Qualifications for Teachers in the New York City Schools," *School and Society* 40(Oct. 13, 1934):484.

(NEA) passed a resolution condemning loyalty oaths for teachers. This resolution attacked the basic premise of the oath supporters as it stated, "We hold that the loyalty of the teachers of America is beyond question."[5] In a somewhat different mood, H. L. Mencken had expressed the same disdain for the supposed threat of radical teachers as he commented on the proposed Maryland oath law: "The Halloway-American Legion Bill is foolish enough to be worthy of its sponsors. Its ostensible aim is to smoke out schoolmarms who poison their pupils with Marxian heresies . . . it is almost as rare for one of them to hatch sedition as it is for one of them to go up in a balloon."[6]

If the opponents of loyalty oaths believed there were too few un-American teachers to make oaths necessary, they even more strongly denied that such oaths would inhibit any of the few disloyal teachers that might exist. Abraham Lefkowitz pointed out that "since these so-called dangerous 'reds' do not believe in bourgeois morality, they will be the first to take such silly oaths and then laugh at bourgeois stupidity and morality."[7] Loyalty oaths could not solve American society's problems, their opponents believed, and the oaths were detrimental to the development of solutions.

Opponents of loyalty oaths contended that the depression had shown that a major responsibility of the schools was to develop students with critical intelligence. They argued that this could be accomplished only by professional teachers who were free from fear. Loyalty oaths would inhibit the development of such teachers, and would be used to retard responsible social change and reduce reasonable social criticism.[8] Florence Curtis Hanson argued that the loyalty oath laws would produce fear among teachers. "Such legislation creates an atmosphere of fear in which it is impossible to develop critical intelligence . . . Effective teaching can be carried on only under conditions of freedom from fear of official discipline for thinking thoughts that may be different from those approved by

---

[5] "Platform and Resolutions," in *NEA Addresses and Proceedings*, vol. 74 (Washington, D.C.: National Education Association, 1936), p. 216.

[6] H. L. Mencken, "Chasing the Reds," *Teachers College Record* 36(May 1935):721.

[7] Abraham Lefkowitz, "Academic Freedom and Progress," *The American Teacher* 19(March–April 1935):11. See also "Teachers' Loyalty Oath," *The American Teacher* 19(May–June 1935):24.

[8] William H. Kilpatrick, "Loyalty Oaths—A Threat to Intelligent Teaching," *Social Frontier* 1(June 1935):10–15.

the guardians of status quo"[9] Opponents believed that the "guardians of the status quo" represented the same selfish business interests that had caused the depression. In a sense, demands for the expulsion of the influence of the guardians of the status quo were not significantly different in nature from demands to eliminate radical influence in the school. The presence of either influence would prevent the teacher from doing the right things to the student, that is, equip him with critical intelligence so that he might understand reality in a way to insure the continuation of the American system.

Perhaps the most interesting, and most visible, of such oaths was the "little red rider" that appeared as an amendment to a June 1935 appropriations bill providing funds for the Washington, D.C., public schools. The amendment stated: "Hereafter no part of any appropriation for the public schools shall be available for the payment of the salary of any person teaching or advocating Communism."[10] The United States controller-general interpreted this to mean that school employees could not discuss communism either in or out of school.[11] Before each payday, every teacher was required to sign a statement swearing that he had not violated this edict. This had the effect of eliminating any discussion or reading material dealing with communism, or the history, geography, and current events of the USSR, in Washington public schools.[12] Representative Thomas Blanton, author of the rider, went so far as to send a questionnaire to the teachers on June 11, 1936, asking if they believed in God, approved of the writings of George S. Counts or Charles A. Beard, were members of the NEA and, if so, who had suggested such membership.[13]

Reactions against such measures were swift and forceful, from both individuals and educational organizations. A concentrated effort against the law resulted in its repeal in May 1937. The most

[9] Florence Curtis Hanson, "Loyalists' Oaths," *Social Frontier* 2(November 1935):47–49. See also Charles L. Bane, "Oaths for Teachers," *School and Society* 42(Sept. 7, 1935):330–331; Franklin W. Johnsen, "The Teacher's Oath," *School and Society* 43(June 20, 1936):832–835; and "Teachers' Loyalty Oath," p. 25.

[10] Quoted in "The Little Red Rider," *School and Society* 43(Apr. 11, 1936):513.

[11] Ibid., pp. 513–514.

[12] Caroline Williams, "Congress Legislates Character," *Social Frontier* 3(January 1937):107–110.

[13] Ellen Thomas, "Sequelae of the 'Red Rider,'" *Progressive Education* 13(December 1936):606–608.

effective arguments against it focused on its debilitating effect on the development of effective, that is, critically intelligent, citizens.

It is interesting to note that the arguments both for and against loyalty oaths were not based on the need for individual freedom. Conservatives who believed that the radical posed the greatest threat to American society wanted the school to produce students whose outlook corresponded to the conservative view. Liberals opposing the oaths based their rationale on the necessity of developing students who viewed selfish business interests as the greatest threat. The rationale for increased teacher freedom was dominated by the desire to utilize this freedom to alleviate a social problem. Concern for the freedom of the individual teacher apart from its social utility did not constitute even a minor eddy in the mainstream of rhetoric.

DEMOCRACY AND NATIONAL UNITY

The World War II era saw a new threat and the development of a different complex of fears on which to focus the academic freedom dialogue. This threat, represented by the fascist dictators of Germany, Italy, and Japan, was both visible and foreign-based. The Garden had been cleansed and a crusade to protect democracy against totalitarianism was sanctioned. This crusade required a unified national effort, and groups and individuals contributing toward that effort consequently were awarded increased esteem. Such groups included American industrialists, women workers, and veterans' organizations. Any activity or idea that seemed to weaken the drive for national unity, the war effort, or "democracy" was immediately suspect.

Within this context, the schools were assigned two somewhat conflicting roles: to extend and protect democracy and to aid in the drive for national unity. Because these roles were somewhat contradictory, their impact on the function of the teacher was felt in contradictory ways. The need to protect democracy lent credence to the arguments for increased academic freedom, while the necessity for unity suggested restrictions.

The most interesting example of the effect of wartime fears on the academic dialogue concerned the development of a rationale for the exclusion of teachers from the profession because of their association with undesirable groups. And this rationale was similar to that produced during the depression era. Since the production of student attitudes conducive to effecting national unity had become a prime school objective, educators now campaigned to purge teachers who might detract from that objective because of their associations with groups that displayed any tendency out of harmony with the norms of "Americanism." It is also interesting to note that this rationale was not entirely dissimilar from the later rationale expounded by professional patriots during the McCarthy era.

The chairman of the NEA Academic Freedom Committee, responding to the pressures of nationalism and fears of European war, declared that "the time has come when we should rethink and rewrite the statement of principles which was adopted of 1937."[14] He accurately forecast the direction the rethinking and rewriting was going to take when he continued:

> There is, we realize, always a danger that certain persons may hide under the cloak of academic freedom and disseminate propaganda in our public schools in behalf of doctrines that will not bear public scrutiny. Occasionally one finds an individual who takes advantage of academic freedom in a subtle way in an effort to undermine the fundamentals of democratic government.
>
> The Committee must not and will not be a shield for Fifth Columnists in the United States of America![15]

The statement of principles drafted by William S. Taylor affected a significant closure on the concept of teacher's freedom in extraschool citizenship.[16] It cautioned teachers that intellectual integrity was indispensable to education and that to qualify as teachers, they must be certain that their associations would not prostitute their integrity. "Any suspicion, therefore, that the teacher is externally controlled or otherwise unduly influenced in reaching his opinions or in expressing them honestly must call into question his intellectual integrity and so work against the desired integrity in all whom he influences."[17]

---

[14] William S. Taylor, "Academic Freedom," in *NEA Addresses and Proceedings*, vol. 78 (Washington, D.C.: National Education Association, 1940), p. 879.

[15] Ibid.

[16] William S. Taylor, "Principles of Academic Freedom," *NEA Journal* 30(May 1941): 142–143.

[17] Ibid., p. 142.

It is important to note that there was no discussion about how to determine whether a teacher was, in fact, "externally controlled." The statement simply said "any suspicion." Not even a *well-founded* suspicion was required to "call into question his intellectual integrity." Significantly, the NEA Committee on Academic Freedom did not find it necessary to even discuss the question of what kind of external control would in fact compromise one's "intellectual integrity."[18] Should, for example, a Baptist, or a Catholic, or a Republican, or a Communist have been disqualified as a teacher because each of them might in some way have been externally controlled? Or did this prohibition apply only to bad external control? If so, who would define "bad"? The problem would surface again at a later time.

The NEA national convention adopted a more precise resolution in 1941. It read: "The NEA is opposed to the employment in any school, college or university, of any person who advocates or who is a member of any organization that advocates changing the form of government of the United States in any means not provided for under the federal constitution."[19] This resolution, while more precise than the Academic Freedom Committee's statement, still made association, rather than acts, cause for summary condemnation and punishment.

The American Federation of Teachers, under the direction of its president George S. Counts, took similar action at its 1941 convention. After revoking the charters of three of its local unions (No. 5, No. 192, and No. 537) for Communist domination, the convention amended its constitution to exclude from membership an "applicant whose political actions are subject to totalitarian control such as Fascist, Nazi, or Communist."[20] The rationale offered by the AFT paralleled that of the NEA point for point and could be subjected

---

[18] It seems from the context in which the phrase "externally controlled" is used that it is meant to indicate control from outside one's own rational decision-making process, such as by some body of dogma or set of preconceptions that would short-circuit the process of inquiry. The context does not seem to indicate control from outside the country as by some foreign power. This lack of preciseness, however, which forces speculation from context, is part of the difficulty with the statement.

[19] "Resolution Committee," in *NEA Addresses and Proceedings*, vol. 79 (Washington, D.C., 1941), p. 906.

[20] "The Twenty-Fifth Annual Convention," *The American Teacher* 26 (October 1941):8.

to the same criticism. It is interesting, however, to discover that during this time such criticism was not voiced in the academic freedom dialogue.

What did appear was an attack on the Rapp-Coudert Committee set up by the New York state legislature in 1939 to examine state aid to education and to investigate subversive activities in the schools. Oddly enough, the same 1941 American Federation of Teachers convention passed a resolution condemning the aims and methods of this committee, charging that teachers should not be dismissed "until legitimate and specific charges for dismissal have been presented and substantiated in a fair public trial."[21]

Although a member of the 1941 NEA Academic Freedom Committee, William H. Kilpatrick also challenged the activities of the Rapp-Coudert Committee.[22] He believed if it was indeed true that Communist teachers had rejected democratic standards of truth and honesty, then this rejection should be scored against their right to remain teachers. He argued, however, that it was important to show that the individual teacher had actually subscribed to the alleged Communist tenets regarding truth and then show that this subscription had adversely affected his teaching. Kilpatrick pointed out that "it is not hated ideas but wrong conduct which calls for penalty."[23] These arguments against guilt by association and demands for proof of wrong actions represented, unfortunately, only a small minority viewpoint. Even Kilpatrick's lonely voice was raised only against legislative committees. Its impact was considerably diminished by the appendage of his name to the 1941 NEA committee report that advocated repressive action.

Moreover, less than four months after his attack on the Rapp-Coudert Committee, Kilpatrick wrote an article defending the American Federation of Teachers' expulsion of the allegedly Communist-dominated locals.[24] He argued that liberal democratic methods demanded free and open discussion as a means to apply intelligence to problems in order to arrive at optimal solutions. Communists, according to Kilpatrick, rejected open discussion and

---

[21] Ibid., p. 23.

[22] William H. Kilpatrick, "The Coudert Investigation," *Frontiers of Democracy* 7(Jan. 15, 1941):102–103.

[23] Ibid., p. 103.

[24] William H. Kilpatrick, "Liberalism, Communist Tactics and Democratic Efficiency," *Frontiers of Democracy* 7(Mar. 15, 1941):167–168.

relied on "obstructive and browbeating tactics so as seriously to hamper the legitimate deliberations."[25] When this happened, he believed, "the bounds of toleration have been passed."[26] In effect, Kilpatrick argued that the Communist locals should be denied entrance to the arena of open discussion because they had not abided by the ground rules and had sought to destroy the process to gain their own ends. This may have been a valid account of the activities of those locals. Difficulty arose, however, as this analysis was generalized from this specific instance and Kilpatrick's argument used against all Communist teachers.

V. T. Thayer presented such a generalization in 1942.[27] He believed the time had come for liberals to rethink their traditional commitment to complete freedom of speech and training, a commitment based on the belief that in the midst of a completely free exchange of ideas man would use his reason to determine truth. According to Thayer, education was the agency charged with instructing future generations with this means of finding truth. Therefore, it must not attempt to inculcate dogmas or beliefs. Its commodity was method, not conclusions.

The teacher who was a Communist or a Fascist could not meet the qualifications Thayer set for membership in the education agency. His first reason indicated his allegiance to that group which saw the teacher as exemplar. He argued that "no conscientious teacher can ignore the fact that there is a relationship between his life outside school and his influence within the classroom."[28] Because his out-of-school behavior was to be an example for his students, it was obvious to Thayer that "conduct becoming a teacher cannot rightfully include membership in any group or party dedicated to a policy of undermining the essential structure of our government or our way of life."[29] Thayer apparently did not think it necessary to show the individual's compliance with or involvement in the organization plans. Nor did he explain what was meant by "undermining our way of life."

[25] Ibid., p. 168.

[26] Ibid.

[27] V. T. Thayer, "Should Communists and Fascists Teach in the Schools?" *Harvard Educational Review* 12 (January 1942):7–19.

[28] Ibid., p. 14.

[29] Ibid., p. 16.

Thayer's second reason for expelling Communists and Fascists from the teaching profession borrowed heavily from Kilpatrick's argument against the three Communist-dominated AFT locals. He contended that the Communist teachers violated the belief that the teacher should be free from dogma and restraint that would prohibit his arrival at undictated conclusions. The key assumption in Thayer's argument was indicated by the statement that "the Communist Party, and doubtless Fascist groups as well, secretly controls the activities of its members for purposes that can properly be termed subversive."[30] Armed with this assumption, which he considered a fact, Thayer believed that it was no longer necessary to demand proof of wrong action before expelling a teacher from the profession. Proof of association with an undesirable group, that is, membership in the Communist or a fascist party, was accepted as sufficient cause for punishment.

Long before the red-baiting, Cold War era, leading educators had developed the guilt-by-association arguments they would again hear from men like Senator Joseph McCarthy and Congressman Richard Nixon. The rationale supporting this closure on academic freedom was based on what the teacher was suppose to do to the student— that is, develop attitudes facilitating the intensification of national unity. It was necessary to expel those teachers whose associations indicated that they might be ineffective examples for the molding of effective citizens.

FEAR AND THE COLD WAR
Several conditions obtaining in the Cold War era produced a new fear. Increasing hostility between the United States and the Soviet Union dashed earlier hopes for world peace that had attended the end of World War II. A series of sensational espionage trials in the United States, Canada, and Great Britain not only informed Americans that their international enemies had acquired the means to destroy American urban areas, but that they had acquired this capacity through the conspiratorial efforts of faceless and silent traitors, some of whom undoubtedly still lurked undetected. Thus, the awesome and constant fear of total annihilation was reinforced by the fear of internal conspiracy.

These fears were reflected in the definition of the school's role. As in World War II, the school was to protect democracy against a

---

[30] Ibid., p. 17.

totalitarian threat. The Communist threat, however, appeared more insidious in that it seemed to involve a significant internal conspiracy. The school had to do more than simply facilitate national unity. Its role now included the preparation of the sentinels of democracy. The teacher's function was to insulate the student from the evil effects of communism and to outfit him for efficient service in the nation's struggle. One significant aspect of the academic freedom dialogue concerned the degree to which teachers should be confined by this role.

An example of this aspect was the demand that the teacher become an instrument of national policy and indoctrinate his students for patriotism and against communism. Writers who supported this idea wanted education to be used as an instrument of social control, and teachers to become agents for obtaining that control. The NEA lent credence to this position when its Educational Policies Commission stated in a 1949 bulletin: "If the schools develop programs that contribute to the nation's needs in this time of crisis, and if they can convince the public that these contributions are useful, then education can command the support it will deserve as an instrument of national policy."[31] This statement suggested not only that education should have been an instrument of national policy, but that it would be less susceptible to attack and perhaps better financed if it was.

When Massachusetts established the position of director of civic education in 1951, Henry W. Holmes, former dean of Harvard's Graduate School of Education, supported the creation by endorsing the statement subscribed to by the Massachusetts Association of School Superintendents. This statement called for the use of the school as an instrument of national policy, and it listed several reasons why a director of civic education was needed. They included the following:

> *First,* the fight against Communism calls for all the weapons in the arsenal. If we neglect education, we are missing an opportunity so important that it may be impossible to make up, later, for what we fail to do now. . . .
>
> *Third,* the Department of Education is the key place for a leader . . . as we see it; *education for citizenship is a grass roots investment in national security; the schools are asking for help*

---

[31] *American Education and International Tensions* (Washington, D.C.: National Education Association, 1949), p. 35.

in meeting this great need; and the Massachusetts plan is to put an experienced leader in a key spot.[32]

Similarly, William F. Russell, dean of Teachers College, Columbia University, asserted that the schools might be more secure if they could convince the public that they were aiding in the national defense. He said, "The basic reason for the attacks on the schools is that many people believe that the schools are not doing as much as they should for the national defense; or that what they are doing is hurting the national defense; or that something else might strengthen the national defense."[33] In a later article, Russell asserted that patriotic history could be one way of aiding national defense. He argued that an analysis of the postwar crisis "points to the supreme importance, in the better prosecution of the cold war, of bringing every American into close relationship with the glorious history of his country. When he knows it he will thrill to it. He will sense that he is a part of it. He will make the sacrifices."[34] This statement left little doubt about the kind of history and the kind of education the dean of Teachers College supported.

Erling M. Hunt also believed that the social studies provided an effective avenue for developing right answers regarding the dangers of communism.[35] Although he argued for a "full study of facts" and contended that "Americans are strong enough and smart enough to compare the theory and the realities of American democracy and Communism, and come out with the right answers," he still favored inoculation.[36] Said Hunt: "So far as Communism is concerned, the schools are, I believe, basically responsible for inoculating young citizens against it. But the serum must be strong enough to be effective. I grant that there are risks in inoculation, but the risks of no inoculation are far greater."[37] Apparently Professor Hunt would support full and open study by American public school teachers

---

[32] "Civil Education: Massachusetts Steps Ahead," *School and Society* 75(Apr. 19, 1952):242.

[33] William F. Russell, "The Caravan Goes On," *Teachers College Record* 54(October 1952):4.

[34] William F. Russell, "Education and the Cold War," *Teachers College Record* 55(December 1953):118.

[35] Erling M. Hunt, "Teaching the Contrast Between American Democracy and Soviet Communism," *Teachers College Record* 55(December 1953):122–127.

[36] Ibid., p. 123.

[37] Ibid.

only when there were guarantees that such study would lead to acceptable answers. This conclusion is supported by his statement: "Perhaps we can safely admit that our democracy has not yet achieved perfection . . . and yet have plenty of margin of attractiveness for our youth."[38] In a "full study of facts," it would seem that the admissibility of a fact should be determined by its validity, not by its effect on the conclusion the teacher wanted his students to reach.[39]

The belief that education should be an instrument of national security did not go unchallenged during the Cold War era. Yet its proponents were the most vociferous and occupied the most prestigious positions in the educational establishment.

Throughout this thirty-year period the academic freedom dialogue was closely related to society's fears. Arguments for increased or decreased academic freedom rested on the function of the teacher, a function determined by the purposes society assigned to the schools. When one examines the history of American education, and particularly its recent history, it becomes clear that most often these purposes have been established in response to fears and anxieties felt in American society. The idea of academic freedom for public school teachers, then, has been shaped by what American society, in response to its fears, has decided the teachers should do to the student to render him a more effective citizen.

---

[38] Ibid., p. 125.

[39] Other writers who also argued that teachers should insure the acceptance by their students of those attitudes and beliefs most beneficial to the national security included Louis William Norris, "The Teacher as Prophet," *School and Society* 71(Jan. 21, 1950):36–39; and Philip H. Phenix, "Teacher Education and the Unity of Culture," *Teachers College Record* 60(March 1959):337–343.

CHAPTER 10

EDUCATION AND
THE COLD WAR:
THE ROLE OF
JAMES B. CONANT

Thomas Grissom

> Education is a weapon whose effect depends on who holds it
> in his hands and at whom it is aimed.
>
> —Joseph Stalin[1]

> . . . The quality most necessary in modern times [is] the ability
> to change the aim when the target moves.
>
> —James Bryant Conant[2]

Probably no single topic in the study of recent American history has
aroused so much controversy and passion as has the reconsidera-
tion of the sources and causes of the Cold War. Stimulated by the
recent availability of governmental documents and diplomatic records, and dissatisfied with official justifications for our present
stance in world affairs, revisionist historians are challenging the
standard interpretation of the Cold War as a necessary, though

---

This essay was originally presented as a paper at the American Educational Research Association meeting in Minneapolis, March 2–6, 1970.

[1] *Phi Delta Kappan* 30(February 1949):back cover.

[2] Speech delivered at the fiftieth convocation of Teachers College, Columbia University, November 1944.

unpleasant, American response to expanding Soviet territorial interests.[3]

This spirited debate has focused on diplomatic and military events, largely ignoring domestic influences on the formulation of policy. So have the standard histories of the Cold War. These have not been concerned with the domestic sources of support and encouragement for the United States's foreign policy and defense posture during these years, nor have they attempted to chronicle the effect of policy formulations on national life or American institutions. This chapter seeks to increase our understanding of the intellectual sources of the justification and rationalization of certain domestic events and developments related to the Cold War. Specifically, it will consider the nation's system of public education and how that system was related to America's political and social objectives during the years just prior to the collapse of the wartime alliance with Soviet Russia.

I will focus attention on the efforts of a single man—James Bryant Conant. And I will argue that those educational "events" designated as Cold War spin-offs—loyalty oaths for teachers, the New York teacher purges, the expansion of federal aid to education, the curriculum reform effort in the sciences and mathematics (before and after Sputnik), and others—were less the result of diplomatic machinations after Yalta or a fear of Communists at home and abroad, than they were the natural extension of a broadly conceived and widely accepted view of the role of education in a modern industrialized nation-state. My concern is not that NEA's Educational Policies Commission issued a document entitled "Point Four and Education" within days after President Truman's announcement of the program, nor with the various state legislative acts to remove Communists from the classrooms. Such an emphasis is misplaced, it seems to me, for it begs the question of why did Americans— parents, educators, politicians—draw a relationship between the nation's political life and the daily operations of its public schools? Toward what ends was American schooling directed and how, if at all, were these ends related to the Cold War?

Answers to these questions, though tentative and incomplete, may provide us with a context for understanding departures in so-

[3] Christopher Lasch, "The Cold War, Revisited and Re-visioned," *New York Times Magazine*, Jan. 14, 1968, p. 26+.

cial policy and changes in domestic institutions without having to rely on specific and tenuous causal relationships between historical events and subsequent responses. Further, such a context allows one to judge whether a series of events is a momentary aberration, a significant departure from the present, or one more accretion to the continuous and preferred view of the past.

A SPOKESMAN'S RISE

James Bryant Conant received his Ph.D. in chemistry from Harvard University at the age of twenty-three. Awarded an instructorship upon graduation, he left Harvard for the army in 1916 and within a year had become a major in the Chemical Warfare Service, directing top secret work on Lewisite gas. He returned to Harvard and moved steadily upward in the chemistry department, becoming chairman in 1931. Two years later, at age forty, Conant became the president of Harvard University.

Within five years, aided and encouraged by his friend Francis T. Spaulding, dean of Harvard's Graduate School of Education, Conant began to articulate a social philosophy of education that has influenced American educational planners for more than three decades. As university president, scientist, liberal democrat, and tactful politician, Conant organized the wartime mobilization of scientists and engineers, advised presidents on the development and utilization of the atomic bomb, aided in the design and implementation of the National Science Foundation, chaired the Educational Policies Commission of the NEA, and acted as president of both the American Association for the Advancement of Science and the American Council on Education before he began his research and writing on educational reform with the support of the Carnegie Corporation in the 1950s. It was during the period 1938–1951, a time of world war, nuclear weaponry, and the "iron curtain," that Conant fashioned a conception of education as an instrument of national policy and the public school as the engine of democracy that would lead to a realization of this country's historic goals.

In the May 1938 issue of *Harper's,* Conant took a critical look at the future of America's colleges and universities.[4] Concerned with antidemocratic tendencies in American education, the perpetuation

---

[4] James B. Conant, "The Future of Higher Education," *Harper's,* May 1938, pp. 561–570.

of a learned class, and the continuation of a privileged group's access to higher education, and turning to his intellectual hero, Thomas Jefferson, Conant called for the cultivation of an aristocracy of talent and virtue. He cited the expanded public school system and the growth and development of American higher education, together with his assumption of a static birth rate, as factors that soon would make it possible to ask the question, Higher education for whom?[5]

Here, and in his report to the Harvard Board of Overseers a few months later, he identified issues that most American educators would not recognize for decades. He saw the need to vary the secondary school curriculum so that it appealed to an increasingly heterogeneous school population. This would entail training for differentiated tasks, educating for citizenship, and increasing standardization of secondary school offerings. Believing that not all could profit from higher education, Conant called for increased efforts in vocational and academic guidance and a scholarship program that would assure that the "right" percentage of American youth went on to advanced education. He sought to eliminate financial ability and geographical location as determining factors in educational achievement.

But one can also find in these initial formulations a sensitivity for issues that were politically and socially controversial. Conant insisted that "selection is not a weeding out process," but rather, "an aspect of educational guidance which has as its objective the direction of every youth into a fruitful field of labor." He assured his readers that he was not calling for uniformity. Rather, "we need to adopt each component part of our educational plan to some end consistent with the general objectives of modern society." He believed there were sufficient numbers of students enrolled in higher education and cautioned against the overproduction and subsequent unemployment of learned persons. He also asserted that education for the professions was a function of the colleges and universities. Vocational education should be carried on elsewhere. Lastly, he decried the absence of any systematic concern for the

[5] Conant mistakenly believed declining enrollments in kindergarten and smaller numbers of graduating seniors in high school were signs of a permanent decrease in birth rates. They probably indicated the effect of the depression on school attendance and enrollment.

problems of public schooling among academecians. He implored scholars in universities to concentrate on the study of education as a social process.

A Call for Social Flexibility

In the spring of 1940 President Conant gave the Charter Day Address at the University of California at Berkeley.[6] Extolling the Jeffersonian tradition in education, he called for a new American radicalism that would lead to the development of a less stratified and more fluid society. Worried about the loss of "opportunity, a gift that once was the promise of the frontier," Conant urges his youthful audience to ignore the Bourbons and the Bolsheviks and instead "look in the direction of the progressive or liberal movements of an earlier period," that is, Jeffersonian thought. He dissented from the view that fascism or socialism, and an accompanying class struggle, were the only choices left to those who would build a better world. His reasons for such a view were clear:

> In my opinion, our newly erected system of public education has potentialities of which we little dream. In this century we have erected a new type of social instrument. Our secondary school system is a vast engine which we are only beginning to understand. We are learning only slowly how to operate it for the public good. But I have hope that it will aid us in recapturing social flexibility.[7]

In a highly industrialized society, Conant argued, jobs do not automatically appear, as in a frontier society. Rather, for each student, "abilities must be assessed, talents must be developed, ambitions guided," so that he or she may find the first rung of an appropriate ladder of opportunity. The schools must educate for both political democracy and vocational utility. With the opening of channels leading to a multiplicity of attractive goals, American society could structure a variety of elites. In the social context beyond the schools, Conant argued for changes in the political and

---

[6] Reprinted in James B. Conant and Francis T. Spaulding, *Education for a Classless Society,* Harvard Graduate School of Education, Occasional Pamphlet No. 4 (Cambridge, Mass.: Harvard University Graduate School of Education, 1940).

[7] Ibid., p. 13.

economic institutions that would hasten the day of a free, classless society.[8]

In introducing the word *class*, Conant made a distinction that affected his entire argument. In America, he stated, the denial of classes is the denial of hereditary classes, not the denial of temporary groupings based on economic differences. Because he believed that the average American equates class with caste, he adopted that usage of the term and asserted that a high degree of social mobility was the essence of the American ideal of a classless society. The uniform distribution of goods is not a requisite for a classless society, according to his view, although power and prestige should be redistributed at the end of each generation so that economic differentiation would always be temporary. To perpetuate a casteless society, said Conant, the nation needed Jeffersonian traditions of freedom of the mind, social mobility through education, and universal schooling.

Clinching his argument, Conant concluded, "If the nation wants to bend its efforts to have as free and classless a society as possible, then for those of us concerned with schools and colleges, our course is clearly plotted. . . . A horde of heterogeneous students has descended on our secondary schools; on our ability to handle all types intelligently depends in large measure the future of this country." Ironically, even as he proposed the rational systemization of schooling based on assessment, selection, and guidance, Conant, in an attempt to attract radical leftists to his cause, warned reformers of the danger of "placing in power the greatest tyrant of all—organized society."

Although in a few months Conant would become an important spokesman for the Committee to Defend America by Aiding the Allies, and later would vehemently articulate reasons for intervention, he was, in 1938 and 1939, a man preoccupied with the public loss of confidence in those American ideals and virtues that had suffered much during the economic dislocations of the thirties.[9] He feared a popular move toward an alien ideology that would over-

[8] Ibid., p. 16. Among the changes he suggested were the revision of methods of perpetual control of many large industries, the overthrow of nepotism and patronage, and the stimulation of small enterprises.

[9] For an examination of Conant's interventionist thought, see James B. Conant, *Speaking as a Private Citizen: Addresses on the Present Threat to Our Nation's Future* (Cambridge, Mass.: Harvard University Press, 1941).

turn historic American values and goals. A free and classless society was preferred to a free but stratified one (England), a classless but unfree one (Russia), or a totalitarian one (Germany). America's system of public instruction, Conant argued, could renew the public's commitment to American values and also serve as the peaceful means for the realization of a more perfect society. In the future, as we will see, Conant's concerns would change. But his metaphors, "social instrument" and "vast engine," would serve well his arguments and, indeed, his interests.

A Philosophy for Wartime

In October 1940, Conant expanded his political and educational philosophy in an address to the Southern College Conference in Memphis, Tennessee. Entitled "What Are We Arming to Defend?" his speech was a ringing criticism of post-World War I disarmament policy and a plea for new directions in American foreign policy.[10] "Must we not," he asks, "accept the responsibility that, fully armed, prepared to fight if need be, and in collaboration with the others who hold our same ideals, we must organize a large portion of the civilized world in such a way that we may continue to prosper as a national unit and develop the potentialities of our nation?" Exultantly, he reminded his audience of their heroic ancestors who courageously fought the French and Spanish for the Mississippi River Valley. It was they "who recognized that the destiny of this country lay in an expanding vision." Daring to believe that the same spirit that moved this country across the continent in the past would once again be awakened to meet the challenge of these times, Conant urged the colleges and universities of America to "think through the implications of all that has happened in these last six months, to evolve a philosophy of action for the dread days ahead."

Then, with unintended irony, Conant criticized Harry Elmer Barnes's view of education as training in criticism of the social order. "The true spirit of liberty," suggests Conant, "is to be found between destructive criticism on the one hand and complacent dogma on the other." Thus, he concluded, the political system we aim to defend is not invariant nor inflexible, but the best possible means of realizing a classless society through open mobility.

---

[10] Reprinted in *Association of American Colleges Bulletin* 26(December 1940):486–488.

Four days later Conant spoke at the inauguration of Howard Lardis Bevis as president of Ohio State University, and an examination of his speech there helps one understand what he meant in Memphis when he mentioned "the true spirit of liberty." The goal of a free and classless society apparently had become a reality if one is to believe his statement: "If we are to continue to have an essentially free and classless society in this country, we must proceed from the premise that there are no educational privileges."[11] Calling for equal access to the schools, he argued for a process of sorting, in each stage in the educational process, those students who can profit from one type of education and those who can profit from another. He warned, however, that the resulting variety of educational channels should not reflect social status, nor should the curriculum represent a hierarchy of preferred disciplines.

What Conant meant by these proposals and how he sought to realize them are questions worthy of our attention. Believing no one could seriously object to the proposition that educational opportunities should be opened to all, he went on to argue that the idea that the United States should be classless reflects a majority point of view. Proof of this, he asserted, lies in American restrictions on hereditary rights to private property. His procedure for the elimination of unpleasant social distinctions between those possessing only a secondary and those blessed with advanced education was to "speak not of higher and lower *planes* of education, but of shorter and longer *periods* of education." Continuing, he argued that this horizontal view of education would differentiate law and medicine from many other vocations only by virtue of the fact that doctors and lawyers require a longer period of training and apprenticeship.

> The social implications hidden in those words "higher education" are obstacles to those who seek to minimize the number who follow the wrong educational road.[12]

Conant had suggested an increase in educational and vocational differentiation. He also proposed to reduce the visibility of this increase by changing vocabulary and playing with the definition of

---

[11] James B. Conant, "The University and a Free Society," *School and Society* 53(Jan. 25, 1941):97–102.

[12] Ibid., p. 101.

words. This concern with visibility reveals the glaring weakness in Conant's thought—he did not deal with wealth or power. That lawyers are paid more than bricklayers, that a B.A. degree has more economic value than a high school diploma, that physics is related to a reward system substantially different from that of home economics were all ignored by Conant. This was not accidental, for his proposals for education in a free and classless society were deduced from an established order predicated on competition, an order, said Conant, "which is the basis of the very benefits of which we might boast." Anticipating the meritocratic arguments of the sixth decade of this century, Conant concluded:

> In a competitive world, society must indicate the opportunities that are open to those of varying talents. With a maximum of persuasion and a minimum of compulsion we can, in education as in public health, direct the lives of many to the better advantage of both the individual and the state.[13]

In June of the following year—1941—President Conant addressed a general session of the NEA convention in Boston. His speech, "Our Country and the World Situation," set forth the goals he desired for the nation, described the enemy threatening the realization of these goals, and suggested the weapons to be utilized to defeat the enemy. Because his remarks contained the seeds of his future thought and encompassed the broad concerns of his political philosophy, the speech is worthy of extensive quotation.

> In short, the future of this country depends on our ability to achieve those goals which have been the national ideals throughout our history. We must continue to strive toward the realization of these ideals—to strive for equality of opportunity for all, for the diminution of hereditary privilege, for the tolerance of all creeds, for the maximum of personal liberty, for the minimum of restraint on individual enterprise. Such are the essentials of the free commonwealth which it is your duty as teachers to secure; such are the essentials of the free commonwealth which is in peril today.[14]

---

[13] Ibid.

[14] *Proceedings of the 79th Annual Meeting*, vol. 79(Washington, D.C.: National Education Association, 1941):39.

The peril facing the nation was a "combination of ideals and weapons."

> To me, communism and naziism are equally detestable. Furthermore, considered merely as ideologies, they are equally inimical to the future of this free nation. But only one of them, naziism, has been backed by a powerful army designed for conquest. Internally, we must fight both communism and naziism as boldly as Jefferson once fought his monarchial opponents. With ideas alone, ideas not backed by force, a democracy must cope by peaceful means. . . . In a democracy what might be called the fair fight, the normal conflict of ideas, is carried on in the long-continued argument and counter argument of public debate. I am convinced . . . in such a fight the American way of life can down the two opposing creeds.[15]

By 1941 Conant possessed well-established credentials as a militant interventionist, but this was the first time he had claimed communism to be as distasteful to American life as naziism.[16] The only difference to him was that Hitler enforced his ideology with massive and aggressive military power. In effect, then, Conant established a criterion for identifying Russia as a peril to the American commonwealth—her military posture. And this just a few days after he argued for what was essentially a world divided between those who share our ideals and those who do not, with such a division guaranteed, if necessary, by military force.

More important for our analysis, however, is Conant's perception of the teacher's role and the function of ideas in the United States. Apparently every teacher had an overriding obligation to secure the essentials of the free commonwealth not just as *citizen,* but also as *teacher.* The tendencies to identify citizenship responsibilities and to merge conceptions of individual health with the health of the state were later to become pervasive themes in Conant's thought.[17] These initial statements were fundamental to the completion of an

---

[15] Ibid., p. 40.

[16] See the complimentary portraits of Conant by his friends Vannevar Bush, "James Bryant Conant," *Scientific Monthly* 62(March 1946):197–200; and Karl T. Compton, "James Bryant Conant," *Science* 103(Feb. 15, 1946):191–192.

[17] Conant, "The University and a Free Society."

intellectual justification for a politically instrumental notion of learning and for the development of individual self-concept within publicly preferred and/or defined limits.

Lastly, despite Conant's insistence that it was the combination of ideas and weapons that made alien ideologies threatening, his distinction was a false one. In fact, ideas were weapons for Conant, though they were distinct from force. Only when the "democratic fair fight" becomes an ideological struggle, will a democracy resort to the employment of force to insure the acceptance of its cherished ideas. Once ideas are perceived or utilized as weapons in ideological disputes, their appeal and acceptance rests not on some discrete knowledge claim, but on their utility in reducing the forces external to the ideas.

THOUGHTS ON THE POSTWAR WORLD

After Pearl Harbor, preoccupied with his work in the Office of Scientific Research and Development, where his efforts afforded him a strategic view of the frightening consumption of intellectual resources and manpower skills in a fully mobilized wartime economy, Conant reversed his prewar opinions. He decided that leisurely education had to be supplanted by revolutionary procedures for the selection and training of all young men.[18] "Education," he said, "like all else, must be refashioned quickly to conform to the imperious needs of a desperate war."[19] Conant also began to justify wartime manpower policies in terms of future peacetime educational objectives that corresponded to his own educational concerns articulated prior to 1941. Citing the need to keep the most promising youth in high school and then send them on to college, he called for a government program that would identify and support intellectual talent so that the very best men will be available to fulfill the nation's needs. The method of selecting army and navy officers would have significance for the postwar period, to the extent that a college education is a road to promotion and privilege based on family finances. If economic barriers obstructing the path

---

[18] James B. Conant, "The Demands of the Market Place: Quiet Privileges of an Ivory Tower." Speech to the Harvard Alumni Association, June 22, 1939. Reprinted in *Vital Speeches* 5(Aug. 15, 1939):647–648.

[19] James B. Conant, "American Youth and the War." Speech to the National Council for Books in Wartime. Reprinted in *Vital Speeches* 8(June 1, 1942):500–503.

to commissioned ranks were removed, Conant observed, the fluidity of the social structure would be increased and the cause for which America fought strengthened.

Choosing his audience wisely, Conant spoke on "Science and Society in the Post-War World" to the New York Academy of Public Education in the winter of 1943 after receiving an academy medal for service to education.[20] He suggested that the relationship of science to industry was symbiotic, and that the prosperity of a free society in postwar times would require technological and scientific progress. In turn, research and development depended on a free society. The conditions for such cooperation were: (1) identification of the exceptional man of talent, (2) scientific competition, (3) flexible and well-equipped research organizations, (4) changes in patent laws to encourage investment and reduce secrecy, and (5) elimination of any peacetime scientific general staff.

The ease with which Conant drew syntheses and listed the conditions for a proper national scientific policy derived from his identification of three major currents in the development of human society since the fifteenth century: industrialism, science, and liberalism.[21] Taken together and understood in the context of the American experience, these currents can be the basis for the construction of a palatable ideology that incorporates all the variant traditions and influences in America's past, creating the impression that democracy and capitalism can exist in this world side by side, ballot box by billfold.

In the fall of 1944 Conant revealed his more fully developed ideas about the relationship between science and national welfare in a speech before the American Chemical Society. Relating generalized encouragement of all learning to the nation's specific postwar responsibilities, he proposed a federal scholarship program in the sciences for eligible high school graduates to be administered by statewide citizens' committees. These scholarships would provide four to seven years of financial support necessary for the training of exceptional scientific talent. Conant went on to say that "the recipient should agree, in return for the opportunity thus provided, to make himself available in time of national emergency for national

[20] James B. Conant, "Science and Society in the Post-War World." Speech to the New York Academy of Public Education. Reprinted in *Vital Speeches* 9(Apr. 15, 1943):394–397.

[21] Ibid.

service under whatever conditions the government should then set."[22] The scholarship program would facilitate the development of additional sources of scientific manpower as well as rationalize, the procedure for utilizing technical expertise in crisis situations. Conant's integration of various interests would be completed when the scholarships were distributed on the basis of merit, thus eliminating geographical and economic barriers to upward mobility *and* national security.

Conant also voiced at this time a deep concern over possible cleavages between the scientist and the nonscientist in American life. Modern man is not always at ease in this new age of science and technology, he noted, and "at times breaks out in fits of nostalgic temper." But a return to the past would be irresponsible and foolhardy, and since "the national welfare depends on science, and likewise, the future of science depends on the national welfare," the task of the scientific profession is to build conciliatory bridges to the polity of laymen.

Three months after Hiroshima, Dr. Conant gave the Julius and Rosa Sachs Foundation lectures at Teachers College, Columbia University. These three lectures, entitled "Public Education and the Structure of American Society," were a comprehensive statement of Conant's view of the relationships between a society's educational system, its economic and social structure, and its dominant political goals.[23] The lectures were significant because in them Conant placed the educational enterprise at the very center of the emerging liberal-scientific-industrial nation-state.

In the lectures Conant argued for acceptance of the following thesis. Equality of opportunity, an important American ideal, implies a minimum of emphasis on class distinction. It is vital to America's future to strengthen the belief in that ideal and work toward its greater realization. While in the last fifty years educational forces have tended to stratify society, they have also created a vast instrument of democracy by virtue of extending universal education to the high school level. Since in a modern industrialized society national educational policy largely determines the social structure,

[22] James B. Conant, "Science and the National Welfare." Speech to the American Chemical Society. Reprinted in *Journal of Higher Education* 15(November 1944): 399–406+.

[23] James B. Conant, "Public Education and the Structure of American Society." *Teachers College Record* 47(December 1945):145–194.

this instrument can be used to restore fluidity in our social and economic life and can make available for the national welfare reservoirs of potential talent now untapped. Furthermore, education can inculcate the political and social ideals necessary for the development of a free and harmonious people operating a free enterprise economic system based on principles of private property and the profit motive but committed to the ideals of social justice. The closer we come to realizing complete equality of opportunity and the better our schools teach and practice the basic tenets of American democracy, the more chance there is for personal liberty to continue in the United States.[24]

Conant's thesis was brilliant, his arguments in its support complex, skillful, and often persuasive. However, the arguments were essentially extensions and syntheses of his observations and thought articulated at other times in other places.[25] The arguments can be summarized:

1. The possibilities for nonrevolutionary development of the nation, despite economic uncertainties, will be assured largely by an educational system that fosters equal opportunity.
2. A social structure that is fluid from generation to generation, that has complex interaction patterns and a low visibility, is desirable in a free industrial society. These conditions can be achieved by consciously created social pressures and artificially cultivated modes of behavior—in short, both by action and by talk. Public education is of prime importance in developing such a social structure.
3. Education underlies our whole economy, and the economy affects the entire social structure of the nation. Geographical and financial barriers to advanced education will result in unequal accessibility to the professional and executive groups in the economy.

---

[24] Ibid., p. 147.

[25] See also *Education for All American Youth* (Washington, D.C.: Educational Policies Commission, National Education Association and the American Association of School Administrators, 1944); *General Education in a Free Society*, Report of the Harvard Committee (Cambridge, Mass.: Harvard University Press, 1945); and W. Lloyd Warner, Robert J. Havighurst, and Martin B. Loeb, *Who Shall be Educated?* (New York: Harper and Row, 1944). Conant endorsed the general policies recommended in these works.

4. Education beyond the high school should be open to all who deserve and *need* it, need being determined by the subsequent vocation.

5. Even though granting a particular occupation academic standing tends to increase its social prestige, and thereby increase social differentiation, education must work toward a society in which a great variety of occupations have equal social status. This goal can be realized by providing two years of post–high school instruction in general, technical, and vocational education at local institutions.

6. A guidance program, based on enlightenment and persuasion, is central to a democratic educational system.

7. It is necessary to acknowledge the reality of intellectual talent and insure the full development of that talent for service in the professions.

8. To that end, the federal government has a special responsibility because social factors influencing the practice and coherence of the professions are to a large extent national.

At the close of his final lecture of the three, Conant anticipated his critics and tried to deal with the major inconsistency apparent in his arguments. He conceded that to argue for minimizing economic and social differentiation by equalizing the value of all labor seemed to contradict his proposal for the recruitment of only those talented youth needed in the professions. But he concluded that his purpose was first to examine public education with an eye on social stratification in America, and then to demonstrate how education could be utilized to change the composition within one level of the existing strata. By suggesting how to reduce rigidity and visibility within one layer, he perceived himself as an analyst of a social process and an advocate of change.

This rear guard defense was not altogether satisfactory. It opened a number of questions for consideration. Why were the professions rather than the vocational trades singled out as an object for change? Why did he not concern himself with the financial reward system that validates, and probably causes, status differentiations between occupations? Although Conant mentioned in the first lecture the "important and explosive problem of racial and religious discrimination," why did he focus on geographical and financial discrimination? (Fifteen years later, it should be pointed out, Conant did return to these other problems in his book *Slums and Suburbs*.)

While these questions suggest a misplaced emphasis, they do not get at the major fallacy in Conant's argument as he makes it—that is, that the elimination of financial barriers by scholarship monies depends for its efficacy as social policy on the responsiveness of the polity to monetary rewards. And since these rewards derive their value in direct proportion to volume, Conant actually strengthened the desire for differentiation and the social forces that encourage it. Worse, he used the professions, already the most highly rewarded occupation group, as the example for his proposal to reduce the visibility of the social structure.

Problems with means and ends, however, are better understood if we again examine Conant's twofold objective. "First, to show how we may examine public education in the light of our knowledge of the present structure of American society; and second, to set goals which we must reach if we are to modify the present structure in the direction I believe essential *in order to stabilize this industrial democracy of free men*" (emphasis added). In other words, the reform Conant advocates is toward a more stabilized, more rational industrial society.

Such reform does not challenge the premises underlying the society in question. In fact, the premises *and* those people whose interests depend on the continued acceptance of the premises are invested with new appeal and vitality when it is demonstrated that they are necessarily and causally related to the society's widely accepted political goals. Intellectual justification for such reform involves two primary tasks. First, the manipulation of the operational definitions for the ideals—that is, a classless society and equal opportunity—and simultaneously arguing that ideals can never be fully realized. Second, the means for achieving these goals will be identified within the given premises of the society *or* in premises acceptable to that society but now ignored or discarded. For example, Conant changed the definition of *class* to approximate what he presumes to be its common usage. His equality of opportunity which, admittedly, can never be reached, has little or no meaning when "applied to adults," and yet, "as long as an ideal represents a goal toward which a community of free men may move by concerted action, the phrase in question has real meaning."[26]

---

[26] Conant, "Public Education and the Structure of American Society."

The vast system of public education we have created can be utilized to achieve these ideals rather than overturn them. The principle of competition, in all forms of human endeavor, is still viable, although we must make it operate as a constructive social force rather than as an excuse for greediness. Although it is true, he admitted, that "there will be ups and downs in our prosperity, varying degrees of employment, difficulties of distribution of consumer goods, conflicting interests between those who seek a 'reasonable return on capital' and those whose rewards are in rates of pay," free enterprise, private property, and the profit motive, if revitalized and made more functional, still were the best means for correcting these problems and resolving conflicts.

Connections with the Past

One is tempted to say, rather wearily, that this approach to school and social reform, unfortunately, simply mirrors the past. Indeed, as Michael B. Katz has ably demonstrated, top-down reform proposals that originate in high places are often replete with unexamined assumptions and values and tend to strengthen the interests of those groups already in controlling roles within society.[27] But beyond this, it must be noted that Conant was concerned with much more than what Katz called the "preservation of domestic tranquility and an ordered, cohesive society." The orderliness and cohesiveness he pursued would come only with the assimilation of science into "our secular cultural pattern." When that was accomplished, he maintained, this nation "would be one step nearer the goal which we so earnestly desire—a unified, coherent culture suitable for our American democracy in this new age of machinery and experts."[28]

Comprehension of this goal provides a context for understanding Conant's testimony urging a national science foundation before a House of Representatives committee in March 1947.[29] "The bottle-

---

[27] Michael B. Katz, *The Irony of Early School Reform* (Cambridge, Mass.: Harvard University Press, 1968), esp. pp. 213–221.

[28] James B. Conant, "The Scientific Education of the Layman," *Yale Review* n.s. 36(September 1946):15–36.

[29] The testimony before the House Committee on Interstate and Foreign Commerce urging passage of H.R. 1815, 1830, 1834, and 2127 is reprinted in full in James B. Conant, "National Science Foundation," *Science* 105(Mar. 21, 1947):299–302.

neck of our scientific advance is essentially a manpower shortage," he testified, and to eliminate that bottleneck in engineering and science is "in the interests of the nation." In conclusion, he stated that we "need a Science Foundation both to forward our domestic economy and to strengthen our military establishment." Moreover, the vitally important document, *Education in a Divided World,* long ignored by historians of this period, becomes a great deal more than a sophisticated anti-Communist tract.[30] It is the final statement of how any nation should utilize its intellectual resources and institutions of learning to secure itself against external threat and internal uncertainty. Schooling is the means for achieving individual mobility, national security, economic prosperity, and free world hegemony. Further, the system of public instruction becomes an agent of total melioration, reducing class consciousness and deliberately obscuring social stratification and cleavage. Conant feared postwar economic upheaval, a return to depression levels of unemployment, and alien class analyses of fiscal instability. And these fears are reflected in his ideas for the integration of *democratic schooling* for scientific and technical competence, the development of technically competent manpower for research and development efforts to strengthen the industrial base of the economy and insure military preparedness, and the need for *economic expansion* and *military posture* as components of the ideological struggle against totalitarianism. Completing his unification, Conant observed that the achievement of these goals would be possible only when a system of schooling democratic in form as well as content existed within a nation.

The issue of "freedom to teach and learn" was of secondary concern, although it remained important. That freedom is valued and must not be compromised precisely because it is an important weapon in an ideological power struggle among nation-states. And, as one would expect, Conant supported this principle. As early as 1947 he wanted to eliminate peacetime secret research from the campus. He testified in 1948 before the Massachusetts legislature against a bill that would provide imprisonment for public school teachers who were Communists. He defended two members of his faculty when their political activities were condemned by Harvard

[30] James B. Conant, *Education in a Divided World* (Cambridge, Mass.: Harvard University Press, 1948).

alumni. On the other hand, he signed a report of the NEA's Educational Policies Commission in 1949 calling for the exclusion of members of the Communist party from employment as public school teachers because Party membership required that they surrender the right to think for themselves.[31]

It is important to attempt to understand Conant's compromise. How could anyone who prized freedom of thought deny someone the freedom to choose the right not to think for himself? (Whether or not that was required of members of the Communist party is not relevant here.) Of first significance is the fact that his endorsement is hidden among nineteen other signatures in a commission report that had no direct consequence in public policy. Second, as the debate following the commission's report revealed, there existed a strong belief that the teaching profession's public image could be greatly improved and a major step taken in the direction of restoring public confidence in the schools if the NEA were to approve such a policy.[32] Internal regulation and the subsequent public confidence insured against a witch-hunt, which Conant feared above all else. Lastly, anyone as perspicacious as Conant must have realized that very few public school teachers were likely to be members of the Communist party. And so, measured against possible benefits, it was an inexpensive compromise for him to make.

CONANT'S INFLUENCE

It has never been clear to what extent thought and policy planning have influenced the development or content of American education. Consequently, one must be cautious in drawing conclusions from the data presented here. And to demonstrate that one man's thought had a direct influence on national policy is doubly difficult. What can be said, however, is that James Bryant Conant was an atypical man whose life experiences afforded him a comprehensive view of his society, a man disposed to articulate a political and social philosophy he believed would reform society in desirable ways. Central to that philosophy was a conception of education as a public instrument to be utilized in the realization of national, political, and economic objectives.

---

[31] *Proceedings of the 87th Annual Meeting,* vol. 87(Washington, D.C.: National Education Association, 1949), pp. 94–99.

[32] Ibid.

During the period under examination, Conant was both educational propagandist and planner. On the one hand he addressed key groups and published articles in journals with varied audiences. On the other hand he developed manpower policies during the war, planned postwar science policy with Vannevar Bush at the Office of Scientific Research and Development, helped write the NEA's *Education for All American Youth,* generated the support for Harvard University's *General Education in a Free Society,* and presided over the American Council on Education's efforts to regulate affairs between higher education and the federal government. And without crediting Conant solely, one can point to the National Science Foundation, the Selective Service's policy on draft deferments, the increase of federal support for education, the National Defense Education Act's provision for guidance institutes, and the development of the comprehensive high school, and agree that there is much in the fabric of contemporary education that reflects Conant's thought of the 1940s.

The fact that his educational proposals were articulated along with and within a larger social and political philosophy several years before Berlin, Korea, McCarthyism, and Sputnik should give pause to those educational historians who have ignored the Conant of pre-Carnegie Corporation days and those observers of education who believe the Cold War to be the primary influence on present-day educational policy.

Most importantly, however, is the possibility that within Conant's views one may identify the basis for a new appraisal of the Cold War. It is true that the legacy of the Cold War has resulted in a blind and unthinking anticommunism and conservative, militant foreign policy. But what my analysis suggests is that the Cold War was the excuse for and the *justification* of our nation's behavior, not the *cause* of it.

In the writings of James Bryant Conant one discovers an ideology born of a pervasive insecurity, one that proposes the reform of certain internal and temporary evils *and,* at the same time, insures against the disruptive influence of *any* alien ideology by identifying in the American nation-state the source and defender of all that is valuable. Conant sought to integrate and unify America's institutions—public and private—its critical and supportive ideas, and its national objectives, both realized and unachieved, into a political philosophy that could describe enemies and prescribe responses. That is the importance of his work prior to 1951.

If it is true that through history those of the past can speak to the present, then one might suggest to those who seek solutions to the crises of contemporary life that they look beyond what the Cold War caused to what caused the Cold War. The malaise that besets our society derives in part from the knowledge that there are few sources of change and resistance. We are all confined by the norms of competition, subtle coercion, achievement, artificial rewards, and loyalty to that which supplies the goods—our government. And the schools, those agents of political socialization, trainers of talent, and repositories of technical and research competence, are as Conant argued they should be, central to the entire process.

CHAPTER 11

YOUTH CULTURE
IN THE
UNITED STATES

Joel Spring

The twentieth century has been marked by change, not the least important of which has been the transition from youth as an age-related social category to youth as an entire cultural movement, transcending the boundaries of age. Youth as a cultural movement is a concept difficult for many people to comprehend, and it has bred a great deal of misunderstanding. The concept's origin can be found in economic and social changes in the late nineteenth and early twentieth centuries, alterations that created conditions allowing adolescents and young adults to live differently from older members of society. By the 1920s there had developed what was known in the popular literature of the time as a generation gap or generational conflict. Young people in the 1920s developed a cultural style associated with their particular age group. After World War II, social and economic conditions that earlier had been peculiar to young people began to affect larger numbers of the population, creating a situation in which youth culture was no longer simply for young people but represented a cultural movement that

This essay was originally presented as a paper at the American Educational Research Association meeting in New York, February 4–7, 1971.

cut across society. Associations of the past caused people to continue to speak of a generation gap, but by the 1960s there existed no longer a generation, but a cultural gap.

DEFINITION OF YOUTH

In discussing the youth phenomenon of the twentieth century it is essential to distinguish between youth as a specific age group and youth as a cultural movement. The problem of defining youth becomes complicated because the two categories have commonly been granted the same meaning. For instance, Jerry Rubin, who was then over thirty years old, tried to express this distinction in *Do It!* when he said: "We're permanent adolescents. We reject careers and middle-class rowboats. Our culture, the hippie long-hair culture, is ageless. Forty-, thirty-, twenty-, and ten-year-olds live together on the same street corners. Age—what's age?—we don't even carry a watch. . . . When we're thirty-five, our ambition is to act like we're fifteen."[1] Rubin was not, of course, referring to a specific physiological stage of development but to those behavioral characteristics American society has come to associate with youth.

In terms of behavior, youth has been popularly defined as a time when intense sexual drives send the young person in pursuit of pleasure and lofty ideals. The romance and idealism of youth supposedly lead to a rebellion against the older generation. This concept of youth gained widespread acceptance after the publication of G. Stanley Hall's *Adolescence* in 1904. Hall concluded, as Rousseau had over a century before in *Emile,* that the flood of passions beginning in puberty developed the social man. "The social instincts," he wrote, "undergo sudden unfoldment and the new life of love awakens."[2] Linking sexual drives and social development created the highly romanticized view of the nature of youth. Jane Addams in *The Spirit of Youth and the City Streets,* published in 1909, called the "divine fire" of youth a "sex susceptibility which suffuses the world with its deepest meaning and beauty, and furnishes the momentum towards all art. . . ."[3]

[1] Jerry Rubin, *Do It!* (New York: Ballantine Books, 1970), p. 89.

[2] G. Stanley Hall, "Childhood and Adolescence" in *Health, Growth and Heredity,* ed. by Charles E. Strickland and Charles Burgess (New York: Teachers College Press, 1965), p. 108.

[3] Jane Addams, *The Spirit of Youth and the City Streets* (New York: Macmillan, 1909), p. 16.

As early as 1912 Randolph Bourne, literary radical and education editor of the *New Republic,* was calling for a League of Youth to revitalize civilization by displacing the older generation whose ideals and beliefs were outdated. Bourne wrote, "How shall I describe youth, the time of contradictions and anomalies? The fiercest radicalisms, the most dogged conservatism, irrepressible gayety, bitter melancholy—all these moods are equally part of that showery springtime of life."[4] The high point of popularization of the romantic idea of youth was Booth Tarkington's *Seventeen,* published in 1915. Tarkington directly linked the sexual drives to a growing social awareness that stimulated the main character of the novel to perform acts of tenderness and nobility and to express himself in poetry. At the book's conclusion, when the summer sweetheart was about to leave, Tarkington concluded that "seventeen needs only some paper lanterns, a fiddle, and a pretty girl—and Versailles is all there!"[5]

This conception of youth might have some foundation in terms of intensity of sexual drives, but there is little in the history of man to suggest that idealism, romance, poetry, and rebellion vanish with physiological maturity. Jerry Rubin could quite justly claim: "One of the yippiest yippies is Bertrand Russell. . . ."[6] The question must therefore be asked, why were these attributes specifically related to youth? Part of the answer can be found in changes in the occupational structure and demography of the United States that made youth marginal to productive forces and allowed youth the leisure and opportunity to appear idealistic, rebellious, and romantic. Growing out of youth into adulthood has popularly meant establishing a career, settling down, and gaining a commitment to the established social structure. Youth within this framework is, in the popular mind, a period of rebellion followed by the conservatism of adulthood. Rebelliousness and idealism have always been attributes marginal to the social structure because they are threats to established institutions. It is precisely because youth was delayed in its entrance to the prevailing social structure that it was either perceived as being idealistic and rebellious or it began to display these characteristics.

---

[4] Randolph Bourne, "Youth," in *The World of Randolph Bourne,* ed. by Lillian Schlissel (New York: Dutton, 1965), p. 3.

[5] Booth Tarkington, *Seventeen* (New York: Grosset and Dunlap, 1915), p. 249.

[6] Rubin, *Do It!* p. 90.

YOUTH AND THE SOCIOECONOMIC SYSTEM

Youth started to become marginal to the social and economic structure before World War I. During the nineteenth century the young had important economic roles to fill on the farm and in the factory. They were viewed as important new hands to be used in farm labor; in the factory, juvenile labor was welcomed as an important part of economic growth because it was energetic, dextrous, and cheap. Parents became heavily dependent on their children's earnings. As working-class youth moved into the factory, middle-class youth moved into white-collar occupations created by the expansion of commerce.[7]

During the early part of the twentieth century in the United States, factors developed that shifted and displaced the young from their economic roles. Improvements in farm technology and rural-to-urban migrations decreased the possibility of the young participating in farm labor. In 1900, 37.5 percent of the total labor force were farm workers. By 1910 this figure had decreased to 30.9 percent, and by 1930 to 21.2 percent. It continued to decline throughout the century. The total farm population reached a peak in 1916 and fluctuated below that figure for many years as the remainder of the population increased.[8] Labor agitation, increased productivity, factory legislation, and technological advances that no longer required dexterity and flexibility all helped to displace the young worker from the factory. These changes in rural areas and in factories caused a decrease in the percentage of youth participating in the labor force. Between 1890 and 1900 the percentage of males between fourteen and nineteen years of age active in the labor force increased from 50 percent to 62 percent. After 1900 this figure began to decline, reaching 51.5 percent in 1920. This percentage, while it represents a slight increase over the 1890 figure, marks a steadily declining participation not broken until the beginning of World War II.[9]

One response to these changes was to seek further institutionalization of all children and youth within the school. There was a general consensus that cramped city streets, the lack of areas for play, and the easy contacts with disreputable persons provided ideal

[7] Frank Musgrove, *Youth and the Social Order* (London: Routledge and Kegan Paul, 1964), pp. 58–76.

[8] Census Bureau, *Long-Term Economic Growth: 1860–1965* (Washington, D.C.: U.S. Government Printing Office, 1966), pp. 178–179, 182–183.

[9] Ibid., pp. 192–193.

conditions for producing juvenile delinquents and future criminals. Combined with this attitude was a feeling that the training in responsibility and industriousness characteristic of the small community and rural areas was lost in the city. John Dewey in his famous "School and Society" lectures in 1899 stressed that in the small communities of the past children engaged in activities that were useful for the maintenance of the community. Modern industrialization and urbanization had destroyed the general usefulness of the child to the family and the community. Dewey believed this had important consequences for the education of children. They must, Dewey believed, be given tasks to perform that would help them gain "training in habits of order and of industry, and in the idea of responsibility, of obligation to produce something in the world."[10] In 1947, at age eighty, Caroline Pratt, founder and director of the City and Country School, reflected in her autobiography on the changes that had taken place because of urbanization. "This is the change I have seen," she wrote, "from a world in which children could learn as they grew in it, to a world so far beyond the grasp of children, that only the school can present it to them in terms which they can understand. . . ."[11]

While problems associated with urban conditions were related to all age groups, there was an increasing concern about unrepressed youthful sexuality. It was believed that the increasing marginality of youth to the economic structure meant that the sexual drives of youth could no longer be channeled through socially meaningful occupations. The romantic interpretation of youth emphasized that the solution of social problems and existence of the social structure depended on directing social-sexual instinctual developments into acceptable and useful channels.

G. Stanley Hall wrote in the introduction to his classic work on adolescence in 1904, "The whole future of life depends on how the new powers of adolescence now given suddenly and in profusion are husbanded and directed."[12] Hall argued that social organizations should utilize the natural instincts of youth and "so direct intelligence and will as to secure the largest measure of social ser-

[10] John Dewey, The School and Society (Chicago: University of Chicago Press, 1963), pp. 10–11.

[11] Caroline Pratt, I Learn From Children (New York: Simon and Schuster, 1948), p. xii.

[12] G. Stanley Hall, Adolescence, vol. 1 (New York: Appleton, 1904), p. xv.

vice, advance altruism and reduce selfishness, and thus advance the higher cosmic order."[13] In a similar fashion, Jane Addams believed that the proper utilization of the sexual energies of youth could bring about the reform of society. She believed that the sexual energies of youth had to be recognized and used for the betterment of society. Parks, playgrounds, parades, education, and national ceremonies were to take the place of cheap dance halls and movie houses that seduced the sexual susceptibility of youth. The divine fire of youth, Jane Addams believed, should be directed toward the problems of the world. The youthful quest for beauty and impatience with the world's wrongs would purify the social order.[14]

High school teachers and administrators evidenced the same concern about channeling the social-sexual instincts of youth into social education programs that included clubs, group activities, and student government. The National Education Association's 1911 report of the Committee on a System of Teaching Morals proposed increased social education at the high school level because it was "the time of life when passion is born which must be restrained and guided aright or it consumes soul and body. It is the time when social interests are dominant and when social ideals are formed."[15]

Irving King, professor of education and social education advocate at the University of Iowa, argued in 1914 that a high school education must provide the adolescent with the opportunity for social service because at sixteen "youth emerges from the somewhat animal-like crassness of the pubertal years and begins to think of his social relationships, his duties and the rights and wrongs of acts." In the same spirit as Hall and Addams, he wrote, "Every youth is . . . an incipient reformer, a missionary, impatient with what seem to him the pettiness and the obtuseness of the adult world about him."[16] This same sentiment was echoed by Michael V. O'Shea, professor of education at the University of Wisconsin, who wrote in *Trend of the Teens,* published in 1920, that the "reformer . . . real-

[13] Ibid., vol. 2, p. 432.

[14] Addams, *Spirit of Youth,* p. 162.

[15] "Tentative Report of the Committee on a System of Teaching Morals in the Public Schools," in *Proceedings and Addresses of the Forty-ninth Annual Meeting* (Washington, National Education Association, 1911), p. 360.

[16] Irving King, *The High-School Age* (Indianapolis: Bobbs-Merrill, 1914), p. 80.

izes that if he would get his cause adopted he must appeal to youth . . . youth longs for a new order of things. . . ."[17]

Youth in the 1920s

As junior high schools developed after 1910, their leaders also claimed for them the function of guiding and directing awakening social-sexual instincts. In 1916, Joseph Abelson, writing in *Education* on the benefits of the junior high, argued that one of the serious defects of the present educational system was the beginning of the high school education after the social instincts had already begun to develop. "To remedy this evil," he wrote, "the Junior High School takes the pupil under its roof at the age of twelve, which is a period of 'fulminating' psychic expansion." The junior high school by providing differentiation and selection of courses would take account of the "nature and upheaval which makes the pubescent ferment."[18]

During the 1920s, as the marginality of youth increased in importance, the sexuality of youth became a central issue in discussions of what was popularly defined as the growth of a generation gap. In the 1920s economic productivity in terms of output per man hour in production increased by 27 percent. Previous to the 1920s, the increase in output per man hour had been 14 percent between 1900 and 1910 and 21 percent between 1910 and 1920. The increase in the amount a man could produce in a given time resulted from new technology and more efficient forms of corporate organization. The effect of increased productivity was not only more material abundance, but also a decreasing percentage of the population required in the work force. Increased productivity was reflected in the percentage of the male population between the ages of fourteen and nineteen years that belonged to the labor force. During the 1920s this percentage decreased by ten percentage points, from 51.5 percent to 40.1 percent. It is interesting to note that prosperity and increased productivity during the 1920s had little effect on the involvement of the over sixty-five age group in the labor force. The percentage of this group in the labor force declined by only about one-and-one-half percentage points, from 55.6 to 54 percent. The

---

[17] M. V. O'Shea, *The Trend of the Teens* (Chicago: Drake, 1920), p. 13.

[18] Joseph Abelson, "A Study of the Junior High School Project," *Education* 37(September 1916):11.

over sixty-five group did not undergo significant displacement from the labor force until after World War II.[19]

The increasing displacement of youth from the labor force brought increased school enrollment. Between 1900 and 1920 school attendance for those between the ages of five and seventeen increased from 78.7 percent to 83.9 percent, an increase of 5.2 percent. For the six-year period between 1920 and 1926 the percentage jumped another 6.5 percent to 90.4. College enrollment for those between the ages eighteen and twenty-one followed the same pattern. In 1900, 4 percent of the eighteen- to twenty-one-year-old group were in college; by 1920 this figure was 8.1 percent, and during the 1920s there was another 4.3 percent increase. The increase in the percentage of the population in these specified age groups enrolled in school and college more than equaled that of the previous twenty years.[20]

The increase in productivity, affluence, and increased school attendance all contributed to what has been called the Flapper Era or the Jazz Age. A youth culture developed around new forms of dress, music, dance, codes of conduct, and technology. The flapper, jazz, modern dance, the new morality, and the automobile all became part of youth culture. Youth fads of the 1920s centered on the consumption of new products of technology. The automobile of the 1920s provided a form of mobility that had not existed for previous generations. Those concerned with the youth problem often traced the decline of morality, as well as the free spirit and rebellion against authority, to the automobile. Lengthy articles and discussions on the automobile and morality appeared in popular magazines. Movie houses, different styles of clothing, new dances, and the gin mill stood along side the automobile as symbols of youth culture. The headmaster of the Lawrenceville School lamented in 1926 about the maelstrom his students would be entering. When he was eighteen, life was less difficult because there was no "prohibition," "ubiquitous automobile," "cheap theater," "absence of parental control," or "emancipation of womanhood."[21]

Many Americans agreed with the headmaster that flapper dress, manners, and morals were leading youth straight down the path to

---

[19] Census Bureau, *Long-Term Growth,* pp. 188–189, 192–193.
[20] Ibid., pp. 196–197.
[21] Mather A. Abbott, "The New Generation," *The Nation,* Dec. 8, 1926, p. 587.

hell, a place or condition defined as one of hedonistic pleasure and liberated sexuality. In 1926, *Forum* magazine published two articles by members of the younger generation under the title, "Has Youth Deteriorated?" The affirmative response to this question reflected concern that unrepressed sexuality led to chaotic and uncivilized disorder. Young people today, one of the youthful authors wrote, ". . . rush in an impetuous, juvenile stampede, not knowing what lies ahead. They have hurled aside all conventions; accepted standards are 'nil'. . . . 'Liberate the Libido' has become, through them, our national motto."[22] The negative response stressed, "Beauty and idealism, the two eternal heritages of Youth, are still alive. It is a generation which is constituting the leaven in the rapid development of a new and saner morality."[23] Both articles referred to youth as "us" and stressed that the central concern with youth appeared to be with sexual standards. As one of the young writers stated, "This tremendous interest in the younger generation is nothing more nor less than a preoccupation with the nature of that generation's sex life. What people really want to know about us, if they are honest enough to admit it, is whether or not we are perverted, whether we are loose, whether we are what they call immoral; and their curiosity has never been completely satisfied."[24]

When in 1922 the *Literary Digest* conducted a national survey on the younger generation, it reported an overriding concern with the decline of sexual morality. The survey questioned high school principals, college presidents and deans, the editors of college newspapers, and the editors of religious weeklies across the country about the plight of the younger generation. The editor of the *Moody Bible Institute Monthly* responded to the survey with the declaration that in both manners and morals society "is undergoing not a revolution, but a devolution. That is to say, I am not so impressed by its suddenness or totalness as by its steady, uninterrupted degeneration."[25] From a college newspaper editor at the University of Pennsylvania came the opinion that "the modern dance has done much to break down standards of morals." Describ-

---

[22] Anne Temple, "Reaping the Whirlwind," *Forum* 74(July 1926):21–26.

[23] Regina Malone, "The Fabulous Monster," *Forum* 74(July 1926):26–30.

[24] Temple, "Reaping the Whirlwind," p. 22.

[25] "The Case Against the Younger Generation," *Literary Digest*, June 17, 1922, p. 40.

ing life on his campus the editor complained, "To the girl of to-day petting parties, cigaret-smoking, and in many cases drinking, are accepted as ordinary parts of existence. . . . She dresses in the lightest and most flimsy of fabrics. Her dancing is often of the most passionate nature. . . ."[26] A writer from the Phi Kappa Psi House at Northwestern University in Evanston, Illinois, summed up the general mood of the survey: "One outstanding reflection on the young set to-day is the reckless pursuit of pleasure."[27]

The 1930s and 1940s

To those who believed that the social order depended on properly controlling directing social-sexual instincts, the new morality of the 1920s represented a direct threat to the foundations of civilization. But the frivolous style of life associated with youth in the 1920s came to an abrupt end with the beginning of the depression. Unemployed youth now became a central issue. Like other marginal groups—such as blacks—youth found itself the last hired and the first fired. Lacking the seasoned skills of older workers, youth found it increasingly difficult to obtain jobs during a time of high unemployment. The 1940 census revealed that by the end of the depression 35 percent of the unemployed were youth under age twenty-five, whereas only 22 percent of the total employable population was within that age range.[28]

In response to the crises of the depression the American Council on Education established the American Youth Commission to investigate the problems of young America. In 1937 the chairman of the council offered the following picture. Defining youth as between sixteen and twenty-four, he described a mythical town of Youngsville with a population of 200 youths. Within this town 76 youths had regular jobs, 40 went to school or college, 5 went to school part-time, 28 were married women, and 51 were out of work and out of school. Half of those out of work received federal aid. The chairman claimed that Youngsville was also experiencing a major decline in personal health. According to the statistics of the Youth Commission, 1 out of 4 among young America had syphillis or gonorrhea and 5 percent were, would be, or had been in an

---

[26] Ibid., p. 42.

[27] Ibid., p. 51.

[28] Harold Rugg, *Foundations for American Education* (New York: World Book Co., 1947), p. 582.

asylum. Added to these problems was the highest crime rate in the country.[29]

One striking characteristic of youth reported during the depression was its lack of idealism and rebelliousness. One of the conditions that created this situation, different from the past, was that marginality in the 1930s was not accompanied by affluence but by a desire for economic security. When Howard Bell of the American Youth Commission surveyed the young people of Maryland in the 1930s as a representative sample of all American youth, he found that 57.7 percent of the youth surveyed named the lack of economic security as the major problem for young people in America. Concern with economic security was accompanied by a realization that youth was a special group in society. Bell found "that only one-fourth of the youth believed that there was *no* youth problem. . . ."[30]

The other important condition affecting youth during the depression was the cultural and social climate. *McCall's Magazine* assigned Maxine Davis to travel around the country and report on the state of youth. Traveling four months and ten thousand miles through cities and backroads of America, she produced not only articles but a book that labeled the youth of the depression as the "lost generation." Within the "lost generation," she reported, "We never found revolt. We found nothing but a meek acceptance of the fate meted out to them, and a belief in a benign future based on nothing but wishful thinking."[31] The major problem among the lost generation was the lack of economic security. The nature of the lost generation, Davis argued, was a product of the psychopathic period in which they grew up. Davis wrote,

> Boys and girls who came of voting age in 1935 were born in 1914. Their earliest memories are of mob murder and war hysteria. Their next, the cynical reaction to war's sentimentality and war's futility. Their adolescence was divided between the crass materialism of the jazz 1920's and the shock of the economic collapse. In effect, they went to high school in limousines and washed dishes in college.[32]

[29] "Outlook for Youth in America: Report of Panel Discussion," *Progressive Education* 14(December 1937):595.

[30] Howard Bell, *Youth Tell Their Story* (Washington, D.C.: American Council on Education, 1938).

[31] Maxine Davis, *The Lost Generation* (New York: Macmillan, 1936), p. 367.

[32] Ibid., p. 4.

It is interesting to compare the attitudes toward the lost generation of the depression with those toward the beat generation of the 1950s. In both cases the general apathy they evinced has been associated with the period of time in which they developed. Jack Kerouac labeled the beat generation in 1950 simply by saying, "You know, this really is a beat generation."[33] Cellon Holmes, author and friend of Kerouac, defined the meaning of the beat generation in a 1952 *New York Times Magazine* article entitled "This Is the Beat Generation." He called it a generation beat from the depression, the war, and the feeling that the peace that was inherited was only as secure as the next headline. "More than mere weariness," Holmes wrote, "it implies the feeling of having been used, of being raw. It involves a sort of nakedness of mind, and, ultimately, of soul; a feeling of being reduced to the bedrock of consciousness. In short, it means being undramatically pushed up against the wall." The new generation, Holmes argued, lived in a world of shattered ideals and accepted the mud in the moral currents; "They were brought up in these ruins and no longer notice them. They drink to 'come down' or to 'get high,' not to illustrate anything. Their excursions into drugs or promiscuity come out of curiosity, not disillusionment."[34]

During both the depression and the 1950s there existed a general uneasiness that youth was not displaying characteristics usually associated with that stage of development. The roots of that uneasiness lay in the fact that during each of these periods people assumed that youth, representing a particular stage of physical and psychological development, should express an idealistic and rebellious nature. That these characteristics did not appear suggests that they are products of social and economic conditions rather than a stage of physiological development. During the 1950s many observers were distressed that youth was security-minded, conformist, and willing to adopt the role of the organization man. During the depression there was a general feeling that youth was a powder keg that might explode at any moment from its general apathy and provide the ranks for a fascist movement. The chairman of the American Youth Commission in the 1930s argued, "It will need education and organization and vigorous action among the young people and those devoted to their care and education to save

---

[33] Cellon Holmes, "This Is the Beat Generation," *New York Times Magazine*, Nov. 16, 1952, p. 10.

[34] Ibid., pp. 10, 19.

America from fascism, and youth from becoming storm troops for an American dictator."[35] Maxine Davis wrote, "This lack of revolt is more ominous than active radicalism, to our mind. Those potential Nazis were not protestors. They were merely sitting, enduring, quiescent. They were unaware of the fact that they were waiting for a leader to galvanize them into action."[36]

The importance of economic conditions in creating the idea of a youth problem and a generation gap became evident during World War II. The war provided a temporary solution to both the youth problem and the depression. War industries and the armed forces solved the economic problems and absorbed the young. Youth's marginality to the occupational structure no longer was a factor, and the young were reintegrated into the mainstreams of social and economic activity in the United States. The proportion of those between the ages of fourteen and nineteen involved in the labor force increased from 44 percent in 1940 to 69.2 percent in 1944. The figure 69.2 percent even exceeded the previous high of 62 percent in 1900. With more places available in the occupational structure there was a corresponding decrease in school enrollments. During the depression, school and college enrollments had continued to climb from 89.7 percent in 1930 to 94.1 percent in 1940 for those members of the population between the age of five and seventeen, and from 12.4 percent in 1930 to 15.6 percent in 1940 for those between the age of eighteen and twenty-one. The increase in school enrollment during the depression reflected the displacement of the young from the occupational structure. The decrease in school enrollment during World War II indicated their reentry into it. Enrollments for those between five and seventeen steadily declined during the war until 1944, when 89 percent of that age group was in high school. College attendance for those between eighteen and twenty-one declined to 11.9 percent in 1946.[37]

After World War II

Following World War II the involvement of males between fourteen and nineteen in the labor force decreased slowly. It did not approximate the 1920 figure until about 1953 when 50 percent of

---

[35] "Outlook for Youth In America," pp. 595–596.

[36] Davis, *Lost Generation*, p. 367.

[37] Census Bureau, *Long-Term Growth*, pp. 192–193, 196–197.

that group participated.[38] The fact that youth could still find employment after 1945 spread alarm among some educators, and they launched a back-to-school campaign in the years immediately following the war. The general secretary of the National Child Labor Committee complained in the early part of 1947, "With jobs still to be had, the young people who left school for work during the war have not returned to school to any noticeable degree and their ranks continue to be augmented by new school-leavers." Interestingly, the secretary concluded that "Short of a depression—and unemployment is a costly price to pay for increased school attendance—most of these young workers are lost to the schools for good."[39]

During the spring of 1949, though, unemployment of both adults and young people increased considerably. The marginality of youth was again apparent, for while the general unemployment rate was 5 percent, it was around 14 percent for youth between sixteen and nineteen years of age.[40] Changes in the job market were again reflected in school enrollment figures. In 1946 the percentage of those between the ages of five and seventeen enrolled in school was 90.3. In 1948 the percentage dropped to 89.5 and by 1950 it increased to 92.6. After 1950 this percentage steadily increased, except for a slight drop between 1958 and 1960, until it reached 97.1 percent in 1965. College enrollments followed the same pattern. Thanks in part to the G.I. Bill and later to the draft deferment system, enrollment in higher education for those between eighteen and twenty-one increased to 22.1 percent in 1947, reached 31.2 percent in 1956, and by 1965 was 43.9 percent.[41]

Economic and social conditions were ripening in the mid-1950s for a repeat of the generation gap of the 1920s, although on a more massive scale. Output per man hour based on an index of 100 for 1929 dropped during the early part of the depression and slowly increased during the latter part of the 1930s until it reached 124 in 1940. During World War II, productivity increased to 159 in 1945 and continued to go up. By 1955 it had more than doubled the

---

[38] Ibid., pp. 192–193.

[39] "The Shifting Problem of Youth Employment," *School Review* 54(January 1947):8.

[40] E. A. Merritt and H. S. Rifkind, "Unemployment Among the Teen-aged in 1947–49," *Monthly Labor Review* 69(December 1949):647.

[41] Census Bureau, *Long-Term Growth*, pp. 196–197.

1929 figure, climbing to 204.8.[42] Increased output per man hour required increased consumption, a requirement met by high consumer spending and massive consumption by the defense establishment. High productivity also required the displacement of portions of the population from production, but not from consumption. The young and the old were directly affected. Locked in school, middle- and upper-middle-class youth could consume the excesses of technological production without contributing to its further increase. Following World War II there was also a rapid decrease among those over sixty-five who could find a place in the occupational structure. Between 1920 and 1945 there was only a decrease of about 5 percent of the population sixty-five and over who participated in the labor force. Between 1945 and 1965 the percentage dropped from 50.8 to 27.9.[43]

The post–World War II child grew up in the richest abundance of technology and mass consumption the world had ever known. "On the surface," Jerry Rubin wrote, "the world of the 1950s was all Eisenhower calm. A cover story of 'I Like Ike' father-figure contentment."[44] As the beat generation moved out of the colleges and universities and achieved its goal of economic security, it was replaced by the children of postwar economic affluence. Almost 50 percent of this generation was to be delayed from entering the occupational structure by continued education after high school. The combination of extended dependency, consumer exploitation, and the sharing of a common social life helped to create the youth culture of the 1960s. And reaction to the youth culture of the 1960s followed the same pattern as that of the 1920s. Sexual permissiveness, dress, music, and lack of respect for authority convinced other members of society that America was on the road to ruin.

Youth Culture Today

The combination of affluence and marginality to the productive structure again set the stage for the return of youthful romanticism and idealism. Locked in institutions of higher learning, youth's only important social functions were preparation for future entrance into the occupational structure and present and future consumption of technology's products. But youth did not remain content with be-

---

[42] Ibid., pp. 188–189.
[43] Ibid., pp. 192–194.
[44] Rubin, *Do It!* p. 17.

ing socially important only in terms of consumption and future production. As a social group freed from concern with working, it could define its social importance in terms of humanitarian crusades. Youth again accepted the labels of idealism and romanticism and joined with blacks in the early 1960s in a massive civil rights campaign. During the middle and late sixties, young people defined their social role by participating in civil rights campaigns, battles against pollution, political campaigns, and a variety of other social projects.

The schools were not prepared for the emergence of this new social role. As custodial institutions they were organized on the assumption that youth had no important social role. Much of the turmoil in the high schools and colleges in the industrial countries of the world during the 1960s and 1970s was the result of a conflict between youth's newly defined social function and the older custodial role of the school. If youth was to be kept in school and maintain its new social role, the school had to change. The school's accommodation had to take the form of allowing for direct social involvement. In high schools and colleges students demanded that their institutions become actively committed to participation in social change. Organizations that had helped create the social status of youth were called upon to reorganize and provide an institutional outlet for student activism.

The important features of the youth culture of the 1960s were the large number of participants and the fact that it did not terminate in a period of economic scarcity as it had during the 1920s. In fact, what had been obscured in the past by economic changes began to assume some clarity by the end of the 1960s. Youth was not idealistic and rebellious because of physiological growth but rather, it assumed these characteristics under certain economic and social conditions. Youth as a special age group was translated into what became popularly referred to as the counterculture. As a cultural movement this transcended age grouping as technology continued to expand through the 1960s. It should be recognized that youth of the 1960s represented the first large-scale attempt to adapt to an economy in which large numbers of producers were no longer needed. Conditions of dependency and delayed entrance into and early exit from the occupational structure were conditions affecting large numbers of the population as productivity continued to increase at a rapid rate.

Relegating rebelliousness and idealism to the age of youth has provided a certain comfort in the past. Defining youth in these terms always allows for the belief that its problems will disappear once youth enters adulthood. Marginality accompanied by affluence allows for romanticism, idealism, and rebelliousness. Aristocrats and bohemians of the past have also shared these attributes. Becoming an adult has meant gaining a stake in the existing social structure so that change will always appear as a threat. What must be realized today is that large numbers of the population will not be required to become adults in this sense. Youth as a cultural movement is no longer related to only a specific age group. It cuts across the entire society. The concept of a generation gap is a myth. What exists is a cultural gap produced by historical, social, and economic forces.

CHAPTER 12

ANARCHISM AND EDUCATION: A DISSENTING TRADITION

Joel Spring

When writing their accounts of the past, historians often overlook or deemphasize those ideas and social movements which, if examined closely, might serve as a source of challenge to the existing social structure. While men can use history to explain and give meaning to their present, they can also forget those parts of history whose recall would drive them from their complacent acceptance of the present. The white man in America could rest comfortably in a racist society so long as the rich tradition of black history was forgotten or ignored. Recent attention to black history has struck at the very heart of the racist social structure by giving the black man a sense of identity and a direction to his own life, and by displaying to the entire society the evolution of black culture and its links to the fabric of American social development. The white man can no longer forget the black man because he is now being forced to see the black as a whole man with a past that he must share. He must now accept the burden of guilt for the past and, more importantly, he is forced to integrate his own identity as an American

This essay was first published at the Center for Intercultural Documentation, Cuernavaca, Mexico, and also appeared in *Libertarian Analysis* 1(No. 4):30–43.

with that of the black man. Black history is expanding the consciousness and self-perceptions of all Americans.

What is being done with black history must now be done with radical traditions of the past. To wipe radicalism from the nation's memory is to attempt to eliminate serious challenges to the present and uphold the present as product of a process of easy growth, facilitated by the idea that all men accepted the development of modern institutions. History that leaves out radical criticism that existed in the past becomes mere propaganda to support the status quo. The majority of American historians, for example, have dismissed anarchists as simply a defective group of bomb-throwing fanatics whose only goals were destruction and chaos. Any person or group that seriously challenged the development of modern institutions has been safely labelled either mentally ill or simply in quest of personal glory and power. Telling the tale of the past in this manner allows the present generation to dismiss radical causes on the same basis.

ANARCHISTS AND AUTONOMY

Educational history has fulfilled its function of propagandizing for the established order of the present. Implications carried by the rise of state-supported schools has been obscured and distorted by an unawareness of a critical tradition. There has certainly been enough internal criticism centering on the form, methods, and goals of public schooling treated in great detail by historians. The exploration of a critical tradition that questions the very existence of state-supported schools and offers an alternative direction for education, however, has been missing. Anarchism as a social and political philosophy concerned with the role and nature of authority in society has, since the eighteenth century, raised serious and important questions about the very existence of state systems of schooling and the possibility of nonauthoritarian forms of education. From William Godwin in the eighteenth century to Paul Goodman in the twentieth, anarchist literature abounds with discussions of education, representing what one might call the dissenting tradition in education.

The central concern of traditional anarchists has been the development of social and economic systems that enhance individual autonomy. Simply defined, autonomy means that a person assumes the responsibility for determining his own actions. At first glance this goal would not appear radical, yet when one begins to work out its implications, it brings into question many of the established and accepted institutions in the modern world.

In the first place, anarchists oppose the existence of the state in any form because it destroys individual autonomy by enacting laws that determine individual action. Anarchists in the nineteenth and twentieth centuries have argued that the state and its laws exist for the protection of the political and economic elite. This rejection of the state includes democratic societies in which the individual is required to sacrifice his autonomy either to the majority or to a representative. The state has also been viewed as a mechanism for protecting economic systems that allow for the exploitation of one man by another. Working from this perspective, twentieth-century anarchists have found themselves in the interesting position of being equally opposed to the political and economic system of both the United States and the Union of Soviet Socialist Republics. Second, anarchists have believed that individual autonomy means an individual who is able to make a choice free from all imposed dogma. This means that to freely determine his actions, a person has to establish his own values and goals. And this has meant the rejection of all institutions that attempt to make the individual into something. Of particular importance in this respect has been the objection to the school and the church as institutions that limit autonomy by molding character.

One of the more important anarchist objections to the existence of national systems of schooling was this: education in the hands of the state would become subservient to the political interests of those in control. Within this context schooling was viewed as a formidable weapon to be used by the state to mold and direct the will and character of its citizens so they would support and maintain existing institutions. Anarchists viewed education linked to the national state as the ultimate form of authority because this limited individual autonomy by directly controlling desires, aspirations, and goals.

William Godwin

William Godwin was among the first writers in the anarchist tradition to voice these criticisms of national education. Godwin's most important work, *An Enquiry Concerning Political Justice and Its Influence on Morals and Happiness,* published in England in 1793, warned that before allowing government to assume the role of educator "it behooves us to consider well what it is that we do."[1] Godwin argued that placing education in the hands of government agencies would allow them to use it to strengthen their positions of power. Said he: "Their views as institutors of a system of education will not fail to be analogous to their views in their political capacity: the data upon which their instructions are founded."[2] Godwin rejected the assumption held by many in the eighteenth and nineteenth century that public schooling would result in individual freedom, although the fact that national schooling could be used for totalitarian purposes did not become clear to the Western world until the twentieth century. "Had the scheme of a national education," Godwin warned, "been adopted when despotism was most triumphant, it is not to be believed that it could have forever stifled the voice of truth. But it would have been the most formidable and profound contrivance for that purpose that imagination can suggest." Even in countries where liberty prevailed, Godwin argued, one could assume the existence of serious social errors that a national education would tend to perpetuate.[3]

Francisco Ferrer

Godwin's criticisms came at a time when public schools were still in their infancy. He was concerned with what might happen as a result of national education. His was not a critique of actual consequences. By the end of the nineteenth century some form of national education had triumphed in most industrialized Western countries, and anarchists could turn to these institutions for more direct evaluation of the relationship between schooling and the national state. One important anarchist critic was the Spanish educator Francisco Ferrer, who founded the Modern School in 1901 in Barcelona. Ferrer's work gained international recognition when in 1909 the Spanish government accused him of leading an insurrection in Barcelona and executed him. His execution struck members of many groups in Europe and the United States as highly unjust, and it sparked interest in his career and educational ideas. In the United States a Ferrer Society was organized and a Modern School established in Stelton, New Jersey. In Europe the International

---

[1] William Godwin, *Enquiry Concerning Political Justice and Its Influence on Morals and Happiness;* photographic facsimile of the third edition (Toronto: University of Toronto Press, 1946), vol. 2, p. 302.

[2] Ibid.

[3] Ibid., pp. 303–304.

League for the Rational Education of Children, which had been founded by Ferrer, was reorganized after his death under the honorary presidency of Anatole France.

Ferrer had pointed out that governments had come to monopolize education. "They know, better than anyone else, that their power is based almost entirely on the school," he stated.[4] In the past, Ferrer maintained, governments had kept the masses in a state of ignorance as a means of controlling them; but with the rise of industrialism in the nineteenth century, governments found themselves involved in international economic competition, and this required trained industrial workers. Schools triumphed in the nineteenth century not because of a general desire to reform society, but because of economic need. Ferrer wrote that governments wanted schools "not because they hope for the renovation of society through education, but because they need individuals, workmen, perfected instruments of labor to make their industrial enterprises and the capital employed in them profitable."[5] At first, Ferrer believed, there was a great hope in the nineteenth century that schooling would become a means of liberating humanity. But that hope had been crushed when it became clear that a national system of schooling by its very organization could only serve the interests of those with political power. School teachers became

> the conscious or unconscious instruments of these powers, modeled moreover according to their principles; they have from their youth up . . . been subjected to the discipline of their authority; few indeed are those who have escaped the influence of this domination . . . because the school organization constrains them so strongly that they cannot but obey."[6]

In Ferrer's mind the schools had accomplished exactly the things Godwin had warned against in the previous century. In becoming the focal points for maintaining existing institutions, the schools depended on a system that conditioned the student for obedience and docility. A variety of critics, of course, leveled this charge at the schools, but from Ferrer's point of view repression was an in-

[4] Francisco Ferrer, "L'Ecole Renovee," *Mother Earth* 4(November 1909):267.

[5] Ibid., p. 268.

[6] Ibid., p. 271.

evitable result of a school controlled by the state. "Children must be accustomed," Ferrer wrote, "to obey, to believe, to think, according to the social dogmas which govern us. Hence, education cannot be other than such as it is to-day."[7] A major goal for Ferrer was to break government's power over education, for reform that tried to work within the system could accomplish nothing with respect to the goal of human emancipation. Those who organized the national schools, Ferrer asserted, "have never wanted the uplift of the individual, but his enslavement; and it is perfectly useless to hope for anything from the school of to-day."[8]

It was inconceivable to Ferrer that a government would create a system of education that would lead to any radical changes in the society supporting that government. It was therefore unrealistic to believe that national schooling would be a means of significantly changing the conditions of the lower classes. Since the existing social structure produced the poor, education could eliminate poverty only by freeing men to radically change the social structure. An education of this kind would not result from national schools because the government would not teach anything that threatened its own stability. Writing in a Modern School bulletin about the mixing of rich and poor in the schools of Belgium, Ferrer stressed that "the instruction that is given in them is based on the supposed eternal necessity for a division of rich and poor, and on the principle that social harmony consists in the fulfilment of the laws."[9] The poor were taught, according to Ferrer, to accept the existing social structure and the belief that economic improvement depended on individual effort within the existing structure. Developing this attitude in the poor reduced the threat of any major social change.

The critical factor that anarchists perceived in a state-controlled educational system was this: the political dogmas expounded and the attempt to shape the individual into a useful citizen undermined the autonomy of the individual by fixing the boundaries and limits of the will. While state and religious schools were recognized as the greatest threat to individual freedom, this did not mean that freedom from these strictures was the sole condition for an anarchist school.

[7] Ibid., p. 272.

[8] Ibid.

[9] Francisco Ferrer, *The Origin and Ideals of the Modern School*, trans. by Joseph McCabe (New York: Putnam's, 1913), p. 48.

Stirner and Authority

The central issue for anarchists was the meaning of freedom and its relationship to education. Most anarchists have agreed with Max Stirner's statement, made in the 1840s, that the major problem with the stress on freedom in the nineteenth century was that it "appeared . . . as independence from authorities, however, it lacked self-determination and still produced none of the acts of a man who is free-in-himself. . . ."[10] From an anarchist standpoint this means that a state might free the individual from direct authority structures but still enslave the individual through a system of schooling. To be "free-in-himself" required that an individual choose his own goals, ideals, and character rather than having them imposed through a planned system of schooling.

Knowledge, in other words, could be both freeing and enslaving. Whether it was one or the other depended on how one gained knowledge. Probably the most cogent statement of this position was made by Stirner in *The False Principle of Our Education*. Max Stirner, whose real name was Johann Casper Schmidt, was a poor German schoolteacher who in the 1840s attended meetings of the Young Hegelians in Berlin with Marx and Engels. Stirner's one and only important book, *The Ego and His Own,* was written during this period and so upset Marx that he devoted a large section of *The German Ideology* to an attack on Stirner's ideas. Stirner wrote his articles on education before he wrote the book, and they were published by Karl Marx in 1842 in the *Rheinische Zeitung.*

Stirner believed that one had to distinguish between the free man and the educated man. The free man used knowledge to facilitate choice. "If one awakens in men the idea of freedom," Stirner wrote, "then the free men will incessantly go on to free themselves; if, on the contrary, one only educates them, then they will at all times accommodate themselves to circumstances in the most highly educated and elegant manner and degenerate into subservient cringing souls."[11] Stirner believed that knowledge should not be taught because the process of absorbing knowledge turned the individual into a learner rather than a creative person. The learner was a subservient person because he was taught to depend on authoritarian

---

[10] Max Stirner, *The False Principle of Our Education*, trans. by Robert H. Beebe (Colorado Springs: Ralph Myles, 1967), p. 16.

[11] Ibid., p. 23.

sources for his beliefs and goals rather than on himself. A learning person was without free will; he depended on learning how to act rather than determining himself how to act. "Where will a creative person be an educated instead of a learner one?" Stirner asked. "Where does the teacher turn into a fellow worker, where does he recognize knowledge as turning into will, where does the free man count as a goal and not the merely educated?"[12]

To avoid producing the mere learner, according to Stirner, the goal of pedagogy should be self-development in the sense that an individual gains self-awareness and ability to act. Existing schools worked against the freedom of the will. In discussing the development of education, Stirner argued that, following the Reformation, education in the humanistic tradition became a means to power. Referring to the humanistic tradition he wrote that ". . . education, as a power, raised him who possessed it over the weak, who lacked it, and the educated man counted in his circle, however large or small it was, as the mighty, the powerful, the imposing one: for he was an authority."[13] The rise of the idea of universal schooling undermined the authority of the humanist scholar, and eventually a system designed to produce useful citizens trained for a practical life was established. Authority under the system of popular education was not that of one man over another, but rather dogmas of what was practical and useful over the minds of men. Stirner wrote that ". . . only scholars come out of the menageries of the humanists, only 'useful citizens' out of those of the realists, both of whom are indeed nothing but subservient people."[14] Education for practical life, Stirner believed, produced people of principles who acted according to maxims. "Most college students," he stated, "are living examples of this sad turn of events. Trained in the most excellent manner, they go on training; drilled, they continue drilling."[15]

Stirner and future anarchists argued that at the heart of education should be the idea of developing a mind able to choose, free of dogma and prejudice, whose goals and purposes are self-determined. Knowledge pursued in this fashion would become a result of self-direction designed to strengthen the will. The individual

---

[12] Ibid.
[13] Ibid., p. 12.
[14] Ibid., p. 23.
[15] Ibid., p. 25.

would not be taught, he would teach himself. This did not mean that the individual might not seek a teacher, but simply that the acquisition of knowledge would be the result of an individual desire and, consequently, directly related to the will of an individual. Stirner, in a statement that would reflect the attitude of later anarchist educators, put the matter in these terms: "If man puts his honor first in relying upon himself and applying himself, thus in self-reliance, self-assertion, and freedom, he then strives to rid himself of the ignorance which makes out of the strange impenetrable object a barrier and hindrance to his self-knowledge."[16]

Leo Tolstoy

This approach to education required that a careful distinction be made between what was normally defined as schooling and what anarchists hoped to accomplish. Leo Tolstoy, Russian novelist and Christian anarchist, who established his own school in Russia in the 1860s, carefully defined this distinction in an article titled "Education and Culture," published in 1862. Tolstoy argued that culture, education, instruction, and teaching had distinct and important meanings. He defined culture as the total of all social forces that shaped the character of the individual. Education was the conscious attempt to give men a particular type of character and habits. As Tolstoy stated, "Education is the tendency of one man to make another just like himself."[17]

The difference between education and culture was over the issue of compulsion. "Education is culture under restraint. Culture is free." He argued that instruction and teaching were related to both education and culture. Instruction was the transmission of one man's information to another; teaching, which overlapped into the area of instruction, taught physical skills. Teaching and instruction were a means of culture, Tolstoy claimed, when they were free, and a means of education "when the teaching is forced upon the pupil, and when the instruction is exclusive, that is when only those subjects are taught which the educator regards as necessary."[18]

For anarchists using Tolstoy's definitions, schooling was to be a process of culture and not education. This meant a school of non-

[16] Ibid., p. 23.

[17] Leo Tolstoy, "Education and Culture," in *Tolstoy on Education*, trans. by Leo Wiener (Chicago: University of Chicago Press, 1967), p. 111.

[18] Ibid., p. 109.

interference and compulsion, where the student learned what he wanted to learn. Tolstoy defined a school as "the conscious activity of him who gives culture upon those who receive it. . . ." In the school, noninterference meant "granting the person under culture the full freedom to avail himself of the teaching which answers his need, which he wants . . . and to avoid teaching which he does not need and which he does not want."[19] Museums and public lectures were examples of schools in which noninterference prevails. They were consciously planned by the institution or lecturer to achieve a certain goal, but the user was free to attend or not to attend. Established schools and universities, on the other hand, used a system of rewards and punishments and limited the area of studies to achieve their particular ends. Tolstoy's example of his noncompulsory school was one without a planned program, where teachers could teach what they wished and their offerings would be regulated by the demands of the students. The school would not be interested in how its teaching was used or what the effect would be on the students. The school would be a place of culture and not of education.

In varying degrees Stirner and Tolstoy reflected general anarchist thought about learning. In the United States, Elizabeth Burns Ferm, writing in the anarchist journal *Mother Earth* in 1907, emphasized the distinction between making the child into something and allowing the child to become something. Using different terms than Tolstoy had, Ferm defined the pedagogue as one who endeavors "to make and leave an impression on the child." Rejecting the pedagogue, Ferm believed that the teacher should aid the individual in gaining an awareness of self and, consequently, autonomy. The role of the teacher would be to act as a mirror for the students' actions, so that the "individual may see how his act reflects his thought and his thought reflects his act. That thought and action are indivisibly, inseparably one—helping the individual to realize this, consciously, by holding him responsible for every word and act."[20] A teacher serving in this capacity would help the individual to become, in Stirner's sense, free-in-himself. Acquisition of knowledge would then become a function of the free choice of the individual.

---

[19] Ibid., p. 143.

[20] Elizabeth Burns Ferm, "Activity and Passivity of the Educator," *Mother Earth* 2(March 1907):26.

Emma Goldman

Most anarchists believe that any form of education would have little meaning unless the family were changed. Emma Goldman, leading spokesman for anarchist thought in the United States in the early twentieth century, declared in 1906, "The terrible struggle of the thinking man and woman against political, social and moral conventions owes its origin to the family, where the child is ever compelled to battle against the internal and external use of force."[21] From Emma Goldman's point of view, the central problem in overcoming the modern authoritarian family structure was to end the subservient role of the woman in modern society. Goldman's career was characterized by a life-long fight for women's liberation.

Francisco Ferrer also recognized the importance of women's social role as a factor in anarchist education. Since women had the major responsibility for child care, free humans could never develop until women were free. Ferrer wrote,

> It is a conspicuous fact in our modern Christian society that, as a result and culmination of our patriarchal development, the woman does not belong to herself; she is neither more nor less than an adjunct of man, subject constantly to his absolute dominion, bound to him—it may be—by chains of gold. Man has made her a perpetual minor."[22]

Coeducation at Ferrer's Modern School in Barcelona was unique not only because it was not generally practiced in Spain, but also because it emphasized the teaching of girls as a means of freeing humanity. He argued that this was crucial because so many of one's ideas were wrapped in the emotions of childhood association with the mother. Ferrer did label the male and female with terms that would later be rejected by ardent feminists, calling the male the individual and the female the conserver. While this identification was not to be accepted by later groups of women liberationists, his recognition of the necessity of changing the status of women as a precondition for any important social change was to become an important argument in that movement.

Freeing the child in the family and the school of all authoritarian dogma created an important dilemma in anarchist educational

---

[21] Emma Goldman, "The Child and Its Enemies," *Mother Earth* 1(April 1906):10–11.
[22] Ferrer, *Origin and Ideals of Modern School*, pp. 36–37.

thought. If the teaching of children was to be free from dogma, what exactly would be taught? For instance, Ferrer searched in vain before opening his school for texts that would meet the criterion of nonauthoritarianism. Interestingly, the Modern School was opened without one book in its library because Ferrer could not find any that met his approval.[23] There was also a concern about an anarchist education forcing the child to become an anarchist since this would be a product of dogmatic imposition. Emma Goldman warned radical parents who imposed beliefs on their children that they would find that the "boy or girl, overfed on Thomas Paine, will land in the arms of the Church, or they will vote for imperialism only to escape the drag of economic determinism and scientific socialism, or that they . . . cling to their right of accumulating property, only to find relief from the old-fashioned communism of their father."[24]

Anarchist discussions of this last dilemma were often resolved in conviction rather than in logic. For instance, the statement of purposes of the International League for the Rational Education of Children, founded by Ferrer, admitted that there was no neutral instruction and argued, "We should not, in the school, hide the fact that we would awaken in the children the desire for a society of men . . . equal economically . . . without violence, without hierarchies, and without privilege of any sort." In the next paragraph the League warned that ". . . we have no right to impose this ideal on the child."[25] The League claimed that if the child's conscience, sense of justice, and reason were aroused, he would work for human emancipation. The conviction underlying this feeling and other anarchist statements regarding education was simply this: reason cultivated free of dogma would create naturally within the individual a desire for the preservation of his own autonomy and that of others.

From this standpoint Ferrer emphasized the presentation of facts from which the child would draw his own conclusions, exhibiting a great faith in the ability of the natural and social sciences to yield objective data with which the human mind could reason. What constituted objective data was, of course, open to judgment. For

[23] Ibid., pp. 76–87.

[24] Goldman, "Child and Its Enemies," pp. 12–13.

[25] "The International League for the Rational Education of Children," *Mother Earth* 5 (July 1910):156.

example, Ferrer argued that arithmetic should be presented without reference to wages, economy, and profit. Its substance would be problems dealing with the just distribution of production, communication, transportation, the benefits of machinery, and public works. "In a word," Ferrer wrote, "the Modern School wants a number of problems showing what arithmetic really ought to be— the science of the social economy (taking the word *economy* in its etymological sense of 'good distribution')."[26]

Objective fact and knowledge therefore had a special meaning in anarchist groups, being objective in the sense that the individual could use them for maintaining his own individual freedom. For Ferrer, arithmetic placed in the framework of existing production systems became a method by which the individual was indoctrinated into those systems. On the other hand, arithmetic presented as a tool for creating a more just organization of the economy became a body of knowledge the individual could use to free himself. It was from this standpoint that Emma Goldman criticized traditional methods of teaching history in the schools when she wrote: "See how the events of the world become like a cheap puppet show, where a few wirepullers are supposed to have directed the course of development of the entire race." History that emphasized the actions of rulers, governments, and great men conditioned the individual to accept a society where things were done to men rather than one in which men acted. From Emma Goldman's perspective, history had to emphasize the ability of all men to act and shape its direction. History presented in the traditional manner enslaved man to authoritarian institutions. History presented as all men acting convinced the individual of his own power to shape history.[27]

As far as Emma Goldman was concerned, men made the Russian Revolution of 1917, but the centralized state of the Bolsheviks defeated its liberating force. While anarchists supported the major surge of revolutionary fervor in Russia, they were quickly disillusioned when their worst fears about the growth of a Communist state and its control of cultural and educational activities seemed realized. Anarchists like Emma Goldman found that in the Soviet state educational institutions were used to bend the will of the people to conform to the needs of the state.

---

[26] Ferrer, *Origin and Ideals of Modern School,* pp. 89–90.
[27] Goldman, "Child and Its Enemies," p. 9.

ANARCHISTS AND COMMUNISTS

Anarchists during the nineteenth century had voiced a constant concern that Communist ideology, by making the state both lawgiver and property owner, would make its control supreme over the autonomy of the individual. During the 1840s Max Stirner had warned Marx and his fellow Hegelians in *The Ego and His Own* that Communist concern with solving industrial problems by making the state property owner would only lead to a highly controlled society where the citizen would become the laborer whose duty was to sacrifice himself for the state. To Stirner, communism meant impressed labor and consumption. He wrote that communism "takes seriously the idea that, because only spiritual and material goods make us men, we must unquestionably acquire these goods in order to be men. . . . Communism compels to acquisition, and recognizes only the acquirer, him who practices a trade. It is not enough that the trade is free, but you must take it up."[28]

When Peter Kropotkin returned from exile after the 1917 Revolution, he was sadly crushed by what he saw. While visiting Lenin in 1919, Kropotkin reportedly told the leader that "local authorities, perhaps even the revolutionaries of yesterday, like any other authority have become bureaucratized, converted into officials who wish to twist the strings of those subordinate to them—and they think that the whole population is subordinate to them."[29]

Emma Goldman returned both willingly and unwillingly to Russia in 1919. She went unwillingly in the sense that the United States government revoked her citizenship in 1919 and placed her, along with some 247 other anarchists, on a ship and sent them to Russia on what must rank among the most curious voyages in history. She went willingly in the sense that she believed the revolution would accomplish libertarian goals. Emma Goldman found "the Bolshevik State formidable, crushing every constructive revolutionary effort, suppressing, debasing, and disintegrating everything."[30] Lenin's deity, she claimed, had become the centralized political state, to which everything was to be sacrificed. All Bolshevik acts and meth-

---

[28] Max Stirner, *The Ego and His Own*, trans. by Steven T. Byington (New York: Libertarian Book Club, 1963):122.

[29] P. A. Kropotkin, *Selected Writings on Anarchism and Revolution*, ed. by Martin A. Miller (Cambridge, Mass.: M.I.T. Press, 1970):327–328.

[30] Emma Goldman, *My Disillusionment in Russia* (New York: Crowell, 1970):p. xii.

ods, she wrote, were "links in the chain which were to forge the all-powerful, centralized Government with State Capitalism as its economic expression."[31] She left Russia in 1921 to publish *My Disillusionment in Russia,* which focused part of its concern on the cultural and educational developments in that country.

Bolshevik cultural and educational activities characterized for Emma Goldman all of the worst fears anarchists had about state-controlled education. She was willing to admit that the Soviet state had increased educational opportunities, but she insisted that critical inquiry and freedom of thought had been sacrificed to quantity and the goals of the state. She found quantity in terms of more schools, more and inexpensive theater, increases in other cultural activities, and an increased support of art. But, she asserted,

> State monopoly of thought is everywhere interpreting education to suit its own purpose. . . . But while the monopoly of thought in other countries has not succeeded in entirely checking the spirit of free inquiry and critical analysis, the "proletarian dictatorship" has completely paralysed every attempt at independent investigation.

To prove her point she cited cases of professors being dismissed from universities for "encouraging the critical faculties" of their students and the use of Communist cells to control activities within the classrooms.[32]

What Proletcult had done to the possibilities of revolutionary art forms accompanying the revolution in Russia was her greatest disappointment. Proletcult was to be the artistic expression of the proletariat supported by the new socialist state. Emma Goldman found that "The mechanistic approach to art and culture and the *idée fixe* that nothing must express itself outside of the channels of the State have stultified the cultural and artistic expression of the Russian people."[33] Not only did she find the richness of the revolution for art destroyed by the state, but also the heritage of the past dismissed because it did not serve the interests of the state. She claimed the discovery of a secret order written in 1920 by the chief of the Cen-

[31] Ibid., p. 247.
[32] Ibid., pp. 222–223.
[33] Ibid., p. 224.

tral Educational Department to "eliminate all non-Communist literature, except the Bible, the Koran, and the classics—including even Communist writings dealing with problems which were being 'solved in a different way' by the existing regime."[34] Goldman summed up her feelings with, "the State monopoly of all material, printing machinery, and mediums of circulation exclude every possibility of the birth of creative work. . . . Russia is now the dumping ground for mediocrities in art and culture."[35]

The rise of Nazi Germany further underscored anarchists' fears of the controlling power of education. And the dissenting tradition of anarchists in the nineteenth and the early twentieth century against granting power to some authority consciously to educate a future generation can be judged correct when one considers the totalitarian regimes of the twentieth century. Americans in particular had disregarded the anarchist argument and plunged ahead with an education planned to turn out the free citizen. A nineteenth-century anarchist could have predicted that by the middle of the twentieth century, American schools would be accused of being racist and business oriented.

AMERICAN EDUCATORS TODAY

One of the problems that beset American educators was a confusion about the relationship of freedom and schooling. That knowledge is an important ingredient of freedom, few people would deny. But as libertarian educators have pointed out, freedom depends on the content and on the method by which the learner receives knowledge. If the state assumes the responsibility of producing good citizens, the nature of freedom becomes highly compromised. It is this fact that many American educators failed to realize. For example, Henry Barnard, one of the great American common school reformers of the nineteenth century, expressed awareness of the problem but dismissed it, insisting that education always provided freedom as the end result.

Barnard expressed his concern in 1853 when he wrote about European systems of education that had attracted the keen attention of American educators: "Everywhere the lessons of the school-room are weakened and in a measure destroyed by degrading national

---

[34] Ibid., p. 226.
[35] Ibid.

customs, by the vicious example of the upper classes and inevitable result of a government which represses liberty of thought, speech, occupation and political action." But he argued that either the school will change the government or the government will change the school. In either case, Barnard said, no matter how much government interferes in education, schooling would inevitably bring about the improvement of the people. In poetic terms he expressed the faith of the nineteenth-century schoolman in the power of learning once it is let loose in a society. "It would be easier," he wrote in reference to the government stopping the well-schooled man, "to return the rain to the clouds, from which it is falling, before it has freshened hill-top and valley, mingled with the waters of every rising spring, and reached the roots of every growing plant."[36]

In general, educational historians have blinded themselves through a sense of devotion to public schooling in the same manner as Henry Barnard. Their failure to remind people of the present that some of those in the past saw grave dangers in creating a vast social machine for the imposition of values and control has left a serious gap in the consciousness of those now faced with a public school that, standing outside the boundaries of community control and functions, seems only to maintain the present social order. The exploration of anarchist attitudes toward schooling is only the first step in restoring the radical tradition in education. It is also a major step in understanding the institution at the heart of the modern industrial state. As the introduction to this volume emphasized, the clearest picture of the present can be gained through a study of the school simply because the school has become the means by which society has attempted to reproduce itself. The school reflects the basic concerns and values of modern society. Understanding schooling means understanding modern society, and this requires a study of both what the school is and what it has done and why people saw it as a potential engine for despotism.

---

[36] John S. Brubacher, ed., *Henry Barnard on Education* (New York: McGraw-Hill, 1931), p. 74.

NAME INDEX

SUBJECT INDEX

Printed in U.S.A.